Evras Press, P.O. Box 465, Rosenberg, Texas 77471

Published 2003
Bound and printed in the United States of America

Library of Congress Cataloging-in-Publication Data

Sakkis, Tony.
Brother, Can You Spare A Dime
Includes index.
ISBN 0-9635305-3-4
1. Cookbook, budget cooking. I. Title: Brother, Can You Spare A Dime?
II. Title: How to Feed Yourself for about $5 a Week

ACKNOWLEDGMENTS

Whether she knows it or not, my mother was the catalyst for this book. She taught me to think of what ingredients were available, not of what the recipe said. It started with buttermilk pancakes—after all, who keeps buttermilk around? She said use yogurt. Not enough sugar? Use applesauce or orange juice. The ideas were endless and they freed me from what the cookbooks told me to do. Buy a kid a fish dinner and you feed him for the evening. Teach him to fish and you feed him for a lifetime. That yogurt-for-buttermilk was the beginning of the fishing lesson. Thanks, Mom.

I also thank my wife, my guinea-pig for all these—among hundreds of other—recipes. Since my kids eat only chicken nuggets and fries, it was she who ended up cleaning the plates. Thanks. I love you.

Thanks, also, to Kathy Kobos for staying with the project, for going over my hieroglyphics, figuring out what I meant to say even when I wasn't quite sure what that was, and for laying it out in a style that would make a full-timer proud—I couldn't have done it without you, Kathy.

And thanks to Hannah Glotz for her fantastic artistry.

And special thanks to José Ngeti. Without your assistance, this work would have never come to fruition. You're a good man.

Tony Sakkis
Rosenberg, Texas
June 2003

CONTENTS

Section One

HOW TO START AND WHAT YOU NEED

Chapter 1

Ramen Noodles

The Foundation of a Good, Cheap Meal

To put it bluntly, if there were a cheaper food with as many possible variations as ramen noodles, we'd use it. But there isn't. Ramen noodles—with the built-in flavoring packet—provide you with one of the best starting points in budget cooking. Eliminate the water; add a touch of cream, the flavor packet, and you've got a very nice meal. To make it special, add an onion, a stick of celery, maybe some chicken—and, well, you get the point. And if you don't, there are some 300 ideas this book that should help.

Noodles have been around for a long time. Marco Polo is said to have traveled to China and brought noodles back to Italy in the late 13th century. After the novelty of the noodle wore off, some intelligent souls realized how inexpensive and versatile it was; hence, it became the base food of Italy. The Irish had potatoes; Italians, the noodle.

Ramen noodles, however, are a relatively new food to the United States. Although pre-packaged noodles have been in Japan and China for some time, they were only brought to this country in the '70s. And for the first ten years or so, they were not sold cheaply enough to have been a serious budget ingredient. In fact, you could still buy spaghetti more cheaply than ramen noodle packages for a long time. And let's face it, because it's made with Durham wheat, spaghetti is a better tasting noodle.

But in the last decade, the proliferation of both ramen noodle manufacturers and the discount stores that sell them have grown tremendously. The little packaged buggers are everywhere. And now, if you walk down the soup aisle of your grocery, you'll pay an average of about 25¢ a package, but you can almost always find specials at 10¢ a package. Brother, can *you* spare a dime?

Eggs Are the Difference

The reason ramen tastes slightly different from, say, spaghetti is in one missing ingredient. Noodles, in general, are made of essentially the same thing—flour, water, salt and some kind of dough conditioner. Where ramen noodles differ from dry spaghetti is in the use of semolina flour, or egg flour. Most ramen is an egg-less, flour/water-only dough. It gives the ramen noodle less flavor, and it also allows it to break down quicker. Leave packages of noodles in water too long and you get a sloppy, soupy mess. Leave the same spaghetti in water and you get soggy spaghetti.

The types of ramen only vary with the flavor packet. The noodles are the same, no matter what the flavoring is. Some types available (and there are others) are:

- Beef
- Picante Beef
- Chicken
- Mushroom Chicken
- Sesame Chicken
- Creamy Chicken
- Teriyaki Chicken
- Cajun
- Vegetable
- Chili
- Oriental
- Pork
- Shrimp

Gimme Some Spice! The Flavor Packet

The difference between ramen and spaghetti, then, (besides price and quality) is the little foil-wrapped packet of soup flavoring. That packet alone can make the ramen into a nice pasta dish. The flavor packet is a convenient way to make a pasta taste unique.

In Mexican kitchens, you'll usually find a canister of Knorr-Suiza chicken bouillon powder or some other brand of chicken soup base. It provides salt and flavor, allowing Mexican cooks to start with a taste—in this case, chicken.

But with ramen, you have ten-cent shrimp, mushroom, tomato, vegetable, and so on. And the good news is that it's already part of the package. With the noodles and the flavoring, you can be like Martha Stewart—without all the insider trading headaches.

Energy Food

Understand this—ramen noodles are mostly carbohydrates, and carbohydrates produce energy. Stored as glycogen in muscle and liver, they function as readily available "people fuel" during exercise. Most nutritionists believe carbohydrates that are high in fiber are the most important nutrient for sports performance.

Okay, so ramen is not exactly high fiber. But it is high in carbohydrates. If you add chicken or beef—or, God help you, tofu—you have protein as well. If you try to remember that along with eating the ramen, it's important also to drink lots of fluid (not just beer) along with pasta. Most sources recommend at least 16 ounces of water per serving of pasta. Otherwise, it can eventually act as a sponge in the system, and create distracting and socially disrupting constipation.

Medical Alert

While we never made it through medical school (which is why we're writing cookbooks to make extra money), we should at least mention that the flavor packet typically contains MSG. If you have adverse reactions to MSG, you'll need to eliminate the flavor packets from your list of ingredients.

We should also mention—just in passing, mind you—that diabetics need to regulate pasta intake. The upshot is that this isn't meant to be a guide for those with special needs ... other than saving cash.

Dieting

Let's face it—most of what's in here won't facilitate weight loss. We're looking for carbs and calories to keep you alive, not to make you skinny. In fact, some of this stuff is downright unhealthy. But what do you expect? We're trying to feed you for 50¢ a meal. We briefly thought about putting in nutritional facts for each recipe then decided it would be too depressing. The upshot is: this isn't a diet book. If that's what you're looking for, find your receipt, take the book back, and have your money returned to you because you're looking in the wrong place.

Improvising

A note about this cookbook: in all cases, we have provided you three versions of the same recipe—one that works as a relatively cheap "real" recipe, one save-a-bunch-of-money price crusher, and one we call "The Big Splurge," for those rare days when you're flush with cash.

Regardless, in all three, all you need is creativity. If you want to make something with shrimp, it's a safe bet you need shrimp. But if you don't have it, use what you do have. The keys to cooking well are to cook so it tastes the way you want it—and knowing how to make it taste similar when you don't have the exact ingredients. Taste combinations are only as good as you think they are—and only as limited as your imagination lets you make them.

Understand that although this is a book based on a ten-cent package of ramen, you can easily go upscale and change the recipes so they're more mainstream. Use fettuccine, penne, rotini, spaghetti, macaroni, or whatever you wish to use to spice up the recipe.

The point is we want you to improvise. By improvising, you'll develop the ability to think outside the, uhh, plastic bag. Find a recipe in the food you have and try something new. Use chicken soup mix and sugar, yogurt and cinnamon, or mango and cilantro in the same recipe. Try it. Try anything; use your imagination.

Flavor Me, Baby

If you're cooking for yourself and some of your goon friends, make your meal by the book if you wish. But if you're cooking to impress a date, have a more open mind.

What follows here is really just a flavor guide for about 200 of what we call food templates. We've tried to give you some of the world's most influential flavors—that you yourself can alter depending on your taste, budget and how well you know your dinner date or dinner companions.

Curries, basil dishes, lamb dishes, and any of the Asian, Italian, Mexican or continental dishes represented here are like form letters that you can address differently. Each recipe provides tips as to what makes the dish unique. And in general, there are only one or two ingredients that make the dish unique—and only one or two ingredients you need to keep. Other than those few important ones, change ingredients as you wish. If you lose one or two you won't screw up the recipe, you'll usually just alter it. But it's okay. Alter away, alter away.

Chapter 2
The Stuff You Need

What You Need To Get Started

You'll need a few things to get your kitchen up to speed. Even on the tightest budget, you'll need at least a few pans and some cooking utensils. You'll be able to find these on the cheap at one of the dollar stores, or on sale at a Wal-Mart or K-Mart or somewhere that has cheap stuff.

Saucepans and Pots

The first thing you need is a pot for cooking the ramen. Since all these recipes are made for four people or more, you'll need a good-sized pot. You should easily find a stockpot or big saucepan for $5 or so. Granted, it won't last for any length of time, but it will keep for a year or two. You won't be able to show off with it, but then we're not trying to make you into Julia Child here.

You should actually have a couple of pots—maybe two deep saucepans, one for, say, boiling a good-sized dead chicken and one for sauces. Or maybe a 12-quart pan and a two-quart pan. You won't need to spend lots of money here either.

By the way, try not to buy a ceramic-coated tin pan. They're not just cheap, they're garbage, and will last literally one meal. If you bend the handle even a little bit, the ceramic stuff flakes off into your food. Although it can actually be quite crunchy when mixed with ramen, it probably isn't too good for you. So look for stainless steel. Or if you can't afford that, buy Teflon-coated.

To Fry

You also need at least one skillet. Cast iron fryers are the best—and also usually quite cheap—but you'll have to have patience to season it. To season the cast iron skillet, rub the pan with cooking oil and set it over a burner, heating the pan until quite hot. Allow it to cool then wipe the burnt oil out with a paper towel or clean cloth. Repeat, frying an onion and salt in the oil. Discard the food and wipe clean again. It will be several months before you get rid of the machined ridges in the pan, but it will no longer taste like machine oil once seasoned.

Whatever you decide, just buy a good-sized—say, about 12–18 inches across—frying pan. A $12–$15 pan should do, but if you can't afford it, you should be able to find a Teflon-coated pan for under $5.

Wok—A Self-Contained Cooking Arsenal

Another way to do this is to buy a wok. They're probably the most efficient way of cooking. They get phenomenally hot, and all recipes are designed for quick preparation, so you won't burn them. Although it's better to make your ramen noodles in a pot, you can also make them in a wok, then set them aside and use the wok to make the rest of the meal.

Best of all—with a wok, to keep it seasoned, you avoid washing it. Once you're finished cooking, just add some water to the hot wok—you have to get the scum out of it—and wipe it out. But that's about the extent of it. You don't need soap. In fact, believe it or not, most wok manufacturers suggest you *not* use soap. It makes things nice and easy to clean. And for guys, it's an excuse to put off the dishes another week or two.

By the way, whether you buy a wok or a fryer, always make sure you get pots and pans with lids so you can simmer food (slow cook on a low temperature).

Utensils

You'll need a few things to chop, dice, mix and serve your food with—like a spatula, a couple of wooden spoons and a knife or two. These you'll want to get at the dollar store since a $4 wooden spoon is no better than one that costs 35¢. And for the most part, the dollar stores will have what you need for a lot less.

Knifes

If you're a bachelor, you'll probably like this part. All guys like knives. This is one time you can by a way-cool knife and get away with it. Try not to get carried away. You really don't need a great knife that will last married people the rest of their lives. In your kitchen, they're good for six months.

Ikea has a few good cheap knives and you can always go to a Wal-Mart or K-Mart and get the same kind of thing. Try not to go to the dollar stores for knives. They're typically crap and will bend. If they break on you, you'll slice your hand off. For about $3–$6 you should be able to find a nice knife that will last you a few years.

Better yet, ask your grandmother for her old knives or steal the oldest one from your mom's knife drawer. She didn't want those old things anyway.

Also get a knife sharpener. You know—the things with six little metal wheels that roll on two separate spindles? (Yeah, they don't look like they'll do any good, but they sharpen knives better than a Boy Scout; truth be told, Boy Scouts don't know what the hell they're doing—which is why adult males can never keep a knife sharp, and why married adults buy way cool knives that don't need sharpening). Although the metal sharpener will eventually ruin your knives, they create great edges for cutting. And since you bought cheap knives, use the metal sharpener. It's easier.

Serving, Mixing And Eating On The Cheap

You'll also have to have a few serving, mixing and eating bowls. For the mixing and serving bowls, go bigger than necessary, since you can always use the extra space. Bigger is better. If you don't have a big enough bowl, you're stuck.

It doesn't matter if they're metal, plastic, or ceramic. If you're on your own for the first time, you'll bend the metal ones, melt the plastic ones and break the ceramic ones, so buy whatever you'll be least angry about when finally destroyed.

If you get a nice ceramic bowl (usually about $6–$8) you can use it to both toss and serve your ramen. Or buy plastic for mixing and a nice one for serving. Okay, if you're really skimping, eat right out of the pot if you want, you slob.

In theory, you can get away with one or two big plastic bowls to prepare your food in, mix, toss your ramen in sauce and eat out of. That's fine, if that's what fits your budget. You can get away with as little as a $1 or as much as $15, depending on what fits your wallet. Both are budget.

A 12-quart pot is a must, as is a cheap skillet and a decent knife and wooden spoon. So for about $11, you should be able to find a cheapy pot or pan, a decent knife and a wooden spoon. Add the plastic bowls and you're in for about $12. Terrific. Now all you need is food to cook.

From Unconventional Sources

What follows will be different from most cookbooks. Although we want to give you a preview of the tastes you'll be encountering in this book, what we ultimately wish to do is give you alternatives.

✱ As we said in the first chapter, with each recipe we've tried to provide an alternative to the ingredients shown. Some work fine, others not so good. Fast food restaurants will have your basic condiments, and in each recipe in the book, you'll find an asterisk (*) next to the ingredients that can be found at any fast food restaurants. You'll find out which ingredients you can scrounge at the local fast food place, and which scrounged ingredients can be used in place of some typically expensive main ingredients. (We call it guerrilla food gathering.) Just remember, all it takes is a few spices to change a meal completely. And if the ingredients are free, that makes it all the better.

If the recipe asks for sour cream, it's actually calling for something with a tangy taste and/or something to bind together the other ingredients. If you don't have sour cream, you can substitute yogurt. No yogurt? Use lemon, water and some egg white. The lemon will give it the taste and the egg white will bind the food and the water will give it the moisture of the sour cream. In some recipes—mostly Mexican—this doesn't work. But in others it's perfectly acceptable.

MINCE, DICE, TWIST AND SHOUT

Throughout this guide, you'll find words like mince, dice, sauté and stuff like that—stuff you may hear on one of those fancy cooking shows, but don't know what the heck any of it means. So what follows is a simplified list of terms you need to know. We have not included some of the really simple ones—we assume you'll know the words "serve" and "eat."

Bake

To cook in the oven. Pretty simple stuff. Instructions as follows: 1) Open the oven and put stuff in it. 2) Close the oven door. 3) Follow cooking directions. 4) Take baked food out (watch out, the pan will be hot). 5) Eat. See? Told you it was simple.

Boil

Look at the water, sauce, etc. in the pan heating on the stove. See the bubbles coming from the bottom of the pan real fast? Yeah, it's boiling. Now turn it down.

Blanch

To flash boil food. Put food in boiling water; just as it gets hot, take it out.

Broil

In this book, it means to put meat in the oven and bake. But for the most part, the source of the heat for broiling comes from above the food rather than below it. Your oven may or may not broil correctly, so think of it as baking.

Chop

Chop is the roughest form of cutting. We are not looking for either uniformity or any perfect size. But for something like spinach, which will usually be too big to eat without altering the natural size of the leaves, you will chop it with a knife until it's easier to work with or eat.

Dice

To cut things into small squares, usually between a quarter to a half inch-square. Salsa chunk-sized is a good way to describe it.

Fry

To place something in a frying pan or skillet and cook through. It is similar to sautéing, but is usually done more just to cook than to flavor.

Grate

Typically what we mean here is to grind things (mostly cheese) into almost a powder; at least something that can easily be assimilated into or sprinkled on food.

Mince

Like dice, but finer. You want to end up with very small pieces, something that will get stuck between your molars, about the size of a sesame seed.

Saute

To fry something in liquid. Once you're done, there should be either no liquid or very little left in the pan, all of it having adhered to the food, imparting the flavor of the liquid (or butter or oil) to the food. Sautéing typically involves a constant stirring or mixing method.

Shred

Use the largest holes on a grater (one of those things with the deformed holes it in). You should end up with 1-inch long slivers of stuff—typically cheese.

But you can also shred radishes or other veggies with some body or substance to them.

Simmer

Cooking, usually with a lid. You're trying to get the food to soften and to take on flavors of the other ingredients in the pot. Simmering is done at lower heat, usually at half-throttle, so to speak.

Sliver

Like it says—make it into slivers, skinny strips. Slivers can be, say, a quarter-inch wide and as long as a sliver can be. Use your imagination.

Stir-fry

To cook while rapidly combining ingredients. You start with ingredients raw (actually, you can also have them pre-cooked) and mix them together while cooking, stirring constantly. Usually done in a wok, stir-frying gets all your ingredients to the same temperature.

Chapter 3

MAIN INGREDIENTS

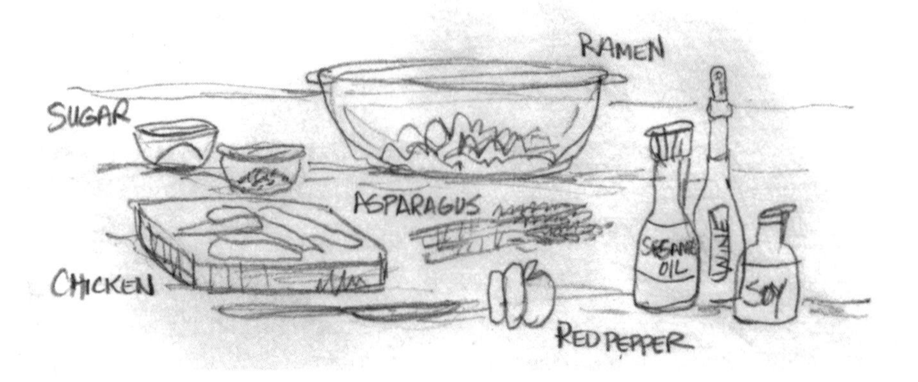

MEAT, POULTRY AND FISH

Beef

Beef, the king of meats, makes the meal. A good cut of beef can stand on its own, without any help from seasoning—or from ramen noodles for that matter.

But if it were that easy to afford a great cut of meat you wouldn't be reading this cookbook, right? So we don't use the best cuts of meat. However, we still use the meat to flavor the dish, not vice versa.

Beef comes in a very wide variety of cuts. In any supermarket, two-thirds of the meat department is devoted to beef, with other meats—lamb, veal, chicken and pork—sharing the remaining third. So which cut do you use? Simple—the cheapest.

Since we are using beef as much as a flavor as a main ingredient, you can flavor your food with inexpensive cuts just as easily as with expensive cuts. Okay, let's not fool ourselves into thinking it will be as good. It won't. But it will save you a lot of money. Compare New York steak to round steak from $8 to $1.98. That's a good savings. And for the most part—not considering how tough or tender it is—the flavor is identical.

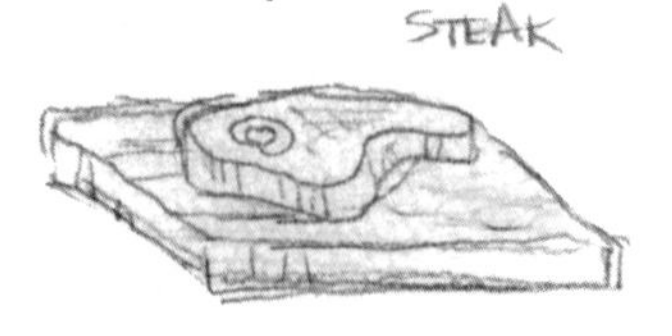

What beef does to food	Gives dishes a hearty, flavorful taste that fills you up
Substitutions	None
Price range	$1.70 a pound, round steak $2.98 a pound, sirloin $3.25 a pound, roasts* $5.50 a pound, T-bone steak *Roasts can be cubed or slivered and sometimes can be found for as little as $1.60 for rib roast

Pork

Pork can mean chops or tenderloins, but it can also mean ham, bacon or sausage. Pork varies as much in taste as it does in packaging. For the most part, what we mean by pork is cubed or sliced pork sparerib or tenderloin cuts. Pork, like chicken, still tends to be relatively inexpensive at around $4 for some of the best cuts available.

Problem with pork is that its reputation as an unhealthy food has been quite exaggerated, and it is still out of favor with a lot of religions. For years one of the most common forms of food poisoning came from trichinosis—an illness that comes from a parasite that lives mostly in raw pork. But if you're a professional bachelor, you've got more toxic stuff in your toilet bowl.

Pork, like chicken, can act as a very nice "canvas" food, which can be altered or changed completely with some spices. In addition, pork has a very nice inherent taste, more subtle than beef, yet still enough that, with only a little salt, it adds a nice base taste to a meal. A lean cut of pork is actually a lot less greasy than most people think, and lean pork shrinks little when cooked. The best way to buy pork is either in center-cut rib meat, chops or tenderloin roast.

Other cuts include ham and bacon, which are both specific cuts of pork. Bacon is smoked and cured and is typically cut into strips. That's the way we use it in this cookbook. Ham, on the other hand, can be served in slices, slabs or cubes. It is characterized with the savory taste of the curing agent—primarily salt and some savory flavoring. By the way, Canadian bacon is more like a ham than bacon (it is in fact a cured pork tenderloin). You can find it in the meat or sometimes deli (pre-cooked) aisle of your grocery store.

Pork sausage is yet another way to serve pork. It is pre-packaged and varies in taste, depending on whether it's breakfast sausage, link sausage, Italian sausage or whatever. Ground pork—which is different from sausage—can be purchased for about $2 a pound. It can easily be made into sausage. For example, if you want to save some money on Italian sausage, add oregano, basil, garlic, fennel and any other spice you desire to ground sausage, mix well and cook.

What pork does to food	Imbues meals with a nice salt/meat quality without overpowering the other flavors of the dish
Substitutions	Chicken can be substituted easier than beef, although chicken is not really the same. For ground pork or sausage substitutes—try ground turkey, but chub pork sausage is often quite cheap.
Price range	$3.18–$3.98 a pound generally $1.50 a pound, butt shoulder roast $ .77 a pound, chub sausage* *Chub means it's wrapped in plastic and sold in rolls

Lamb

If beef flavors food perfectly, lamb is unpopular in the United States for the opposite reason—it is too flavorful. Lamb gives a flavor that is sharper than beef and gamey in taste.

Lamb chops or rack of lamb is popular in the U.S. because it has the least amount of lamb flavor. Leg of lamb, or lamb roast, has the most flavor.

We have few lamb dishes in this cookbook because it's tough to find in most grocery stores; few people know a good cut; and fewer know how to cook it. And it's more expensive than either beef or pork, plus a lot of people just don't like the taste.

What lamb does to food	Gives dishes a sharp gamey taste similar to beef, but more complex in flavor
Substitutions	Beef or pork
Price range	$1.99 a pound, untrimmed leg of lamb $3.99 a pound, trimmed leg of lamb $16.00 a pound, a rack of lamb (which you obviously won't be using—at least not with this cookbook)

POULTRY

Chicken

Chicken is the ultimate canvas of main ingredients. When boiled and served unsalted, it is almost tasteless. But add a spice or two, and you have a great ingredient.

Chicken, therefore, is the *Brother, Can You Spare A Dime?* featured ingredient.

It is the easiest to work with, the toughest to screw up, the cheapest of all main ingredients and the easiest to find. On the harshest budget, you can still use the same basic proportions and come up with something tasty and filling.

The question is—how do you buy it?

Chicken comes in different packaging, from whole to skinless and boneless. Without a doubt, the best bargains come from doing the work yourself. Fryers, or whole young chickens, are typically around 70¢ a pound. That means you'll have to chop and remove the skin and bones on your own.

Or you can frequently find specials for 10-pound bags of thigh quarters for very low prices—sometimes as little as 29¢ a pound. Again, you'll have to bone and skin them yourself. But what you come up with for $3 will feed you for several weeks.

The prized part of the chicken is the white meat, or the breast. It is juicy, but not oily, and is easiest to flavor. It is also the most expensive part of the chicken. But even then, skinless, boneless chicken breasts are still relatively inexpensive at an average of $3 per pound. Or, as mentioned previously, if you buy either a whole chicken or breast-on-bone pieces you can knock that amount in half—but you must do the work of the butcher.

Thigh meat, on the other hand, is brown, meaning it has more natural fat in it. Therefore it tends to be greasier and is slightly more difficult to flavor because of the inherent "waterproofing." No matter, it is still a lot less expensive, and you're trying to make simple meals here, not gourmet art works.

By the way, drumsticks are pretty much off limits in this book. They are difficult to work with, and for the price you'll typically pay, it's easier to buy breasts than to find the meat on a drumstick.

What chicken does to food	Gives you a very adaptable main ingredient
Substitutions	Turkey
Price range	$3.00 a pound, breasts $1.97 a pound, boneless thighs $1.19 a pound, thighs with bone and skin $ .69 a pound, whole fryers By the way, you can also get canned breast meat for about $2.20 a 10-ounce can

Turkey

Turkey, like chicken, is more of a "canvas food" than a food that creates a taste on its own. But turkey, unlike chicken, has more flavor and is typically juicier. A lot of that has to do with how it is packaged and how it is cooked.

Typically, you bake a turkey and that allows the juice to settle into the bird. A trend toward selling turkey parts—drumsticks, wings, breasts—is beginning to evolve. But for the most part, you still buy turkeys whole—usually around the holidays—and bake them that way.

Most of the recipes in this cookbook call for pre-cooked turkey, meaning you can easily use leftover turkey you stole from your mother after Thanksgiving.

What turkey does to food	Gives a chicken-like flavor and does well with spices
Substitutions	Use chicken in a pinch
Price range	$1.19–$1.39 a pound During Thanksgiving, you can find specials for as little as 9¢ a pound

SEAFOOD

Fish

Twenty years ago, fish was the great budget food. It was easy to find fresh whitefish at a great price, often less than $2 a pound, and it was always flavorful. Now, however, fish of any kind is tough to find truly fresh at a normal grocery store, and it hardly ever goes for less than $4.

We don't have a lot of fish recipes in this book, and even then they are mostly reserved for catfish (which does not crumble or fall apart easily) and canned tuna or salmon. Catfish farms are springing up all over the place and catfish nuggets can often be found for about $2 a pound. Other than that, there are too many variables to include in this cookbook.

Fish, in general, vary in taste, with one lone similarity—the fresher the fish, the less fishy the flavor. Unless you love the taste of fish (and most people, given the choice, like the less fishy taste of fresh), you'll be priced out of the ball game.

What fish does to food	Gives a light, usually flaky texture with a nice (depending on freshness) seafood taste
Substitutions	Chicken—obviously tastes nothing like fish, but it can typically be used in the same recipe with good results
Price range	$2.00 a pound or less, catfish $1.49 a pound, whiting $1.78 a pound, pollock $ .40 a can, canned tuna

Shrimp

Rich, chewy and almost fatty-tasting, shrimp doesn't exactly overpower with its taste, but you'll know if it's in the dish and in what abundance. Its subtle flavor appeals to seafood lovers and those who avoid seafood with equal aplomb. It is one of the few types of seafood (lobster being another) that crosses over to the turf lover's plate. Almost everybody eats shrimp. And perhaps that's what makes it so expensive.

Shrimp ranges from about $3 per pound all the way up to $20 for the extra large variety. Typically, the bigger the shrimp the richer and more buttery the taste; the smaller the more fishy the taste and the less meaty.

Yet if you order pasta with shrimp at a restaurant, you'll notice that they don't give you a lot of shrimp—no matter what the size. So it has become more of a seasoning than an actual ingredient. And for the purposes of this book, you won't be asked to use great portions of shrimp. Like a good Chinese restaurant, you'll use the shrimp as a lure, with the object of the dish being to evoke the taste of shrimp without spending a lot on the actual shrimp.

How do you do that? The problem with shrimp is their size and shape. The shelled and de-veined shrimp tends to be thick and crescent-shaped. And due to its size, it is a single bite's worth of food. By cutting the uncooked shrimp in three pieces, you'll have the taste of the shrimp in better proportions. Usually, for under a dollar per dish, you can cut the shrimp and still come out with a great tasting meal.

By the way, shelling the shrimp is as easy as peeling it and removing it from the semi-soft shell. De-veining is the process of removing the "guts" of the shrimp by slicing up the center of the shrimp and removing the black waste tract of the shrimp before cooking.

What shrimp does to food	Adds a buttery richness not found in most seafoods
Substitutions	Crawfish come close and are inexpensive. In the certain parts of the country, however, they can be as expensive as shrimp.
Price range	$1.19–$19.99 a pound

Mussels, calamari, clams and crab

Even though mussels and clams are both shellfish, they each have a different taste. But typically they can be interchanged. It isn't so much the exact taste of the mussels or the clams, but the consistency of the meat of either that makes them unique as ingredients. If using whole clams or mussels (meaning still in the shell), make sure you scrub them with a stiff brush to get off all the iodine and algae.

As for crab, the meat tends to be stringy and dry if not fresh. Although the taste of fresh crab is better than (some) sex, cheap or bulk crab is usually not worth the money. Use fake crab instead of cheap crab. Mixed with ramen, it will taste better.

Calamari is a great way to get a seafood taste without the cost. It's cheap, tasty and readily available. To clean squid, you remove the plastic-like inner pieces and the guts, saving the tentacles if you can tolerate the chewiness. Cut it into rings and maybe even tenderize it, using a metal or wood meat tenderizer.

What mussels, calamari, clams and crab do to food	Add a tang and taste not found in chicken or beef
Substitutions	Whitefish—the fresher the better
Price range	$1.99–$12.99 a pound

Vegetables

Asparagus

Although there are several recipes utilizing asparagus, there shouldn't be. For the most part, asparagus is far too expensive. Asparagus, sold in spears for about $3 a pound, is very unique in texture and taste, but is not so unique that you need to spend $3 on it for one meal. You can use less. Or substitute it for something cheaper. It smells up the bathroom afterward anyway.

What asparagus do to food	Adds bulk; gives a slightly tangy taste that goes well with rich sauces
Substitutions	String beans taste different, but also hold sauces well
Price range	$2.98–$3.98 a pound, fresh asparagus $1.57–$2.45 for a 15-ounce can

Bamboo Chutes

Bamboo chutes are not so much a taste as a texture. Chewy and tender—almost like the center of a pineapple—they taste a little like sweet corn and add volume and depth to any Asian meal. It's difficult if not impossible to get fresh bamboo chutes—even in an Asian grocery. So for the most part, you'll have to buy canned. Canned chutes are available at most big supermarkets and at any Asian market. Drain and rinse before use since they tend to taste like formaldehyde right out of the can. Any leftovers can be stored in fresh water in a jar for weeks in the refrigerator.

What bamboo shoots do to food	Mostly used for texture; gives a crunch and a chewiness that is unique in vegetables
Substitutions	Celery hearts—taste nothing like bamboo chutes, but the texture is approximate, and they cost less
Price range	$1.19 for an 8-ounce can (unless you find an Asian grocery)

Beans

Beans, like potatoes and ramen, are the life sustainers of the world. They are cheap, fill you up and provide complex carbohydrates to give you a great energy source. Despite their reputation for creating a rank-stinky by-product, beans are great additives to your ramen. Just try not to cook them for a date—unless both of you like that sort of thing.

What beans do to food	Fill out a dish, giving an almost bread-like density
Substitutions	Why bother?
Price range	33¢ for a 15-ounce can of kidney beans 38¢ for a 15.5-ounce can of pinto beans

Bean Sprouts

Eaten raw or stir-fried until just hot, bean sprouts give a flavorful crunch that is light and slightly sweet. Available fresh in most grocery stores, bean sprouts fill out a dish when there is nothing to be gained by adding a more flavorful ingredient.

What bean sprouts do to food	Add filler without changing the taste of the recipe
Substitutions	Celery strips
Price range	$ .97–$1.59 per pound

Bell peppers

Sold in red, green, yellow and orange varieties, bell peppers are the big, non-explosive pepper available in most grocery stores. The flavors vary, but the prices keep you to one color—green. Although red, yellow and orange peppers are sweeter and look nicer, they tend to be almost four times the price of green. Due to price and versatility, the green pepper is the best supporting vegetable nominee for BCYSAD.

What bell peppers do to food	Fill out a recipe for very little money; adds a nice touch of color and a great texture
Substitutions	Onion, although bell pepper is much better for you
Price range	$ .25–$ .65 a piece, green $ .75–$2.00 apiece, red, yellow and orange

Broccoli

George Bush Sr. didn't like broccoli. But what the hell did he know? He only lasted four years and broccoli has been popular a lot longer. Broccoli can be used easily as a main ingredient, and for about $1 for a bunch (roughly 1-2 pounds of the stuff) it will fill you up and give you energy. The florets hold sauce like no other vegetable, and the taste goes as well with seafood as with beef, lamb or chicken. The tender florets are the sought-after part, but strip the stems of the tough sinewy covering, and you have an unbelievable taste—almost like a very crunchy cucumber.

What broccoli does to food	Fills out a meal and provides nutrition
Substitutions	Cauliflower, while not as nutritional as broccoli, is quite similar in its versatility (but usually more expensive)
Price range	$1.00–1.50 a bunch (about 1.5 pounds), fresh $ .88 per 1-pound bag, frozen

Cabbage

Hard as a rock and almost as tasty, cabbage is a good filler vegetable that functions as a digestive aid as well. The roughage from cabbage is legendary. It is also dense, so you'll have a hard time eating a great deal of it, making it probably the most filling vegetable in the grocery store. It is cheap and quite versatile. Even though cooked cabbage is quite popular in most parts of the world, cooking does little to help its taste. Red or green, we use it in salads and serve it raw for most of our recipes.

What cabbage does to food	Adds a tasty filler
Substitutions	Lettuce in cold recipes; spinach in hot ones
Price range	$4.00 a head for green cabbage $ .77 a head for red cabbage

Cauliflower

Cauliflower, like broccoli, can also be used easily as a main ingredient. Also like broccoli, the florets hold sauce quite well and the taste goes as well with seafood as with beef, lamb or chicken. Cooked, however, it has a sweeter, creamier, more complex taste than broccoli.

What cauliflower does to food	Fills out food and acts easily as a main ingredient for vegetarian dishes
Substitutions	Broccoli usually works as well for less money
Price range	$1.97 a head (about 2.5 pounds), fresh $1.19 per bag, frozen

Carrots

Unlike a lot of vegetables, carrots absorb more taste than they add. Sauces are lost on shredded carrots. For the most part, carrots provide color and give something more to chew on, but you'll find most of the recipes in *Brother, Can You Spare A Dime?* use carrots sparingly. Nevertheless, they are cheap and plentiful.

What carrots do to food	Add another texture and fill out a meal
Substitutions	Celery—does the same without the greediness of the carrot
Price range	43¢–75¢ a pound, fresh

Corn

Corn adds a sweet, chewy taste to meals, adding volume for not a lot more money. It gives you a nice splash of color, and few people dislike corn.

What corn does to food	Adds another texture and fills out a meal
Substitutions	Peas can be used with about the same result — except kids will eat corn a lot quicker than peas
Price range	10¢–50¢ an ear, fresh 42¢ for a 15.25-ounce can 88¢ a one-pound bag, frozen

Cucumber

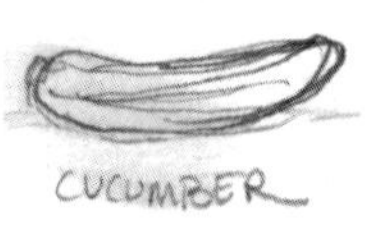

Cool as a cucumber? This veggie gives us the icy cool that no other vegetable has. It is seldom cooked, because when drained of its natural water, it becomes tasteless and limp, no more appetizing than an old piece of soggy bread. But in salads, it gives a taste that's hard to ignore.

What cucumbers do to food	Add to volume and take nothing away from the original flavor
Substitutions	Green apples can pass if used in a salad
Price range	25¢–67¢ each, fresh

Eggplant

With a taste that's a cross between zucchini and mushroom, eggplant cooked correctly has a taste and a feel like no other vegetable. But poorly prepared eggplant is no more appetizing than shoe rubber.

Eggplant tends to be fairly expensive and loses its size once cooked, so you'll need to be careful if you experiment. Cooked right—with olive oil and a few subtle spices—eggplant makes a great vegetarian dish. That's if you're still trying to be politically correct with less than two bucks in your pocket.

What eggplant does to food	Fills it out, can be used on its own and is very versatile
Substitutions	Cored zucchini can be used in a pinch
Price range	$1.27-$2.15 each; typical size is about a pound

Green Onions

As one of the cheapest vegetables in the supermarket, you'll find nearly half the recipes in this book use green onions. And no wonder—they fill out a dish, add color and give a nice flavor that yellow onions can't. You can do green onions the American way and toss out anything above the white part of the stalk, or turn Japanese and use the entire thing (less about three inches of the top). Either way, they add a nice savory taste to any recipe.

What green onions do to food	Give the onion flavor without the heaviness of the yellow or white onion
Substitutions	They're so cheap, why bother?
Price range	25¢–60¢, but usually closer to 25¢ a bunch year round

Green Beans

Fresh, frozen or canned, green beans are a great main ingredient for any vegetarian. Or use them as a filler to meat, chicken or fish dishes. Unless you're cooking them *al dente* (so they're flash cooked and hot on the outside, but crunchy inside), canned and frozen beans are just as good and a lot cheaper—plus, you won't have to clean them. They hold sauces well, so you can add them at the beginning of the cooking cycle without worrying about them soaking up all the liquid.

Green Beans

What green beans do to food	Fill out meat dishes or make a great main ingredient
Substitutions	Snow peas if no green beans available (snow peas will be more expensive, though)
Price range	$1.27 to $1.99 per pound, fresh $ .42 for a 14.5-ounce can $ .78 for a 1-pound bag of frozen green beans

Green Peas

Sweet peas, stripped of their pods and sprinkled through a dish, are a typical American veggie. They sweeten and add color—in addition to adding nutrition. You can buy them fresh, but if you cook them anyway, why bother? They're cheaper and usually as good canned or frozen.

What green peas do to food	Add volume and taste, giving a sweetness that is almost fruit-like
Substitutions	Garbanzos, although different in taste, fill out a recipe as well, adding a similar sweetness
Price range	$1.67 to $2.80 for 2-pound frozen bag $ .50–$ .90 for a 15-ounce can

Lettuce—Iceberg, Red-Leaf, Boston and Romaine

Crunchy but mostly tasteless, lettuce is a good fluff vegetable. Prized in most cold salads, it doesn't do much in the taste department except act as a vessel for dressings and additives. The differences in the types of lettuce lie in the way they feel or crunch as opposed to how they taste—although they do, in fact, taste slightly different. Iceberg lettuce is the round head lettuce that is most common. It is the coolest and the crunchiest throughout, yet it is also the blandest. Romaine is the one that looks most similar to spinach and is essential to a good Caesar salad. And Red Leaf, also known as butter lettuce, tastes the way it sounds, buttery and thin.

Lettuce

What lettuce does to food	Adds filler and crunch
Substitutions	Spinach, kale, mustard greens or any other leafy green (but for a veggie that doesn't have a flavor, stick to lettuce)
Price range	$ .67 for iceberg lettuce $1.98 for Romaine Average price $1.00 for either

Mushrooms

Depending on the mushroom, these creatures of the dark and damp will add either volume or taste (or both). All supermarkets will carry white mushrooms—the popular American variety that run about $2.00 a pound. Like most mushrooms, they are slightly buttery in flavor and act as sponges in most meals, soaking up the moisture and adding some of their own flavor.

Although canned mushrooms have a different (slightly mediciney) taste than real mushrooms, there are some advantages when using them. They are typically soaked in water, so tend not to shrink. That means you don't have to constantly figure out how much the meal will contract. They're also cheaper than real mushrooms. Just know that they're not as flavorful as fresh mushrooms and should only be used if budget or supply is a genuine problem.

The other types of mushrooms sold (the ones used in this cookbook at any rate) are porcini, portobello and shiitake, all available in specialty markets and, in the case of shiitake, at Asian markets. Porcini and portobello have a thick, smoky taste and are much bigger and meatier than most mushrooms. Since they're Italian, you'll find them mostly in Italian dishes. Shiitake is more delicate in flavor, but also has the buttery, smoky taste. By the way, psilocybin is not a part of *any* food group, so forget it.

What mushrooms do to food	Add volume and taste
Substitutions	Dried mushrooms, like white or Chinese dried mushrooms, or use canned mushrooms
Price range	$ .78–$1.98 for a 12-ounce pre-packaged, plastic-wrapped carton $ .50 for a 4-ounce can of mushroom pieces

Onions

Since at least 75% of all recipes in this book are made using onions, it is fitting that there be a few paragraphs about BCYSAD's mascot ingredient, the onion.

First and foremost, onions are cheap—which is why they are our favorite ingredient. They also have a very capable and strong flavor, which can vary from subservient to dominant, depending on how you use them.

Onions, with their pungent taste and sharp bite, can easily overpower. Dry them and they become sweet and tangy.

Onions can be fillers or they can be the key ingredient. The more they are cooked, the more tender and mild-flavored they become. You want more onion taste, throw them in at the end of the cooking process. For just a milder taste, start cooking with them.

ONION

Yellow onions are the harshest, then red, and then white. You also have green onions and bulb onions, which are lighter still.

Onions are cheap and can be found in any grocery store with any kind of produce department.

What onions do to food	Give a pungent, savory taste to foods; also add some sweetness
Substitutions	No suitable substitutes
Price range	19¢–67¢ a pound, for red, white or yellow onions, depending on the supply and the store 38¢–89¢ a pound for white and red onions

Potatoes

The great tuber, potatoes are about as versatile and life-sustaining a food as can be found on this earth (besides, of course, ramen noodles). In fact, if it weren't for ramen and the sauce that comes with it, the potato would be the ten-cent ingredient of choice.

The potato is cheap at about 25¢ a pound. It has loads of carbohydrates, which will give you energy for prolonged work. Now, as in past cultures, the potato is a filler ingredient. Put it in a dish to gain volume. Or put it in to soak up some of the sauce without adding anything of its own except some starch.

Potatoes

What potatoes do to food	Add volume and carbohydrates at a very popular price
Substitutions	Ramen noodles
Price range	$3.00 for a 25-pound bag, on sale $2.49 for a 10-pound bag* *New potatoes are more than double that amount

Radish

The heart of a radish tastes both cool and spicy-sharp at the same time. It can be used as a filler, or it can help shape the food's flavor by giving it a slight bite. Sold in bunches, radishes add a lot for not a lot of money. If the sharpness bothers you, reduce the amount. By the way, try not to use radishes for a date; radishes make you belch out something that smells like burnt plastic.

Radish

What radishes do to food	Give it a slightly spicy taste, but also make it cool and fresh
Substitutions	Celery—gives the same fresh cool taste without the spice
Price range	50¢–89¢ for pre-packaged 6-ounce bags or fresh bunches

Snow Peas

Used frequently in Chinese dishes, snow peas are tender and tasty and can be used as a main ingredient. They are best when stir-fried so they still crunch, but they can also be served boiled—although with far less appetizing results. They do not soak up sauces, so are really just an accessory to the sauces. Unfortunately, they tend to be expensive. We suggest you reduce the amount the recipe calls for and substitute the rest with either onion or celery or both.

What snow peas do to food	Add a fresh vegetable taste that doesn't overpower the meal
Substitutions	Either reduce the amount and add celery or onion pieces instead
Price range	$1.98–$3.48 per pound (less at an Asian grocery)

Tomatillos

Not just underdeveloped red tomatoes, these small green tomatoes (which come fresh and still wrapped in their natural papery, dry skin) are much more flavorful, but not nearly as sweet as red tomatoes. In most green hot sauces, tomatillos are the main ingredient. They're good raw, imparting a lemony tang to salads; or they can be cooked with some chicken stock and puréed jalapeno to make a great hot sauce.

What tomatillos do to food	Fill dishes out, giving a slightly lemony taste
Substitutions	No good substitutes
Price range	$1.25–$2.15 a pound ($1.98 is common)

Tomatoes

Tomatoes, the staple of Italian and Mexican cooking, do pretty much everything. You want to create a sauce, start with a tomato. Tomatoes add a tang and a sweetness that hold many different spices. Add basil, onion, fennel, garlic and olive oil, and you have one of the great recipes of the ages.

Tomatoes are used in many of dishes in this book and are a basic ingredient for a lot of cultures in the world. Yet the tomato doesn't seem to have been harvested or grown in any significantly cheaper form in the last three decades. So in a lot of cases, you'll see that we've substituted canned tomatoes or tomato sauce for fresh.

What tomatoes do to food	Create a liquid structure that can be used as a base for other spices; bind food and give flavor
Substitutions	Fresh tomatoes are nice, but if there aren't any good ones, use canned
Price range	$ .69–$1.29, fresh (more at specialty stores) 78¢ for a 28-ounce can of crushed 50¢ for a 14.5-ounce can of diced

Sun-dried Tomatoes

Although made from regular tomatoes, sun-dried tomatoes have a completely different taste than fresh. The drying makes them sweeter yet tangy at the same time. And once dried, the tomatoes also develop a completely different texture, almost like dried beef jerky. Thus, a few sun-dried tomatoes can change the way your food tastes, providing small flavor bits as you discover them mixed in with your meal.

What sun-dried tomatoes do to food	Give a chewy tangy flavor when sprinkled into food
Substitutions	No suitable substitutes
Price range	$6.00 a pound for dried $8.00 a pound for tomatoes soaked in olive oil

Spinach

Popeye could have picked broccoli, but he didn't. He picked the leafy, dark green, rich, flavorful spinach plant. Full of iron and the epitome of a vegetable, spinach finds itself a main ingredient in a lot of salads nowadays. We think it really tastes better raw than cooked, but you can use it any way you like. In a lot of parts of the country, finding a good bunch of fresh spinach is tougher than finding a rap song you can whistle. If you can't find it in top shape for a salad, omit it. For cooked dishes, you'll do fine with frozen or canned spinach.

What spinach does to food	Adds a nice green, leafy texture and fills out a meal
Substitutions	Kale and Swiss chard
Price range	69¢–98¢ a bunch, fresh 88¢ for a 1-pound bag, frozen 60¢ for a 15.5-ounce can

Watercress

Watercress, sold fresh only, adds a slightly tangy, peppery, almost basil-like taste to salads. It is eaten raw, providing a cool sensation similar to cilantro without the aromatic aftertaste. It's kind of highbrow, so if you're trying to impress somebody, use it. Better yet, say you used it and try cilantro or parsley instead.

What watercress does to food	Adds a peppery-cool tang to salads
Substitutions	Basil is okay, but is almost overpowering and is far more expensive than watercress
Price range	39¢–89¢ per bunch

Water chestnuts

Water chestnuts have a benign or subtly soapy flavor, but do more for the texture of a dish than for the flavor. Whether precooked, stewed or cold, they remain crunchy while chewing a forkful of ramen. They chew like pieces of apple and help with the volume of a meal. They are not cheap, but will work in a lot of BCYSAD recipes without breaking $2. Don't look for them in the produce section; look for them canned in the international aisle or in an Asian supermarket.

What water chestnuts do to food	Give food a chewy crunch
Substitutions	Green apple, in a pinch—or better yet, use celery. It has the same essential feeling in the palate and the taste is also benign, just along for the ride, so to speak.
Price range	From 87¢ for a 5-ounce can

Yams

Yams are mostly seasonal food. They don't appear at the table unless it's a holiday—although they are grown year round and sold canned, too. Fresh yams—or sweet potatoes—add a nice filler-type quality to foods and provide complex carbs for energy. They are relatively cheap and easy to get even during months other than November and December.

Yams

What yams do to food	Add a starch and filler to most recipes
Substitutions	Regular potatoes with brown sugar will do fine
Price range	25¢ a pound during Thanksgiving $ .55–$1.10 a pound during off-season

Zucchini/Squash

Zucchini and squash have a natural sweetness and do well in dishes that need a sweet vegetable flavor. Squash is definitely sweeter, and therefore, more of an oddity. As a red-blooded American, you probably tend to like your sweet things at dessert, not during dinner. But either or both give a filling and nutritional base to a good meal.

Zucchini

What zucchini/squash does to food	Adds filler and some sweetness
Substitutions	Eggplant works okay, but is more expensive Try well-cooked sweet potatoes
Price range	77¢ a pound, butternut squash 20¢–25¢ each (or up to $1.00 a pound), zucchini (double that in an expensive store)

Chapter 4

SPICES, SAUCES AND OTHER FLAVORS

Anise

Anise, a licorice tasting herb, adds a complex, heady taste to your food—kind of like adding cough syrup to a main course. It gives a subtle, almost-menthol aftertaste that adds not just a different taste to food, but a different quality. Anise has been used for thousands of years, as a flavoring, breath sweetener, digestive aid and cough suppressant.

What anise does to food	Gives a licorice or camphor-like aftertaste
Substitutions	Fennel (good, but slightly milder) and a number of licorice flavorings* *In a pinch, you can use mint, which gives the same type of complex, heady aftertaste, but which tastes entirely different
Price range	$4.77 for a 1.25-ounce spice jar
Freebies (*)	No

Balsamic Vinegar

Balsamic vinegar is made by aging high-quality red wine vinegar in barrels. The result is a hearty vinegar that bites less and tends toward sweet. Once quite expensive, far more varieties now exist and many are really quite cheap—but still usually 2–3 times more than distilled or cider vinegar. Balsamic vinegar is a common ingredient not just in salads and cold pastas, but also in Italian cooking.

What balsamic vinegar does to food	Gives foods a nice warm tang that is not as harsh as most distilled or red wine vinegars
Substitutions	Mix regular vinegar, brown sugar and salt. For one cup, mix 7 ounces of distilled vinegar, one tablespoon brown sugar, with a ½ teaspoon of salt (or use half of a beef ramen flavor packet).
Price range	$1.70 for a 12-ounce bottle; typically, $2.75 for a pint
Freebies (*)	No

Barbecue Sauce

Barbecue sauce provides a sweet tang that mixes well with meat. Sauces range in taste from smoky-sour to honey-sweet and from 75¢ to $8 a bottle, depending on the brand. For the purposes of this book, cheaper is better. Free is best.

What barbecue sauce does to food	Sweetens and gives a unique hearty tang (depending on the brand)
Substitutions	Ketchup with some honey, pepper, vinegar and garlic or onion powder added
Price range	$ .79 to $4.99 for a 16-ounce bottle
Freebies (*)	Yes (check any fast food place that serves chicken strips or barbecue beef)

Basil

Fresh basil is a fleshy, sweet, green plant that is both sweet and tangy at once, and delicate in flavor in either case. When blended, the juices come out quickly, and it can be overpowering—as in pesto. Fresh basil goes very well with tomatoes and can stand alone in almost any chicken or fish dish. It is also good with bouquets and garnishes. When dried, basil leaves change flavor dramatically. Gone are the subtle tang and sweetness, and instead what remains is more of a dried oregano-like woodiness. For pesto and dishes that whine for a dominant basil taste, use fresh. For a hint of basil, use dried.

What basil does to food	Gives a unique, tangy, lemony flavor if fresh; gives a warm woody flavor if dried.
Substitutions	No substitute for fresh For dried, use Italian spice or oregano
Price range	$2.48 or more for about a cup's worth of fresh 50¢ for a 2.25-ounce cheapy spice jar of dried $2.86 for a nice spice jar of expensive dried stuff
Freebies (*)	No

Bay Leaf

Bay is a pungent, slightly bitter flavor that steeps in soups, casseroles, stews, fish and marinades. It gives off an oil that mixes with food to give it personality. You'll typically find bay leaves whole—that's how you will see them listed as ingredients in this cookbook—and usually you'll be asked to add 1 or 2 whole bay leaves to a dish, removing them when the dish is ready to be served. Unlike something like anise, fennel, chili or ginger, bay leaves are not as complex and can be dropped much easier from the recipe.

BAY LEAF

What bay leaf does to food	Adds a pungent, slightly bitter savory flavor
Substitutions	Slightly similar to rosemary, but use only a very small bit of rosemary in the place of bay leaf—rosemary is stronger and can easily overpower
Price range	$2.48 for a cup of fresh Up to $4.98 for dried leaves
Freebies (*)	No

Bean Sauce/Bean Paste

Bean sauce, also called bean paste, is a sweet paste that's available in jars in Asian markets—or at larger grocery stores. It adds a base flavor that tastes like sweet soy sauce. The two types that are most available are yellow bean and black bean. Yellow is sweeter than the black, but either can be used.

What bean sauce does to food	Imparts a cream-like sweet carbohydrate base to foods
Substitutions	Mix a few tablespoons of water-thinned refried beans, sugar, garlic and either cayenne or crushed red chilies, with chicken ramen flavoring to taste
Price range	From $1.79 for a 13-ounce jar
Freebies (*)	No

Black Pepper

Pepper is, oddly, the only spice (salt is not a spice) found on the table of the average American family. It is so commonly considered a regular additive to food that most people don't even consider it a real ingredient. In fact, in many recipes here, it is listed "to taste," almost meaning "use it if you want."

But pepper is a fantastic spice. In a white sauce, the correct amount of pepper will make or break the sauce. In a cheese sauce, it brings out the flavor. Without salt, it isn't as powerful, but add a little salt, some garlic or some sugar and black pepper comes to the front. In larger proportions, pepper is as hot as chili.

For the most part, it is readily available. And that is important here. It means you can usually find black pepper free somewhere. Use it for your own recipes by picking up extra pepper at a restaurant and taking it home.

What pepper does to food	Adds a subtle-hot earthy flavor
Substitutions	None
Price range	As cheap as 50¢ for a 4-ounce spice jar to $3.48 for 1.87 ounces
Freebies (*)	Yes—everywhere to-go food is served

Capers

Capers are small, roundish olive-green vegetables that resemble juniper berries. They are, in fact, the pickled, unopened flower buds of the caper plant. They remind you of herb-flavored lemon pieces with a slightly bitter aftertaste. Native to the Mediterranean, most dishes in this cookbook using capers are also Mediterranean. Capers make a good addition to salads and can kick butt in any chicken or fish dish.

What capers do to food	Give a unique texture and appetizing sour-bitter combination
Substitutions	Although difficult to substitute because of size, texture and flavor, you can use green olive pieces or diced green pickle in a pinch
Price range	$1.29 to $2.59 for a 4-ounce jar
Freebies (*)	No

Caraway Seeds

Caraway seeds (the seeds you find in rye bread) are sharp and slightly peppery with a slight anise aftertaste. They are seldom ground, but used as a visible, almost garnish-like ingredient. Although they are more difficult to eliminate than a lot of other spices, they are not a dominant flavor, but more of a layer of flavoring. They can usually be left out without disrupting the overall experience of the food.

What caraway seeds do to food	Add a slightly peppery, aromatic flavor
Substitutions	Very little has the peppery taste of caraway. You can use cumin seeds if nothing else is around. They will be a similar texture and feel, but the taste will change.
Price range	$3.78 for 1.75 ounces
Freebies (*)	No

Cardamom

Cardamom, a seed and seedpod that are ground into a powder, has a smoky, aromatic flavor. Grown and used mainly in India, cardamom has a 4,000-year history. It is used mostly in Indian dishes (go figure) and is a staple of curries. In this cookbook, you'll find it only in Indian dishes adapted to the ramen noodle.

What cardamom does to food	Gives a heady aromatic flavor
Substitutions	None
Price range	$1.99 for 1.75 ounces
Freebies (*)	No

Cayenne Pepper

Dried ground cayenne, like most dried chili, has little aroma. In fact, other than the heat, all that lets you know cayenne is in the dish is a slightly bitter aftertaste. But add a teaspoon and you'll definitely know it's there. A fiery spice that instantly adds chili-heat to any food, cayenne is great for quick fixes. You screw up, add some cayenne. It'll still be screwed up, but it will be so hot nobody will know. If you're out of crushed red pepper or jalapeno or whatever fresh chili you're using, try a pinch of cayenne. Or sprinkle on top of a finished meal to add some pain to it.

What cayenne pepper does to food	Burns the tongue and makes you forget every other flavor
Substitutions	Crushed dried red chilies are actually better and easier to control in terms of heat, so you should use them first anyway
Price range	As low as 50¢ for a 2-ounce spice jar
Freebies (*)	No

CHEESE

Cheese

Cheese is a binding agent, a flavor enhancer and has enough of a presence to be a main ingredient in most cases. It tends to be more expensive than most meat and therefore, must be thought of in this cookbook as a flavor more than a main ingredient. Cheese is made of milk (either cows', sheep's or goats') and carries a good amount of fat within it. If you want a low-fat, inexpensive diet, the simple answer is to eliminate cheese.

But since it's so rich and since it adds so much to foods, it's more appropriate to reduce the amount and still leave it in. But what cheeses add the most flavor, and what do they cost? Read on, milk breath.

Parmesan Cheese

This is the most prolific cheese in this cookbook, mostly because a little cheese goes a long way and also because you can find it free in a lot of places. Parmesan is inexpensive in dry form and can be purchased grated for less than a lot of other more common cheeses. It has a sharp flavor and can easily overpower the other tastes in the recipe, so be careful how much you use. It is without a doubt, the strongest cheese in this cookbook. And because of that, a little goes a long way.

What Parmesan does to food	Enhances the flavor of food
Substitutions	Dry packaged Parmesan or use Romano cheese
Price range	$2.27–$3.67 for an 8-ounce shaker can $2.50 and higher for fresh 5-ounce wedge
Freebies (*)	Yes—try a pizza place

Romano Cheese

Same basic taste as Parmesan, but plays second fiddle to Parmesan. It's also available dried and grated but can easily be substituted with Parmesan.

What Romano does to food	Enhances the flavor of food
Substitutions	Dry packaged Romano or use Parmesan cheese
Price range	$2.27–$3.67 for an 8-ounce shaker can $2.50 and higher for 5-ounces fresh
Freebies (*)	Yes—try a pizza place

Cheddar Cheese

Cheddar cheese is an American specialty, which tends to run as the cheapest cheese in the dairy case at around $3 a pound. In that respect, your money is better spent on meat rather than cheese. The problem with Cheddar is that, even with extra sharp Cheddar, you still don't really have a good taste of the cheese, just the bulk and the binding agent. For the most part, you'd do better by using Parmesan—and using a lot less of it.

What Cheddar does to food	Enhances the flavor of food; binds food
Substitutions	Reduce the amount and use dried Parmesan
Price range	$2.99–$4.99 for fresh
Freebies (*)	No

American Cheese

Okay, let's face it, American cheese is highly processed and always looks, compared to other more natural cheeses, as if it's created from some kind of plastic-composite material. But American cheese is nice to work with because it melts easily and evenly. Other than that, it is not the most flavorful of cheeses and tends to be expensive. If you need to use it, use the real cheese (not the individually wrapped "cheese foods" available).

What American does to food	Enhances the flavor of food
Substitutions	Reduce the amount and use dried Parmesan
Price range	$2.99–$4.99 for a pound of sliced or a 2-pound box of Velveeta, or another suitable American cheese loaf
Freebies (*)	No

Monterey Jack Cheese

Like Cheddar, Monterey jack runs around $3 a pound. Again, your money is better spent on meat rather than cheese. But where Cheddar gives a very mild taste, Monterey jack is even milder and mainly acts to affect the way the meal sticks together. For the most part, you'd do better by using Parmesan—and using a lot less of it.

What Monterey jack does to food	Enhances the flavor of food; binds food
Substitutions	Reduce the amount and use dried Parmesan
Price range	$2.99–$4.99
Freebies (*)	No

Muenster Cheese

Again, like Cheddar, Muenster has a slightly sharper taste than Monterey jack. It's less sharp than sharp Cheddar and goes for more than $5 a pound. Your money is better spent on meat. Use dry shredded Parmesan.

What Muenster does to food	Enhances the flavor of food; binds food
Substitutions	Reduce the amount and use dried Parmesan
Price range	$3.99–$5.99
Freebies (*)	No

Swiss Cheese

Swiss cheese gives you a flavor different from Cheddar and different, in fact, from Parmesan. It is sharper than Cheddar (less sharp than Parmesan) but much creamier and richer than both, making it more difficult to eliminate than the other cheeses. Nevertheless, it can be substituted by using Cheddar and Parmesan together.

What Swiss does to food	Enhances the flavor of food; binds food
Substitutions	Reduce the amount and use dried Parmesan
Price range	$3.99–$5.99
Freebies (*)	No

Feta Cheese

This sharp goats' milk cheese is nice in that it takes a very little to make the flavor come out. It is very sharp and as expensive as fresh Parmesan—usually about $6–$8 a pound. But for just a few cents, you can give food a unique flavor. Crumble a few tablespoons of the cheese over the mixed food, and you have something very unique.

What feta does to food	Enhances the flavor of food
Substitutions	None
Price range	$1.78 for a 4-ounce package of crumbled feta, enough for 6–10 dishes
Freebies (*)	No

Blue Cheese

No feta available? Try Blue cheese. It tastes different, but with its moldy ash flavoring, this sharp cheese also can flavor a dish for only pennies. Crumble the cheese over the mixed food. Use blue cheese dressing as an alternative to real cheese.

What blue cheese does to food	Enhances the flavor of food
Substitutions	Blue cheese salad dressing
Price range	$1.78 for a 4-ounce package of crumbled blue $3.99 for a pound of fresh Danish blue cheese
Freebies (*)	No, but fast food places offer blue cheese dressings

Ricotta and Cottage Cheese

Both Ricotta and cottage cheese provide a creamy, slightly tangy taste to cooked foods and casseroles. Baked, they create a firm not-quite-cheesy taste that is lighter than aged cheeses. Ricotta is saltier and has more taste, but is also quite a bit more expensive than cottage cheese.

What ricotta and cottage cheese do to food	Enhance the flavor of food
Substitutions	None
Price range	$2.29 for a 15-ounce container of ricotta $1.59 for a 12.6-ounce container of cottage
Freebies (*)	No

Chili

Chili is a bad-ass spice that starts life, oddly enough, as a fruit. For recipes here, we use it mostly as ground red chili peppers, as chili powder, as chili oil, as canned or pickled chili and as fresh. And there are hundreds of types of chilies—from the paint-peeling habanero to stomach-rotting jalapeno and tear-jerking serrano—all of which taste different, but with the same characteristic of the heat.

In general, the chili adds the dominant characteristic of the dish. Whether it's cayenne or dried crushed red, it will not actually drive the taste, but the sensation. In other words, when you feel your cheeks melt into your gums, when your mucus membranes begin bleeding, when you can't see through the tears, you've added quite enough, thanks.

The heat you feel in your mouth comes from the chili. That heat does something more than make your eyes water and your sphincter burn. It creates another layer of complexity to the taste. If you hate the heat, use something milder. Red bell pepper has a bit of a bite, but doesn't sting. Only problem is that it is expensive. Really, the best way to do this is—if you don't like the heat, just omit the chili.

Also, and this is important, so listen up—it changes your appetite. Therefore, you'll typically need less hot food to fill you up. Chili also eliminates the need for other flavor enhancers. If you're on a low-sodium diet, a bit of chili with some garlic or onion will give you more than enough taste without the salt.

Chili is an essential ingredient of Mexican food, Thai food, some Chinese food and Indian curry. Other chilies include paprika, pimento, sweet pepper, red pepper and cayenne pepper. And the general view in Mexico is that if you take out the seeds the chili will have less impact on your poor tongue. And if you use the flat of your hand to roll it firmly, pressing down on the whole raw chili, on a flat counter or table top, you'll release the oils, and together with the seeds you'll have a more potent chili on your hands (literally).

By the way, you'll need to be careful when handling raw chilies. If you're cutting them by hand and have the urge to scratch your eyes, you'll be like putting chemicals in them. You'll literally be in pain for 30 minutes or more (... and you don't want to know what happens if you forget to wash your hands before going to the bathroom). Watch out.

What chili does to food	Heats it up!
Substitutions	Red bell pepper
Price range	$ .49–$2.59 (use the cheap stuff; it's basically the same)
Freebies (*)	Use crushed red chili pepper from a pizza place in a pinch

Chili Powder

Chili powder is the fine powder of relatively mild red chili. It has an earthy, tomato-ey taste that also packs some heat. It is the main ingredient in the dish called chili. Chili powder is inexpensive these days, running as little as 50¢ for a 2.9-ounce spice jar. Use it mostly in Mexican and Southwestern dishes.

What chili powder does to food	Provides spicy heat that flavors food
Substitutions	Use either paprika or cayenne or both in place of chili powder (use a lot less cayenne!)
Price range	$ .50 for a 2.9-ounce spice jar to $3.48 for a 2.12-ounce spice jar
Freebies (*)	No

Cilantro

Cilantro produces the qualifying smell that tells if you're eating authentic Mexican food. It is pungent and aromatic, yet very flavorful and cooling to the palate at the same time. It counteracts the heat of the chilies and binds all the flavors in a nice juicy manner. Cilantro is also very cheap—and now available in just about every large grocery store (and some small ones). Biggest problem with cilantro is that it doesn't keep for more than a couple of days. Use it immediately, or lose it. And that goes for finished foods. If it's in the dish when it goes into the refrigerator, it should be eaten pretty quickly afterward.

What cilantro does to food	Imparts a pungent, aromatic cooling taste to food
Substitutions	None suitable
Price range	25¢–40¢ a bunch (which yields about 1½ cup)
Freebies (*)	No

Cinnamon

Not just for your buttered, sugared toast. Cinnamon interacts well with other tastes. By itself, cinnamon has a sharp and slightly peppery taste. Ground cinnamon enhances many curries and meat stews. Primarily known in the U.S. as a spice that goes with sweet dishes like cakes, breads, fruity desserts and hot drinks—and, okay, your buttered, sugared toast—most of the uses for cinnamon in this cookbook will be for sweeter dishes. But don't be surprised if you find it in other places, since it is a good complement to other flavors.

What cinnamon does to food	Provides an exotic base taste to savory foods and a familiar, earthy taste to sweet dishes
Substitutions	Clove will work in a pinch. Although it tastes different, it will still give you that spice-island taste you seek.
Price range	50¢ at a discount store $3.57 for 1.87 ounces at an upscale supermarket
Freebies (*)	No

Cloves

Cloves are the small dried, unopened flower buds of a Southeast Asian myrtle tree. The taste is what's known in candy as a "red hot cinnamon" taste. It's not the same taste as cinnamon, however. It's clove. In the US, cloves are used mostly in desserts. But in fact cloves, because of the intense flavor, are also good in complex curries and sauces.

What cloves do to food	Gives an aromatic, nutty taste
Substitutions	Use cinnamon in a pinch (yes, we just said it's not the same, but nothing else is anything near the taste of clove)
Price range	$6.96 for 1.1 ounces of dried whole cloves
Freebies (*)	No

Coconut Milk

Available in canned form, coconut milk is a staple of Thai and Indonesian food and is completely peerless in the taste department. It is both cool and creamy at the same time, adding its own salt and sweetener concurrently. If you've had Thai food and wondered how they got it to taste that way, the secret is coconut milk. It's sold in most grocery stores (although you'll have to look for it). By the way, look for the creamy coconut milk in the Asian foods aisle, not the Hispanic coconut milk (which is too watery).

What coconut milk does to food	Gives food a sweet, salty, creamy flavor
Substitutions	Use fresh coconut milk, or better yet, buy a bag of flaked, sweet baking coconut and soak a few teaspoons a day before using, then dump it all in—including the shredded coconut
Price range	$1.48 for a 14-ounce can
Freebies (*)	No

Coriander

Coriander is the dried fruit of cilantro, but tastes completely different from cilantro. Where cilantro is parsley-like, with a tangy pungent flavor that seems to make your taste buds open up, coriander is a smoky, musky flavor that adds a heavy layer of taste to foods. If you drink Earl Gray tea, most of what you like is the taste of coriander. For this book, coriander is used almost exclusively in Indian dishes.

What coriander does to food	Gives an earthy, smoky flavor
Substitutions	No suitable substances, but you might try tearing open a bag of Earl Gray ... (at your own risk; we've never tried it)
Price range	$2.76 for 1.1 ounces
Freebies (*)	No

Cornstarch

Cornstarch is the Chinese secret to a good sauce. It thickens cooked liquids and becomes a clear glaze once mixed in a hot saucepan. Amateur cooks add cornstarch to the pan with a teaspoon—and they get unappetizing lumps. The way to add the white powder is to first mix it with an equal amount of cool water in a separate glass or cup, then add the mixed liquid to the saucepan. It will prevent lumping and make you look like a superstar in the kitchen.

What cornstarch does to food	Binds, thickens and glazes
Substitutions	Use flour, but not too much because it adds an earthy taste you don't want
Price range	$ .67–$1.24 for a 16-ounce box
Freebies (*)	No

Cream

Cream does what it advertises—it adds a creamy base to foods, a base hard to duplicate with any non-dairy ingredient. Its main asset is its fat level, which serves not just to make food smoother and oilier, but also binds, creating thick, rich sauces. Alas, cream is expensive—around $1 cup. And because of that, you'll have to improvise. Use milk, sour cream or yogurt and flour for something similar. Or find it free. Almost any place that serves coffee will have the small sealed cream packages. Use them. But do not use non-dairy cream, which is made of gasoline or some such derivative and will screw up any dish you add it to.

What cream does to food	Binds and adds a very rich base to sauces and gravies
Substitutions	Milk and flour (just don't add too much flour or you'll make the food taste bland and dry)
Price range	$ .87–$1.55 for an 8-ounce carton
Freebies (*)	Yes—anywhere coffee is served (DO NOT USE NON-DAIRY CREAMERS!)

Cumin

The dried fruit of a small Mediterranean plant, cumin has a very unique taste. Although few recipes in this book call for cumin as the dominant ingredient, it always emerges as one of the strongest in the stew, to employ a corny metaphor. Cumin looks very similar to caraway (the seed in rye bread), but tastes quite different. It is far more musky or savory than caraway. It is mostly used in this cookbook as an Indian curry additive, but is also very popular in Mexican dishes. Once you have identified cumin—which is mostly used in this book in powdered form—you'll recognize it in a lot of dishes.

What cumin does to food	Gives food a musky, aromatic flavor
Substitutions	None
Price range	$3.28 for 1.5 ounces
Freebies (*)	No

Currants

Currants used here are basically dried wine grapes. For the difference in name, they cost a lot more and are more difficult to find. Like raisins, they add a chewy fruitiness to foods that is difficult to find in non-dried fruits. If you're having a hard time finding them, go ahead and use raisins.

What currants do to food	Add a complex flavor and texture to foods
Substitutions	Raisins or dried cranberries work just as well
Price range	$4.99 per pound
Freebies (*)	No

Dill

Dill is a tangy or sweet spice that comes from the parsley family. Because it has a flavor that tends to stand alone, it is often used as a main spice. With lemon, sugar or salt, you can bring the flavor of dill out so it encompasses the main ingredients and flavors them completely. Fish and chicken are especially good main courses for dill, since unlike beef, they have little natural flavor to begin with.

What dill does to food	Gives food an aromatic, almost sweet flavor
Substitutions	No really no great substitutes for dill, but you can try sage or oregano. Neither taste like dill, but both have the same sort of dominant, individual flavors that can go well with a lot of other ingredients.
Price range	$3.98 for a .5-ounce spice jar $2.48 for a pre-measured package of fresh (that yields about a cup)
Freebies (*)	No

Eggs

Unless used as a main dish, eggs are used to bind and stabilize foods. The cooked egg provides natural cement around which everything else sticks. You can't bake a cake without eggs, nor can you hold together a soufflé. If you want something to be more solid, add an egg. Separately, eggs are also great as a main ingredient, in omelets and fried or hardboiled. They are cheap—usually around $1 a dozen, and even most corner liquor stores have eggs.

What eggs do to food	Bind, stabilize and solidify food
Substitutions	None
Price range	7¢ each if bought in quantities of 2½ dozen
Freebies (*)	No

Fennel

Fennel, like anise, is a licorice-flavored spice that is used as an after-meal breath freshener in Indian restaurants. It is used frequently in Italian sauces and meat dishes to add a level of complexity and taste. Use it in tomato dishes or sauces and in sausages and Indian dishes to create diversity. Fennel is typically sold as the whole seed, and that's the way this cookbook calls for it—in whole-seed form.

What fennel does to food	Gives food a pleasant, understated licorice flavor
Substitutions	Use anise or licorice flavoring
Price range	$2.98 for 1.5 ounces
Freebies (*)	No

Fenugreek

Fenugreek is a dried spice that has a strong, pleasant and quite peculiar odor that some have described as a subtle maple flavor mixed with old socks. The good news is that it sounds grosser than it is, and there are only a couple of recipes in this book that call for it. Fenugreek is used in this cookbook in Indian recipes, adding yet another layer to the traditional Indian flavor complexity.

What fenugreek does to food	Adds complexity and a slightly savory-sweet flavor
Substitutions	None
Price range	$3–$6 for a 2-ounce spice jar
Freebies (*)	No

Five-Spice Powder

Five-Spice is another super-secret powder available through Asian stores. It's nothing more than a combination of fennel, star anise, clove, cinnamon and chili pepper. Different places sell it in different proportions—although it is supposed to be all the same. You can buy each spice individually, put them in a coffee grinder or food processor and grind them to as fine a powder as possible. Use anise seed if you have no star anise (which is less flavorful, but costs a lot less, too). Or just add the five spices to your food in proportion.

What five-spice powder does to food	Adds a complex base flavor
Substitutions	Make your own
Price range	$3.99 for a 1.5-ounce spice jar
Freebies (*)	No

Flour

Like cornstarch, flour thickens when cooked with liquid in a hot saucepan, so you can use it to thicken sauces and gravies. Unfortunately, it also clumps together like cornstarch. So instead of adding it to the pan with a teaspoon, first mix it with an equal amount of water in a separate glass or cup then add the mixed liquid to the saucepan. It will prevent lumping.

What flour does to food	Binds, thickens and glaze
Substitutions	Cornstarch is actually better than flour, but flour can be used in a pinch
Price range	$ .97–$1.30 for a five-pound bag
Freebies (*)	No

Garlic

Other than giving you breath that will melt tempered glass, garlic makes your dish. It adds so much flavor and taste to a bland ingredient that it becomes the ingredient itself. It is used as easily in vegetable, meat and poultry dishes as in noodle dishes (oh, yeah!) and marinades.

One medium-sized head weighs less than four ounces, and each head contains a dozen or so cloves. Oddly enough, the garlic bulb—or the cloves in the bunch—is almost odorless. But cut or bruised, the individual cloves produce a big stink. Drive through California's Salinas Valley (specifically Gilroy) during the late spring, and you'll think you've been dropped into a pot of Italian soup. Eat a big, garlicky meal at night, and the next morning you still smell like you swam in the stuff.

Unfortunately, it also overpowers in a lot of ways. It knocks out the more subtle flavors of, say, a cumin, caraway or a dill dish. But it is cheap, it is sweet—so it needs very little else to spice up a bowl of noodles—and it is healthy. You'll find it a large percentage of the meals in this cookbook. Just try to limit conversations to the phone after a big garlic-fest meal.

What garlic does to food	Hides flaws in the main ingredient; overpowers all other flavors
Substitutions	None—and you wouldn't want to try either
Price range	$1.78 to $2.45 per pound
Freebies (*)	No

Ginger

Put a slice of raw ginger in your mouth, and your taste buds will go from sweet to sour to bitter, with the odd sensation of licorice at the same time. Mostly, however, ginger runs sweet and earthy—and that's what you're using for flavor.

Ginger, a root, is considered in India and China as a fresh vegetable and a spice at the same time. It can be used sliced and cooked and added to most noodle dishes as a main vegetable. Or it can be chopped and added, like garlic, as an ingredient that typically characterizes the entire dish. Or, as you will find quite commonly in this cookbook, you can substitute dried ginger for fresh and use it as a spice. Although it will not be the same, it is closer than, say, using dried for fresh basil.

What ginger does to food	Adds a lemony tang along with an earthy savory flavor
Substitutions	None
Price range	$3.98 for 1.62 ounces
Freebies (*)	No

Herbes de Provence

Herbes de Provence—also known on the spice rack as "French Herbs," or in England as "Froggy Spice" (... okay, so we made that last part up)—is a spice that, in fact, is a combination of basil, fennel, lavender, marjoram, rosemary, savory, tarragon and thyme. They are mixed in a variety of proportions (mix to your own taste if making it yourself), but are concocted to be a great addition to roasts, from chicken to beef or pork. It tends to be expensive, so try to make your own (although you'll have trouble finding the lavender).

What Herbes de Provence do to food	Add a unique, heady taste to foods
Substitutions	Make your own, using proportions of whatever spices are available—basil, fennel, lavender, marjoram, rosemary, savory, tarragon or thyme
Price range	$4.29 for a 1-ounce spice jar
Freebies (*)	No

Hoisin Sauce

Hoisin sauce is another of the secret sauces you're supposed to buy prior to cooking any Asian meal, yet a substitute is very simple to make (see below). It tastes like a heavy, pasty soy sauce and adds a nice salty-sweet base flavor to meals. If you make your own, it may not be perfect, but, considering the different interpretations of hoisin sauce, it will be close enough.

What hoisin sauce does to food	Adds both concentrated salt and sweet
Substitutions	Take a jar of Gerber's (or any other brand) prune baby food and add one packet of beef ramen flavoring, 2 teaspoons of soy sauce, ½ teaspoon garlic powder, a tablespoon flour and some ginger. Bingo—you have hoisin sauce for about 40¢.
Price range	About $1.89 for a 15-ounce jar
Freebies (*)	No

Horseradish

Prepared horseradish has a hot, pungent, almost ammonia taste that clears out your sinuses and makes you wish you were dead. It comes from a plant in the mustard family, made by grinding the root and drying it in a controlled environment. It is commonly used as a condiment for roast beef, but finds its way into cocktail sauces and garnishes. Wasabe, the green sushi sauce, is a form of horseradish.

What horseradish does to food	Changes the way you taste food by heightening the taste buds
Substitutions	If no powdered horseradish is available, use large red radishes, which tend to have a similar yet far more benign taste

Price range	Typically between $ .87 and $1.44 for a 9-ounce jar
Freebies (*)	Yes—try any fast food restaurant that specializes in roast beef or that has roast beef sandwiches

Hot Sauce

Like barbecue sauces, hot sauces vary depending on the brand and ingredients. For the most part, you'll pick your favorite. And for the most part, you should be able to find some place that has your favorite flavor free. If not, just buy a cheap Louisiana hot sauce—usually sold for about 35¢ a bottle—and add your own spices to it. Careful how you use it, though.

What hot sauce does to food	Adds heat and some tang to food
Substitutions	Any hot sauce that suits you
Price range	$ .44–4.30 for a 6-ounce bottle
Freebies (*)	Yes. Most fast food restaurants have it. But if you want the best, go to Mexican fast food places.

Ketchup

Few recipes in this book have ketchup as an ingredient—although there is at least one where it is essential. The reason is simple—if you want something cheap, easy and that tasted like you threw it together, you could have thought of it yourself. You didn't need our help. Since tomato sauce is dirt cheap (about 20¢ an eight-ounce can), try to avoid ketchup if possible.

What ketchup does to food	Gives a sweet tomato flavor
Substitutions	Tomato sauce, which is a far better ingredient
Price range	From 78¢ for a 24-ounce bottle
Freebies (*)	Yes—everywhere take-out food is sold

Lemon

The juice of real lemon is one of the most versatile flavors you can use when cooking. It can make a dish tangy or sour, depending on the ingredients or how much sugar you use. It is a very pure sour sensation, unlike either vinegar or lime, which each add more respective flavor. Certainly you know how it tastes already.

What lemon does to food	Adds a sourness to food that can vary toward mildly tart and quite sour depending on the sugar content in the other ingredients
Substitutions	Lime is a decent substitute, although lime adds a taste you may not want
Price range	As little as 5¢ to 33¢ each, depending on store and supply 10¢ a lemon is what you should expect to pay at a competitive store
Freebies (*)	Yes—any fast food restaurant that serves iced tea

Lemon Grass

Lemon grass is a key ingredient for Asian dishes, giving food a sweet lemony taste. Its stems are far more complex than the fruit it is named for and, therefore, quite important in dishes that need the flavor of lemon with more than just the tart. You can buy it in bunches at many grocery stores.

What lemon grass does to food	Gives a sweet lemony taste—like a cross between ginger and lemon
Substitutions	Use green onion and lemon
Price range	About $2.98 a bunch, about the same as a bunch of green onions
Freebies (*)	No

Lime

Lime, like lemon adds a sourness that creates a tang when combined with sugary foods. But lime is a subtler flavor, with a bit more citrus taste than lemon (which tends more toward a perfect sour). It gives foods a bit more depth than lemon.

What lime does to food	Creates a tart that is difficult to create with lemon or vinegar
Substitutions	Lemon
Price range	Depending on supply and store, expect to pay about 10¢ a lime; but don't be surprised to see them for 20 for a dollar or three for a dollar
Freebies (*)	No

Marjoram

This gray-green leaf looks a lot like fresh oregano, but marjoram is sweeter and more delicate, with hardly any of the tang of oregano. It has a pleasant flavor with a slightly bitter aftertaste. It is compatible with a lot of foods, but is most often used to spice lamb and veal—neither of which are big BCYSAD ingredients (in fact, there are no veal dishes in here). But marjoram also blends well, so it can be used in a lot of other dishes, too.

What marjoram does to food	Gives food a bittersweet aromatic flavor
Substitutions	None
Price range	$2.58 for a .25-ounce spice jar
Freebies (*)	No

Mint

What we find in the United States is mostly spearmint, but peppermint is also an indigenous plant. The taste is familiar to anyone who has tried Certs or any other breath freshener—although we recommend that you not flavor your food with Certs. It has a cool, complex aftertaste, similar to anise, but altogether different in flavor. Use fresh mint for more of the aftertaste—dried for more of the mint flavor.

What mint does to food	Gives food a camphor-like taste
Substitutions	None
Price range	About 99¢ a bunch—which yields about three-quarters of a cup
Freebies (*)	No

Mustard (dry)

Mustard—the ground powdered spice and not the yellow stuff you squeeze onto your hot dog—is sharp and chili-like. It interacts well with other spices (seldom on its own) and sharpens up tastes in stews and salads (and is most famous for its role in making a Caesar salad a Caesar salad). Mustard is used in soups, stews, salad dressings and, as you know, prepared as a condiment for hot dogs and hamburgers.

What dry mustard does to food	Adds a peppery, savory taste
Substitutions	Try a little pepper mixed with some horseradish, if you have it. If no horseradish is available, use black pepper and a bit of dried ginger.
Price range	$3.80 for a 1.75-ounce spice jar
Freebies (*)	No

Mustard (prepared)

As with ketchup, hardly any recipes in this book have prepared mustard as an ingredient—because if you make something with mustard, it tastes like it was made with mustard … and as if you threw it together. And you're less shallow than that. Avoid prepared mustard if possible.

What prepared mustard does to food	Gives a sour tangy flavor and adds a bright yellow color
Substitutions	Lemon and salt are always better
Price range	From 50¢ for a 16-ounce bottle to $1.19 for the same size bottle
Freebies (*)	Yes—everywhere takeout food is sold

Nutmeg

Oddly, nutmeg, the seed of an evergreen tree, is produced on the same branch and pod as mace. The tree's fruit split into an outer membrane—mace—and the seed—nutmeg.

Although powdered, both taste similar, nutmeg is more pungent and sweeter than mace. Nutmeg, with its perfume-sweet aroma, has an almost chalky flavor when alone. But add sugar or salt and it comes alive. For that reason, we see it most in the U.S. as a spice used in baking and deserts rather than in savory dishes. But you'll also find it in many complex spiced dishes like curry.

What nutmeg does to food	Provides an earthy, perfumed base to dishes
Substitutions	Mace
Price range	$4.97 for a 1.81-ounce spice jar
Freebies (*)	No

Olives

Olives are the fruit of the olive tree, which are typically grown in hot arid regions and are primarily associated with Greek, Spanish and Italian food—where coincidentally, most of these country's climates are hot and arid. Olives have a very earthy, slightly bitter taste that changes depending on how the olive is cured. Spanish olives tend to be cured in oil and are usually sweeter than Greek and Italian olives, which are usually cured in brine. The olives you see at most stores are black olives and are the blandest of the group but also the cheapest. Unless otherwise stared, most recipes use black olives. But if you mince a cured Kalamata olive you'll get a lot more taste—just use significantly less than black olives and you'll stay within the budget.

OLIVES

What olives do to food	Add a different, grainier texture and a concentration of salt If using good olives, gives a bitter, tangy taste
Substitutions	Capers
Price range	$ .97 for a 6-ounce can $3.32 for a 5-ounce jar of fancy olives
Freebies (*)	No

Olive Oil

Olive oil is different from vegetable oil in that it is not only nutritionally better for you, but also adds a flavor most other oils can't (with the exception of sesame or chili oil). Italians use olive oil as a dip for fresh bread. And you can use it to turn a ten-cent package of ramen into something pretty amazing.

Bad news though—it is quite expensive, often as much as $8 a pint for extra-virgin olive (the first pressing of the olives). But if you look carefully, you should be able to find a 3-liter can of decent olive oil (not extra-virgin, of course) for $7-$9. And treated with respect, it can last you almost a year. Prego.

What olive oil does to food	Coats, keeps foods from sticking and adds a unique earthy flavor
Substitutions	Vegetable oil if you must, but realize that you're losing a lot of taste
Price range	$7 for a 3-liter can to $8 for a 16-ounce bottle
Freebies (*)	No

Orange/Orange Zest

Oranges are some of the best citrus fruits for cooking. Their flavor is obviously different than that of lemons and limes. Oranges have a robust flavor that gives a very unique twist to food; they sweeten and give tartness at the same time. For the most part, the recipes in this book are composed with orange zest, which is utilized more as a spice than the juice flavoring.

Orange zest—the skin of the orange—gives not just the essence of the orange, but the sharpness of it as well. The way you get the zest is to use a fine cheese grater and scrape the orange stuff off the skin of the orange, letting it fall into the dish you're preparing. Another way is to remove the skin of the orange and slice it thinly (make sure to get rid of most of the white pulpy stuff between the orange and the skin). Try it someday with just some cream and ramen.

What oranges and orange zest do to food	Add a unique sharpness that is more spicy than fruity
Substitutions	Although different, use lemon, lime or grapefruit zest (reduce the amount)
Price range	From 49¢ a pound (one good-sized naval orange can weigh a pound) to 8 oranges for a dollar
Freebies (*)	No

Oregano

This Mediterranean plant is a staple spice of southern European cooking. Italians and Greeks use it more than anybody else, but it is also used in French and Mexican cooking (the taste of Mexican oregano is slightly different).

Oregano provides a natural tang, without being sour. As a dried spice (you'll get it packaged as small bits of dried leaves, each piece about ¼-inch or so), it is typically slightly sweet and woody tasting and adds to flavors already in the dish as opposed to changing the flavors. Fresh oregano is still more an additive than a main flavor, but it will certainly be a stronger, more intense flavor when fresh. In dishes with lemon or lime, oregano really shines.

What oregano does to food	Gives a nice earthy tang
Substitutions	Italian spice or dried basil in a pinch
Price range	$ .50–$2.79 for a 1.25-ounce spice jar
Freebies (*)	Yes—try a pizza place

Oyster Sauce

Another secret Asian sauce you can't do without. But just try to find a recipe for it. It is essentially a sauce made from oysters and, again, soy sauce.

To make your own, you should start with about a cup of fresh oysters, a cup of clam juice, a few slices of fresh ginger, a ¼ cup of green onions, two cloves of minced garlic, and a ¼ cup of soy sauce. Since you won't have the oysters, leave them out. If you don't have the clam juice, use a shrimp flavor packet from a package of ramen noodles instead. Boil and let simmer. Add cornstarch to a small bit of cold soy sauce, stirring until thick. Store in the refrigerator until cool. Voila—oyster sauce.

What oyster sauce does to food	Imparts a sweet seafood taste to food
Substitutions	Try making your own (see above)
Price range	$1.90-$3.00 for an 11-ounce jar
Freebies (*)	No

Paprika

Paprika comes from a mild red pepper and is really a kind of sissy spice used mostly for looks, as opposed to taste. Its brilliant red color makes dishes attractive, but the spiciness is not substantial. In Eastern Europe, where chili peppers don't often grow in abundance, it is used more as a flavoring. So for traditional Polish or Hungarian dishes, you'll find paprika. But for Indian, Mexican, Jamaican or any other regional dishes where real chilies are required, you'll use something more masculine such as cayenne or chili powder.

What paprika does to food	Gives food a semi-sweet chili flavor—without as much hot taste
Substitutions	Chili powder, chili ramen flavoring or cayenne
Price range	$ .50–$3.48 for a 2-ounce spice jar
Freebies (*)	No

Parsley

Yes, you eat parsley, too. Mostly known as a garnish, parsley is also used frequently in dips or marinades for shrimp or fish. It has a light flavor and does well as an enhancer of flavors.

You can buy it dried or fresh. But frankly there's no reason to buy it dried. It's usually 25¢ or less for a cup's worth of fresh parsley; even more than that for a few tablespoons of dried parsley. And fresh parsley keeps for a couple of weeks in the refrigerator without going bad.

What parsley does to food	Gives food a slightly peppery, fresh flavor
Substitutions	If you must change something, try dried oregano, which is entirely different
Price range	25¢ for a fresh bunch $ .50–$2.28 for a 2-ounce spice jar
Freebies (*)	No

Peanut Butter

Forget the grape jelly. Peanut butter in this book is used primarily in two or three recipes that are Indonesian or Thai in origin. And if you've had sate or Asian peanut sauce, you'll realize it is indispensable. It instantly provides the thickness needed for the sauce. But you can always use fresh peanuts mixed in a very thick brown sugar-and-water mix.

What peanut butter does to food	Binds and gives a workable alternative to fresh minced peanuts
Substitutions	A few chopped fresh peanuts mixed with brown sugar and water
Price range	$2.20 for a 28-ounce jar
Freebies (*)	No

Raisins

Chewy and sweet, raisins are often used to liven up a primarily sour dish, or to sweeten up one that is already sweet. They may make the other flavors too dull, however, so you may easily eliminate them.

What raisins do to food	Add a sweet, filling base to savory or sweet foods
Substitutions	Currants or dried cranberries
Price range	$1.37 for a 15-ounce box
Freebies (*)	No

Ramen

Would we say anything mean about the little dry, wormy-looking noodles in the dime bag? No chance. Ramen, our secret weapon, our self-contained meal within a meal, our raison d'être (our way to make a buck), is easy to find, dirt-cheap and reasonably tasty if you follow the directions on the plastic bag. If, however, you follow our recipes, you'll have yourself a culinary masterpiece. You should be able to find this tidbit of fine dining at almost any store that sells food—from 7-Eleven to Albertsons—and at almost every gas station/convenience store in between.

Although we don't say it in every recipe, if you boil the noodles and then fry them in oil, they take on a different texture. They become firmer and more like good-quality pasta, more, uh, noodlish. Whatever—ramen is a good, cheap, filler food at its best.

By the way, we are typically liberal in our measurement of water to boil your ramen. Since you'll toss the water for most recipes anyway, we didn't think it was critical to say how much water to use in each recipe. As a rule of thumb, use about 2 cups of water per package of ramen noodles.

What ramen Noodles do to food	Fill it out for a bargain-basement price
Substitutions	Sure, but then you wouldn't need us, would you?
Price range	As low as 8¢ and as high as 30¢ per package (they're basically all the same in taste)

Rice Vinegar

Rice vinegar is deep, flavorful vinegar that tends toward sweet, but not as sweet as balsamic vinegar. It enhances the flavor of quite a few dishes in this cookbook, but like most vinegars, it is a luxury and not a necessity.

What rice vinegar does to food	Gives food a warm rice-tasting tartness
Substitutions	Any vinegar
Price range	Around $2 for a 12-ounce bottle
Freebies (*)	No

Rosemary

Resembling overgrown pine needles, rosemary tastes remarkably like pine—although who actually ate pine to know? Not us. At any rate, rosemary enhances lamb, pork and chicken and tends to be overpowering if you use too much; so be careful. Fresh rosemary, like any fresh herb, is preferred to dried.

What rosemary does to food	Gives a piney, aromatic taste
Substitutions	None
Price range	$2.57 for a .5-ounce spice jar
Freebies (*)	No

Saffron

Long used for dye, truly good-quality saffron comes from the stigma—the slender, dried, reddish-brown center—of what is essentially a small iris flower. It has an aromatic smell and an exotic bitterness that reminds you slightly of old bay leaves. Yet saffron is, in fact, a highly prized ingredient. If truffles go several hundred dollars a pound (relax, there are no recipes with truffles in this book), good quality saffron goes several thousand dollars a pound. To get one pound of saffron threads, you'd have to hand pick nearly 50,000 flowers. When buying real quality saffron, you'll spend $6–$8 for about an eighth of a gram, ranking it right up there with brown heroin in cost. McCormick charges around $13.47 for .06 ounces of the stuff—that equals a pretty stiff $225 an ounce. It's more expensive at specialty food stores.

So we won't be using *that* saffron in this cookbook. What we will be using is the cheap and low-qualify stuff sold in Mexican groceries for about a buck for a four-ounce bag. It tastes almost completely different, but gives food the proper color and still yields a unique taste. Saffron, for the purposes of this book, is like wine. Recipes are enhanced dramatically by wine or saffron, but don't lose all palatability without them.

What saffron does to food	Gives food a bittersweet taste and a yellow color
Substitutions	Don't substitute anything (unless you're looking just for the color; then use a pinch of turmeric)
Price range	$1 for 4 ounces of the cheap stuff $13.47 for .06 ounces of a brand name
Freebies (*)	No

Sage

In its fresh form, sage is a long, gray-green leaf that has a velvety appearance. As its name suggests, sage is a dry-tasting and earthy herb that is used quite extensively in sausage and poultry stuffing. In fact, it is one of the few truly American herbs.

What sage does to food	Imparts an earthy, slightly aromatic taste
Substitutions	Use black pepper instead (use about 1/8 of the proportion of pepper to sage)
Price range	$2.48 for a pre-packaged container of fresh (which yields you about a half-cup); dried is from $.50–$3.44 for .43 ounces
Freebies (*)	No

Salad Dressing

A few recipes within these pages call for bottled dressings. And for the most part, it's your call as to which one to use. Again, with prepared dressings and sauces, your cost and quality can vary greatly. If you have a favorite in any category, use it. The dressings vary from ranch and blue cheese to Italian and vinaigrette. You'll have to choose which one is best in each category. Most dressings seem to add distracting flavors (from stabilizers and preservatives), so with the exception of Italian—which seems to be pretty difficult for manufacturers to screw up—you'll have more tastes than you asked for. So try to go easy on the dressings.

What salad dressing does to food	Adds an oil-based coating that flavors food
Substitutions	Oil, milk, cream and appropriate spices mixed with either vinegar or lemon will usually get pretty close. Better yet, find a freebie.
Price range	$1.07–$4.88 for an 8-ounce bottle of pre-made dressing
Freebies (*)	Yes—anywhere to-go salads are sold

Salt

You'll notice that there is no mention of salt in any recipe in this book. The reason for it is you probably don't need it. Typically the flavor packets included in your ramen will provide plenty of salt. If not, then add salt at will.

What salt does to food	Brings out the flavors and livens up the taste of the food
Substitutions	Sugar also livens up the food, but in a more interesting way
Price range	Usually around 30¢ for a 26-ounce carton

Freebies (*)	Yes—everywhere

Sesame Seed

Sesame seeds have a mild, buttery, nut-like flavor. They are used equally in desserts and main dishes because they tend to enhance flavor without dominating. Typically sprinkled over vegetables and finished dishes, sesame seeds can also be cooked. Sesame oil or sesame paste is used in place of sesame seeds when the flavor of the sesame is intended to dominate the flavor of the meal. Sesame seeds are readily available in the spice section of your supermarket.

What sesame seeds do to food	Provide a nice buttery, nutty texture; doesn't dominate
Substitutions	None
Price range	$ .99–$2.49 for a 4-ounce spice jar
Freebies (*)	No

Sesame Oil

Used more to flavor than to keep food from sticking, sesame oil is available in the international aisle of most large supermarkets or Asian markets. It tends to be expensive—more so than even olive oil—so you'll find it constantly eliminated in the substitutions and omissions area of each recipe in this cookbook. If you have it, use it—especially in Asian dishes—because it will add a very nice flavor to your food. But if you don't want to spend the cash, use sesame seeds and stick to cheap vegetable oil.

What sesame oil does to food	Gives food an earthy, buttery flavor
Substitutions	Forget the taste and add vegetable or olive oil
Price range	About $2.99 for a 6-ounce bottle
Freebies (*)	Yes, but tough to find (some Chinese restaurants with to-go menus use sesame oil with the pot stickers)

Shallots

Shallots are the more flavorful brethren of green onions. They tend to be a lot more expensive, but have a less harsh, more flavorful, almost sweet taste. They give you the onion flavor without the associated overkill. They still give you bad breath, though.

What shallots do to food	Provide a savory flavor that goes well with a lot of foods
Substitutions	Green onions are harsher, but will work in a pinch
Price range	$1 a bunch at Asian markets to as much as $2.79 for 4 ounces prepackaged, trimmed pieces
Freebies (*)	No

Sour Cream

Sour cream adds a tangy coating to recipes—one that serves to sharpen the overall taste. It also binds food together nicely. The cost of sour cream tends to vary, depending on where you buy it, so you should comparison shop until you find it for about $1.25 for a 16-ounce tub.

What sour cream does to food	Sharpens flavor, adds tang and binds foods
Substitutions	Cream mixed with some lemon
Price range	$1.00–$2.75 for 16 ounces
Freebies (*)	No

Soy Sauce

Soy sauce, the equivalent of Asian ketchup, is found in almost every Asian dish in this cookbook and gives a savory, beefy taste, but is also highly salty. There are a couple of types of soy sauce sold—"light soy sauce" and "dark soy sauce." The light soy sauce, which is actually quite dark and the most readily available, is the more flavorful of the two. The dark sauce is sweeter and imparts a reddish color to food. Both are relatively cheap. This cookbook uses mostly light soy (again, it will still be very dark). If you don't have soy sauce, you need to get some.

What soy sauce does to food	Imparts a salty, hearty taste
Substitutions	Use a beef flavor packet, some water and just a drop or two of vinegar (make sure the graininess of the packet is dissolved in the water)
Price range	From $1.48 for a 15-ounce bottle to $1.18 for a 5-ounce bottle
Freebies (*)	Yes—try any to-go Chinese restaurant

Sugar/Brown Sugar

Sugar is the most underrated flavor enhancer in the cooking world. On every table, you find salt and sugar, but most people only use sugar for coffee and breakfast cereal. In actuality, it can be used in far more places. Instead of salt, try sugar. Sugar brings out flavors better than salt, and it creates a taste that is very unique. Not to say you can use it in place of salt. But when making a sauce that doesn't have quite the flavor you want, add some sugar. You'll often find it will give it just what you need.

Brown sugar, on the other hand, gives you a syrupy taste that is associated with the molasses in which it is soaked. It sweetens, but also adds the heavy tastes of molasses. It is used to make heavy sauces even heavier.

What sugar does to food	Sweetens and heightens the flavors already in the food
Substitutions	Any fruit with natural sugar
Price range	Around $1.57 for a 5-pound bag of white sugar about $1 for a 2-pound bag of brown
Freebies (*)	Yes—any place that serves coffee

Tamarind

Tamarind is almost unknown in the U.S.—but it shouldn't be. With an appearance that borders on a look of old rotting fava beans (meaning it looks like an oversized brown string bean), it appears to be something you'd throw away as soon as eat. The bean cover is brown and leathery. And while sitting in the bin at the grocery store (you might have to search for it; it isn't in all grocery stores), the pods will crack and look like a compost heap. But when stripped and made into a paste, it becomes delicious.

Having the intensely tart flavor of lemon mixed with a savory, mild saltiness, it is a very unique natural spice. It is one of the key ingredients of A1 Steak Sauce and Worcestershire sauce. The tamarind seed itself is as hard as a rock and is useless as anything but a projectile. What you'll do with the tamarind is to put it in warm water (peel the hard skin of the bean pod first) and separate the seed from the pod. Then mash the gummy brown meat of the tamarind pod in a half-cup of water until it has is dissolved completely. Because of its tartness and tang, it goes unbelievably well with shrimp and chicken.

Some places sell prepared tamarind in square plastic packages. Try to find it where it's loose, thereby guaranteeing relative freshness.

What tamarind does to food	Imparts an intensely tart, earthy flavor of lemon mixed with a savory, mild saltiness
Substitutions	In a pinch, use tamarind drink mixes (which often use too much sugar) found in some Mexican food stores, or use lemon mixed with a beef ramen noodle flavor packet
Price range	$3.00 a pound for pre-packaged and about $1.40 for bulk
Freebies (*)	No

Tarragon

Tarragon has a slightly bittersweet flavor, with a slightly aromatic aftertaste—vaguely similar to anise or mint. It's commonly used as a flavoring for vinegar and is used in pickles, mustards, and sauces. It goes well with fish, meat and soups and sometimes is sprinkled over fresh fruits.

What tarragon does to food	Gives a slightly bittersweet flavor with an aromatic aftertaste
Substitutions	None
Price range	From $3.66 for a .37-ounce spice jar
Freebies (*)	No

Thyme

Thyme for dinner? Thyme (pronounced *time*) has a vibrant flavor that brings out the best in poultry and pork and works well in baking or broiling. It has a smoky, savory taste that makes it a great ingredient when barbecuing as well. Rub it on chicken or fish, making sure to use salt to bring out the flavor. Thyme to eat.

What thyme does to food	Gives a smoky, savory taste
Substitutions	None
Price range	$2.57 for a .62-ounce spice jar
Freebies (*)	No

TOFU

Sorry if we can't hide our disdain for tofu. Made with puréed and pressed soybeans, this whitish bean curd that resembles packing material is quite nutritional—high in protein and low in fat. But we'd sooner eat live grubs or bat guano than tofu. Not that you should adopt this attitude, mind you. Typically you'll buy it in chunks of about three inches square, and it is now available in most large supermarkets. Once opened, it will keep in the refrigerator for a few days if submerged in a container of water.

WHAT TOFU DOES TO FOOD	Fills it out
SUBSTITUTIONS	Who'd want to try?
PRICE RANGE	$ .99–$2.99 a pound depending on where you buy it
FREEBIES (*)	No

TOMATO SAUCE

Tomato sauce is the official sauce of BCYSAD. It is extremely cheap (usually 20¢ a can or less on sale), very versatile (can be thickened to a paste or thinned to a soup) and can be flavored from spicy and meaty to fruity and tangy. It is readily available and comes in convenient 6-ounce cans. Anything that calls for tomatoes can be substituted with tomato sauce, and anything that calls for tomato sauce can be made quite inexpensively. By adding just a few spices, you can dramatically alter its final character—and if you goof up, it doesn't cost a lot to toss it and start all over.

WHAT TOMATO SAUCE DOES TO FOOD	Coats, seasons, binds and adds a base flavor to meals that can be enhanced simply by tossing in a few spices
SUBSTITUTIONS	Ketchup if you're really desperate, but why? Tomato sauce is cheaper and doesn't taste like ketchup.
PRICE RANGE	20¢ for an 8-ounce can 33¢ for a 15-ounce can $1 for 8 cans on sale
FREEBIES (*)	No, but it's cheap enough—why bother?

TURMERIC

Turmeric gives mustard its color. It also gives curry its yellow hue and will be essential in most Indian dishes. Closely related to ginger, turmeric was introduced by Marco Polo as a substitute for saffron. It has a woody, earthy, slightly peppery taste. But the truth is, it's mostly used to color foods.

What turmeric does to food	Colors food and gives it a peppery seasoning
Substitutions	For flavor there is no substitute. For color you can try saffron if you have it available (although not the good stuff, please).
Price range	$3.28 for a 2-ounce spice jar
Freebies (*)	No

Vegetable Oil

Vegetable oil keeps food from sticking to the pan and provides an agent that helps assimilate different types of ingredients. Types of vegetable oil include corn oil, safflower oil, canola oil, peanut oil and a blend, labeled simply vegetable oil.

What vegetable oil does to food	Keeps it from clumping and sticking and adds a rich, tasteless, warm base to foods
Substitutions	Butter or margarine work as well, but cost more
Price range	Usually $1.47 or so for a 32-ounce bottle
Freebies (*)	No

Vinegar

Vinegar, as opposed to lemon, gives a hearty tart taste that is in itself a flavoring. The reason there are so many types of vinegars in this and other cookbooks is that they all flavor differently. Lemon and lime add more of a tartness that still needs some flavoring. What all this basically means is that if you use cheap vinegar, you need to hide it with something else. Otherwise you'll want to use more expensive vinegar. The way around the expense is to flavor the vinegar yourself. You can usually find distilled vinegar, the cheapest kind, for 40¢ for 12–16 ounces. A good way to flavor it is to put in garlic or a fresh spice like dill or tarragon. Makes you feel like a chef already, doesn't it?

What vinegar does to food	Gives foods a sour tangy flavor
Substitutions	Lemon or lime with salt (adding a small bit of wine also enhances the lemon flavor)
Price range	38¢ for a 16-ounce bottle of regular distilled vinegar
Freebies (*)	Yes—look in Chinese to-go restaurants that serve pot stickers

Wine/Liquor

Different wines and liquors flavor food differently, but the one common thread is that once the alcohol is burned off, the underlying distilled flavor lingers in the food. If you use wine, you end up with the woody flavor of the wood in which the wine was aged and the fruitiness of the grapes. If using white wine, the flavor will be dry and slightly sour; if red, it will be hearty and fruity. If using gin, whiskey, cognac or vodka, you get the slightly bitter flavor of juniper, grain or mash or distilled sweet wine. It imbues food with a savory flavor base that is hard to identify, but which is important. It also makes cooking so much more fun when you sample the ingredients as you go.

What wine and liquor do to food	Give an aromatic base flavor
Substitutions	None
Price range	From $2 for a cheap bottle of wine to $80 for a decent bottle of cognac
Freebies (*)	Boy, wouldn't that be nice?

Worcestershire Sauce

As savory as beef broth, Worcestershire sauce adds a tartness that is very complex and very unique. Created from soy, tamarind and assorted spices, it compliments a variety of sauces and is essential in a good Caesar salad. It is relatively cheap and will last years in your refrigerator.

What Worcestershire sauce does to food	Gives an aromatic base flavor
Substitutions	None
Price range	Around $1.17 for a generic 12-ounce bottle
Freebies (*)	No

Yogurt

Dairy based, yogurt gives foods a creamy taste without the associated fat or cost. Made from cultured milk, yogurt, like cheese, gets its creaminess from bacteria—similar to the slime in your sink, but without the associated health risks. But it also serves to bind foods as well as flavor and thicken sauces. Unlike cream or milk, it also adds a cool sensation to foods.

What yogurt does to food	Coats and adds a fresh, cool flavor to food
Substitutions	Sour cream works best, but you can also use milk or cream mixed with some flour
Price range	40¢–79¢ for an 8-ounce container
Freebies (*)	No

Section Two

THE RECIPES

Chapter 4

SALADS

MEATLESS SALADS

ANTIPASTO RAMEN SALAD

Serves four

Notes: *Artichokes are likely expensive, so eliminate them if you must. Or use olives.*

Ingredient	Cost
3 packages mushroom ramen	.30
1 cup roasted peppers, cut into strips	1.50
1 12-ounce jar marinated artichoke hearts	1.25
1 cup Monterey jack cheese, shredded	1.00
1 cup mushrooms, sliced	.75
½ cup onion, chopped	.25
½ cup fresh basil, chopped	.50
¾ cup Italian salad dressing	.75
Total:	$6.30

Open both packages of ramen. Cook the noodles 2–3 minutes in boiling water. Add both packets of seasoning. Drain, set aside and allow to cool.

Peppers can be purchased pre-roasted, or you can roast them in one of two ways—bake at 375° on a baking sheet for 20 minutes; or place the peppers on a gas stove and allow skin to blister and brown, then microwave on high for two minutes. In either case, slice into strips once cool.

Combine pepper strips, artichoke hearts, cheese, mushrooms, onion and basil in a large bowl and toss in cooled ramen noodles. Cover and refrigerate at least 1 hour before serving.

SUBSTITUTIONS & OMISSIONS

Get rid of the artichoke hearts, use a fraction of the amount of Parmesan cheese for Monterey jack and use dried for fresh basil.

3 packages mushroom Ramen	.30
3 roasted green peppers, cut into strips	.75
3 tablespoons Parmesan cheese	*
½ cup mushrooms, sliced	.40
½ cup onion, chopped	.25
2 teaspoons dried basil	.10
½ cup Italian salad dressing	*
Total:	$1.80

$$$ BIG SPLURGE $$$

Use skiitake mushrooms instead of white mushrooms and fresh crumbled Parmesan cheese. Replace ramen noodles with fettuccine.

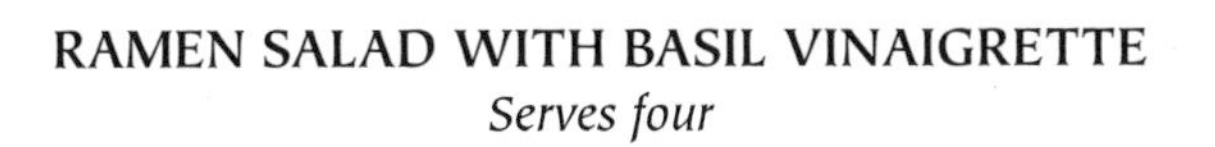

RAMEN SALAD WITH BASIL VINAIGRETTE

Serves four

Notes: As long as you don't mess with the basil (in other words, keep in some proportion), you have the essence of this dish. The rest you can modify.

3 packages chicken ramen	.30
4 cloves garlic, minced	.10
2 teaspoons basil	.10
2 teaspoons sugar	.05
1 teaspoon mustard powder	.10
3 teaspoons lemon juice	.30
¼ cup red wine vinegar	.30
1 cup olive oil	1.50
2 zucchinis, sliced	.50
2 tomatoes, diced	1.00
3 green onions, chopped	.15
¼ cup Greek olives	1.00
¼ cup toasted pine nuts	.50
black pepper to taste	.05
Total:	$5.95

Open both packages of ramen. Boil the noodles without the seasoning packets, cooking the noodles only two or three minutes. Drain and dry. Set aside.

Mince garlic with a fork or in a food processor. Add basil, sugar, mustard, lemon juice, one flavor packet and pepper, then the oil.

Boil zucchini until just tender, about five minutes, then dice. In separate bowls, toss zucchini, ramen noodles, green onions and tomatoes with dressing.

Serve salad into individual bowls. Sprinkle olives and pine nuts on top.

SUBSTITUTIONS & OMISSIONS

Omit the vinegar, Greek olives and pine nuts. Reduce the amount zucchini. Use less than half the tomato amount. Add a package of ramen.

4 packages ramen	.40
4 cloves garlic, minced	.10
2 teaspoons basil	.10
2 teaspoons sugar	*
1 teaspoon dry mustard	.10
3 teaspoons lemon juice	*
¼ cup vegetable oil	.05
1 zucchini, sliced	.25
2 medium tomatoes, diced	.50
3 green onions, chopped	.10
black pepper to taste	.05
	Total: $1.65

$$$ BIG SPLURGE $$$

Use rotini in place of ramen noodles and balsamic vinegar in place of red wine vinegar.

RAMEN BEAN SALAD

Serves four

Notes: Beans are cheap and high in nutrition—not to mention the fact that they fill you and give you hours of post-dinner entertainment. This recipe will definitely last a long time. Or it will feed more than a couple appetites.

3 packages chicken flavor ramen	.30
2 cups canned red, pinto or pink beans, drained	1.00
½ cup mayonnaise	.40
¼ cup green pepper, diced	.15
¼ cup celery, diced	.15
¼ cup carrots, chopped	.15

¼ cup green onion, chopped	.15
2 tablespoons sweet pickles, diced	.30
2 tablespoons pine nuts, toasted	.50
½ cup fresh spinach, torn	.50
	Total: $3.60

Open all packages of ramen. Cook the noodles without the seasoning packets. When done, drain and set aside.

Combine the cooked noodles with the beans, mayonnaise, green pepper, celery, carrots, green onion, pickles and pine nuts in medium-size mixing bowl. Sprinkle in one flavor packet and toss with cooked noodles.

Cover and refrigerate until well chilled. Just before serving, toss in the spinach.

SUBSTITUTIONS & OMISSIONS

Reduce the amount of beans and add another ramen noodle package. Use relish for sweet pickles.

4 packages chicken flavor ramen	.40
½ cup cooked or canned red, pinto or pink beans, drained	.30
4 tablespoons mayonnaise	*
¼ cup green pepper, chopped	.15
¼ cup celery, chopped	.15
¼ cup carrots, chopped	.15
¼ cup green onion, chopped	.15
2 tablespoons sweet pickle relish	*
2 tablespoons peanuts, chopped	*
½ cup fresh spinach leaves	.25
	Total: $1.55

$$$ BIG SPLURGE $$$

Add one pound grilled chicken breast and lose the ramen altogether.

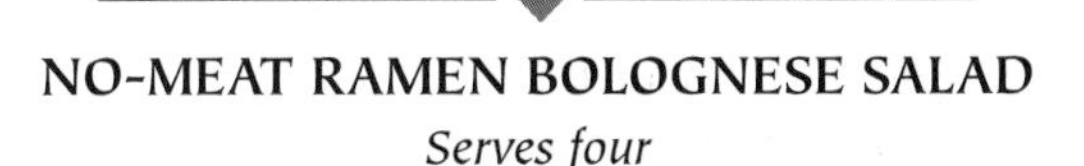

NO-MEAT RAMEN BOLOGNESE SALAD

Serves four

Notes: This is a simple ensemble that has been enhanced by a cup of cheese, which also can be left out. Without the cheese—or with just a hint—this is cheap and easy to do.

3 packages beef ramen	.30

3 tomatoes, diced	1.25
1 cup Cheddar cheese, shredded	2.00
2 cucumbers, diced	.50
1 cup green onions, diced	.25
1 green pepper, diced	.25
	Total: $4.55

Cook the ramen noodles in boiling, slightly salted water until *al dente,* 3–4 minutes, omitting the flavor packets. Drain well and rinse under cold water. Set aside.

Add all ingredients, including two flavor packets, with the cheese going in last. Mix well. Let stand at least 2 hours before serving.

SUBSTITUTIONS & OMISSIONS

Leave out the cheese, reduce the tomatoes and add another package of ramen.

4 packages tomato ramen	.40
1 tomato, diced	.40
2 cucumbers, diced	.50
1 cup green onions, diced	.25
1 green pepper, diced	.25
	Total: $1.80

$$$ BIG SPLURGE $$$

Use spaghetti instead of ramen noodles.

CHILI-GARLIC RAMEN NOODLE SALAD

Serves four

Notes: Again, one of the super-secret Chinese sauces (actually two if you consider the oyster sauce). Find it if you can, or improvise and do it yourself (see page 56).

3 packages spicy shrimp ramen	.30
¼ cup green onions, julienned	.25
¼ cup carrots, shredded	.25
1 clove garlic, minced	.10
¼ cup soy sauce	.30
¼ cup rice vinegar	.30
2 tablespoons oyster sauce	.30

2 tablespoons chili sauce	.50
1 tablespoon sesame oil	.20
2 teaspoons sugar	.05
	Total: $2.55

Boil water in a large pot. Add ramen noodles and return to a boil for one minute, then reduce heat and cook another 2-3 minutes. Drain and set aside until cool.

Combine soy sauce, rice vinegar, oyster sauce, chili sauce, garlic, sesame oil, sugar and one ramen flavor packet. Toss with the noodles to coat. Garnish with julienned green onions, carrots and cucumber.

SUBSTITUTIONS & OMISSIONS

Make your own oyster sauce (see page 56).

3 packages spicy shrimp ramen	.30
¼ cup green onions, julienned	.10
¼ cup carrots, shredded	.10
¼ cup soy sauce	*
¼ cup rice vinegar	.30
2 tablespoons homemade oyster sauce	.10
2 tablespoons hot sauce	*
3 teaspoons sesame oil	.20
2 teaspoons sugar	*
	Total: $1.10

$$$ BIG SPLURGE $$$

Use angel hair pasta for ramen noodles.

CREAMY RAMEN SALAD

Serves four

Notes: Good as an inexpensive main course or an auxiliary salad. Fresh basil will make this taste like a million bucks, even though, as usual, we don't have a million bucks to work with. Dried basil is just fine.

3 packages creamy chicken ramen	.30
1 cup mayonnaise	.40
2 tablespoons lemon juice	.20
4 green onions, chopped	.15

1 6-ounce jar artichoke hearts, drained and sliced	**1.25**
1 tablespoon basil (fresh or dried)	**.10**
Total:	**$2.40**

Open both packages of ramen. Boil the noodles without the seasoning packets for three minutes. When done, drain and set aside.

Stir the mayonnaise and lemon juice into the ramen. Add the green onions, artichoke hearts, basil and one seasoning packet and mix well.

SUBSTITUTIONS & OMISSIONS

Reduce the amount of mayo.

2 packages creamy chicken ramen	**.30**
¼ cup mayonnaise	*
2 tablespoons lemon juice	**.20**
4 green onions, chopped	**.15**
1 6-ounce jar artichoke hearts, drained and sliced	**1.25**
1 ½ tablespoons basil (fresh or dried)	**.10**
Total:	**$2.00**

$$$ BIG SPLURGE $$$

Use a half-cup cream in place half of the mayonnaise, and use angel hair pasta for ramen noodles.

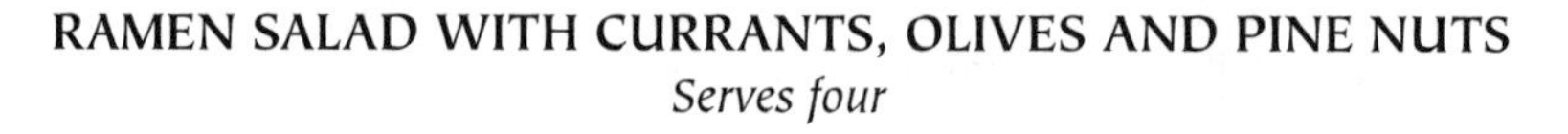

RAMEN SALAD WITH CURRANTS, OLIVES AND PINE NUTS

Serves four

Notes: You may not like the sweetness of the currants, but it's what makes this dish unique. Omit them if you wish, but change too much else and you lose the character of the recipe.

3 packages vegetable ramen	**.30**
1 clove garlic, minced	**.10**
1 cup fresh parsley, chopped	**.25**
¼ cup lemon juice	**.50**
¼ cup red wine vinegar	**.40**
1 teaspoon curry powder	**.10**
1 teaspoon sugar	**.05**
1 teaspoon ground cumin	**.10**
1 cup olive oil	**.75**
1 red onion, diced	**.50**
1 cup Kalamata olives, pitted and sliced	**1.50**

½ cup dried currants	**1.00**
½ cup toasted pine nuts	**1.00**
pepper to taste	**.05**
	Total: $6.60

Cook the ramen noodles in boiling, slightly salted water until *al dente*, 3-4 minutes, omitting the flavor packets. Drain well and rinse under cold water. Set aside.

Blend garlic and one ramen flavor packet with a fork, adding lemon juice, vinegar, curry, sugar, cumin, parsley and pepper. Gradually add oil. Pour mix over ramen.

Add onion, olives, currants and pine nuts to ramen and toss. Cover and refrigerate until chilled.

SUBSTITUTIONS & OMISSIONS

Use a small half-box of raisins for currants, omit the vinegar and the pine nuts, use yellow onion for white and get rid of the olives. Add a fourth package of ramen noodles for volume.

4 packages vegetable ramen	**.40**
1 clove garlic, minced	**.10**
1 cup fresh parsley, chopped	**.25**
¼ cup lemon juice	**.40**
1 teaspoon curry powder	**.10**
1 teaspoon sugar	*
1 teaspoon ground cumin	**.10**
½ teaspoon pepper	*
½ cup vegetable oil	**.20**
1 yellow onion, diced	**.25**
3 tablespoons raisins	**.20**
	Total: $2.00

$$$ BIG SPLURGE $$$

Use a few tablespoons white wine and use shell pasta for ramen noodles.

FIRE-STARTING RAMEN SALAD

Serves four

Notes: This one isn't for the weak at heart. Jalapenos and green chilies make a potent combination that heats up any lunch break. You can lighten up on the chilies, but don't get rid of the cumin. Keep plenty of Kleenex on hand.

3 packages spicy chicken ramen	.30
1 cup red onion, diced	.75
1 cup red bell pepper, diced	1.00
1 cup corn (canned or frozen is fine)	.50
¼ cup green chilies, diced	.40
1 tablespoon jalapenos, diced	.10
¼ cup cilantro, chopped	.10
1 tablespoon chili powder	.10
2 teaspoons cumin powder	.10
1 cup Italian salad dressing	.80
	Total: $4.15

Cook ramen in boiling water for 3-4 minutes or until tender. Drain and refresh under cold running water. Set aside.

In a large bowl, combine pasta, onion, red pepper, corn, chilies, jalapenos and cilantro. In a small bowl, whisk together salad dressing, chili powder, one flavor packet and cumin. Pour over pasta mixture, tossing to coat well. Chill.

SUBSTITUTIONS & OMISSIONS

Use green pepper for red, yellow onion for red. And if your stomach isn't cast iron, lighten up on the chilies.

3 packages spicy chicken ramen	.30
1 cup yellow onion, diced	.25
1 cup green bell pepper, diced	.25
1 cup corn (canned or frozen is fine)	.25
½ cup green chilies, diced	.40
1 tablespoon jalapenos, diced	.10
¼ cup cilantro, chopped	.10
1 tablespoon chili powder	.10
2 teaspoons cumin powder	.10
2 tablespoons Italian salad dressing	*
	Total: $1.85

$$$ BIG SPLURGE $$$

Use rotini for ramen noodles and add some Mexican *queso fresco*.

GARDEN FRESH RAMEN SALAD

Serves eight

Notes: Basil makes this one, so use fresh if possible. For a variation, roast the peppers.

5 packages vegetable ramen	.50
1 teaspoon lemon juice	.10
1 pound broccoli, cut into 1-inch pieces	1.25
4 carrots, sliced or shredded	.25
3 leeks, sliced into 1-inch pieces	.50
1 large red pepper, diced	1.00
1 large yellow pepper, diced	1.00
½ cup fresh basil, chopped	.50
1 egg yolk	.10
1 tablespoon Dijon mustard	.20
1 tablespoon balsamic vinegar	.20
1 cup vegetable oil	.40
½ cup olive oil	.50
1 tablespoon dried thyme	.10
1 tablespoon orange zest, finely grated	.10
black pepper to taste	.05
	Total: $6.75

Cook the ramen in boiling salted water until semi-tender. Do not overcook. Drain thoroughly and place in a large mixing bowl.

Cook the broccoli and carrots separately in boiling water just until tender. Drain and combine with the ramen.

In the same water, blanch the leeks (boil them until just hot) one minute. Drain. Add the blanched leeks, red and yellow peppers and fresh basil and toss to combine. Whip the egg yolk, lemon juice, mustard and vinegar together, pouring the oils into the mix. Add the thyme, orange zest, one flavor packet and pepper to taste.

Pour the dressing over the salad and toss to coat thoroughly. Serve chilled.

Substitutions & Omissions

Substitute green onions for leeks, green peppers for red and yellow. Use spinach for broccoli and eliminate the olive oil. Dried basil is also okay in place of fresh.

5 packages vegetable ramen	.50
1 teaspoon lemon juice	*
1 cup broccoli florets, frozen	1.25
6 carrots, shredded (canned is fine)	.25
1 bunch green onions, sliced	.25
2 cups green peppers, diced	.50
1 tablespoon basil	.10
1 egg yolk	.10
1 tablespoon Chinese hot mustard	*
1 tablespoon balsamic vinegar	.20

1 cup vegetable oil	.40
1 tablespoon dried thyme	.10
1 tablespoon orange zest. finely grated	.10
black pepper to taste	*
	Total: $3.75

$$$ BIG SPLURGE $$$

Toss in some asparagus and serve over rotini instead of ramen noodles.

RAMEN GREEK SALAD

Serves four

Notes: For the most part, this is the only way to make this dish. The ingredients are all here, you just need to play with the proportions. Keep the feta, if even just as a hint of the flavor. Also keep the onions and cucumber because they're authentic... and cheap.

3 packages vegetable ramen	.30
8 ounces feta cheese, crumbled	2.50
2 tomatoes, cut into one-inch chunks	1.00
1 green pepper, diced	.25
1 cucumber, cut into one-inch cubes	.25
1 white onion, cut into one-inch chunks	.40
¼ cup dried oregano	.10
¼ cup olive oil	.50
1 teaspoon sugar	.05
juice of 3 lemons	.30
	Total: $5.65

Cook the ramen noodles in boiling, slightly salted water until *al dente*, 3-4 minutes, omitting the flavor packets. Drain well and rinse under cold water. Set aside.

Mix lemon juice in cup with oil, two flavor packets and oregano. Toss cucumbers, tomatoes, green onions and onions together, then add ramen, mixing thoroughly. Pour the lemon-oregano mixture in and mix well. Opa!

SUBSTITUTIONS & OMISSIONS

You can omit all but about three tablespoons of feta. And if you buy it fresh at a deli, you can easily get away with even half that very small portion. Use one tomato instead of two, lose the green pepper, use a yellow onion in place of white and add another package of ramen.

4 packages vegetable ramen	.40
1 ounce feta cheese, crumbled	.30
1 tomato, cut into one-inch chunks	.40
1 cucumber, cut into one-inch cubes	.25
1 yellow onion, cut into one-inch chunks	.25
¼ cup dried oregano	.10
¼ cup vegetable oil	.05
1 teaspoon sugar	*
juice of 3 lemons	*
	Total: $1.75

$$$ BIG SPLURGE $$$

Use more feta, use very good extra-virgin olive oil and use fettuccine in place of ramen noodles.

GRILLED PASTA SALAD

Serves four

Notes: This is a million-dollar recipe that costs only a few bucks. Since it will taste like you spent a lot more, it's a good date recipe. If you're chronically single, it will also keep a couple days, so you can enjoy it later.

4 packages ramen: two tomato, two spicy chicken	.40
4 zucchinis, halved	1.00
1 onion, cut into large chunks	.25
¾ cup red peppers, roasted and diced	1.00
juice of two lemons	.20
	Total: $2.85

Prepare ramen by boiling for two to three minutes, then removing from heat and draining. You do not want the ramen overcooked. Set aside.

On broiler pan, arrange zucchini and onion side by side. Take both spicy chicken flavor packages and combine with juice of two lemons, about three tablespoons water and ¼ cup oil. Mix. Brush the zucchini and onions with this mix. Bake for 20 minutes at 425°. Remove, let cool and dice.

In bowl, toss cooked pasta, roasted vegetables and vinegar. Serve at room temperature.

SUBSTITUTIONS & OMISSIONS

Green pepper for red, yellow onion for red.

4 packages ramen: two tomato, two spicy chicken	.40
4 zucchinis, sliced	1.00
1 yellow onion, cut into large chunks	.25
¾ cup roasted green peppers, diced	.25
juice of two lemons	*
	Total: $1.90

$$$ BIG SPLURGE $$$

Add some portobello mushrooms, some flank steak and use orzo instead of ramen noodles.

RAMEN AND LENTIL SALAD

Serves four

Notes: Lentils are great nutrition-wise and are filling, too. Leave out a few things and you still have a great tasting and filling meal.

3 packages vegetable ramen	.30
½ cup olive oil	.40
3 tablespoons wine vinegar	.30
1 tablespoon Dijon mustard	.20
1 large garlic clove, minced	.10
2 cups lentils, cooked	1.25
1 cup carrots, grated	.15
½ cup green onion, sliced	.15
1 cup celery, diced	.30
1 cup red bell pepper, diced	1.00
½ cup parsley, chopped	.25
	Total: $4.40

Cook the ramen noodles in boiling, slightly salted water until *al dente,* 3-4 minutes, omitting the flavor packets. Drain well and rinse under cold water. Set aside.

In a large bowl, combine the oil, vinegar, Dijon mustard and garlic. Season with one flavor packet and toss to blend.

SUBSTITUTIONS & OMISSIONS

Reduce the lentils by half (you have enough carbs with the ramen) and add another package of ramen. Add lemon juice, lose the vinegar, use Chinese mustard for Dijon, reduce the parsley and use green pepper for red.

4 packages vegetable ramen	.40
½ cup vegetable oil	.10
1 tablespoon Dijon mustard	*
1 large garlic clove, minced	.10
1 cup cooked lentils	.45
1 cup carrot, grated	.15
½ cup green onion, sliced	.15
1 cup celery, diced	.30
1 cup green bell pepper, diced	.25
¼ cup parsley, chopped	.10
1 teaspoon lemon juice	*
	Total: $2.00

$$$ BIG SPLURGE $$$

Use fettuccine for ramen noodles and roasted or marinated pimento for bell pepper.

MANGO SUMMER SALAD

Serves four

Notes: Mango mixed with spices creates a taste more like a sweet lemon salsa than a fruit salad. Cumin makes this is a very savory combination. The other spices are along for the ride. This one will make you look quite sophisticated.

3 packages vegetable ramen	.30
1 mango, diced	.75
1 cup pineapple with juice, diced	.50
½ cup onion, diced	.25
1 jalapeno pepper, diced	.10
½ red bell pepper, diced	.50
2 tablespoons cilantro, chopped	.10
1 tablespoon cumin	.10
1 teaspoon sugar	.05
	Total: $2.65

Bring about five quarts of water to boil in a large pot. Drop in ramen noodles and boil for a minute, then reduce heat. Cook another 2–3 minutes, or until tender. Remove from heat, drain and set aside.

Mix all other ingredients, plus one flavor packet, in a large bowl and toss in ramen noodles. Refrigerate before serving.

SUBSTITUTIONS & OMISSIONS

Use green pepper for red and reduce the pineapple by half.

3 packages vegetable ramen	.30
1 mango, diced	.70
½ cup crushed pineapple with juice, diced	.25
½ cup onion, diced	.25
1 jalapeno pepper, diced	.10
½ green bell pepper, diced	.15
2 tablespoons cilantro, chopped	.10
1 tablespoon cumin	.10
1 teaspoon sugar	*
Total:	$1.95

$$$ BIG SPLURGE $$$

Add a shot of pineapple schnapps and serve over spaghetti instead of ramen noodles.

COOL MELON AND RAMEN SALAD

Serves four

Notes: A fairly expensive recipe, you can still do it on the cheap by mid-August, when both honeydew and cantaloupe are in season. Leave out the chili powder if it bothers you. If you're eating alone, reduce the amounts; this will spoil quickly.

3 packages ramen (don't use flavor packets)	.30
2 cups honeydew, cut into ½-inch chunks	1.50
2 cups cantaloupe, cut into ½-inch chunks	1.50
1 medium cucumber, peeled, seeded and cut into ½-inch chunks	.25
½ cup limeade concentrate	.40
2 tablespoons vegetable oil	.05
1 teaspoon chili powder	.10
Total:	$4.10

Bring water to a boil in a large pot, and add ramen noodles. Cook for approximately four minutes, or until tender. Drain and set aside. Let cool.

Toss the honeydew, cantaloupe and cucumber together in a large bowl. Then, in a small mixing bowl, whisk together the limeade concentrate, oil, chili powder and salt. Add the dressing to the fruit mixture.

Toss pasta with fruit and dressing and serve.

SUBSTITUTIONS & OMISSIONS

Omit either the honeydew or the cantaloupe, use lemon juice and sugar for limeade. Add another package of ramen for volume.

4 packages ramen (don't use flavor packets)	.40
1 ½ cups honeydew, cut into ½-inch chunks	1.20
1 medium cucumber, peeled, seeded and cut into ½-inch chunks	.25
½ cup limeade concentrate	*
2 tablespoons vegetable oil	.05
1 teaspoon chili powder	.10
	Total: $2.00

$$$ BIG SPLURGE $$$

Use bow tie pasta for ramen.

MEXICAN RAMEN WITH SALSA

Serves four

Notes: Hot and cool at the same time. If you can't find tomatillos or green tomatoes (and you should do yourself a favor and find them), you can use red tomatoes instead. Orale.

3 packages spicy chicken ramen	.30
6 tomatillos, cut into wedges	.75
2 jalapeno chilies, chopped	.10
1 tablespoon cilantro, chopped	.05
2 tablespoons vegetable oil	.05
juice of two limes	.20
zest from one lime peel	.00
	Total: $1.45

Prepare ramen by boiling for two to three minutes, then removing from heat. Drain well and set aside.

Mix the ramen noodles, tomatillos, chilies and cilantro. Mix in one flavor packet with the lime and zest and toss. Cover and refrigerate until chilled, at least 2 hours.

SUBSTITUTIONS & OMISSIONS

Don't have tomatillos? Use regular tomatoes if you must.

3 packages spicy chicken ramen	.30
1 large red tomato, cut in wedges	.75
2 jalapeno chilies, diced	.10
1 tablespoon cilantro, chopped	.05
2 tablespoons vegetable oil	.05
juice of two limes	.20
zest from one lime peel	.00
	Total: $1.45

$$$ BIG SPLURGE $$$

Crumble some *queso ranchero* on top and use orzo for ramen noodles.

MINESTRONE RAMEN NOODLE SALAD

Serves four

Notes: Navy beans and vegetables make this an old favorite. Use your choice of vegetable or chicken ramen flavoring and recreate it on the cheap.

3 packages chicken ramen	.30
1 16-ounce can navy beans, drained	.75
3 carrots, shredded	.25
1 ½ cups celery, chopped	.50
¼ cup parsley, chopped	.15
¾ cup mayonnaise	.30
½ cup vegetable oil	.20
2 tablespoons vinegar	.10
black pepper to taste	.05
	Total: $2.60

Boil about six cups of water and toss in ramen noodles. Cook one minute, then reduce the heat. Cook another 2-3 minutes, drain and set aside.

In a large bowl, combine navy beans, carrots, celery, parsley, oil and one flavor packet. Mix with the ramen noodles and toss in mayonnaise, cider and pepper. Stir well. Refrigerate and serve.

SUBSTITUTIONS & OMISSIONS

Use half the posted amount of navy beans and one-third the amount of carrots. Add another package of ramen.

4 packages chicken ramen	.40
½ 16-ounce can navy beans, drained	.35
3 medium carrots, shredded	.25
½ cup celery, chopped	.20
¼ cup parsley, chopped	.15
¾ cup mayonnaise	*
½ cup vegetable oil	.20
2 tablespoons vinegar	.10
¼ teaspoon pepper	.05
	Total: $1.70

$$$ BIG SPLURGE $$$

Lose all pasta but a half-pound a half of angel hair and make it soup. Or substitute a pound of penne for the ramen and make it a casserole.

RAMEN NICOISE SALAD

Serves four

Notes: You need the olives and the garlic, but the remainder can be changed. Capers help this a lot but can be omitted.

3 packages Oriental ramen	.30
2 large tomatoes, quartered	1.00
1 red bell pepper, diced	1.00
½ cup green beans	.50
1 cup black olives	.50
1 teaspoon capers	.30
4 tablespoons olive oil	.30
2 tablespoons white vinegar	.30
2 cloves garlic, minced	.10
	Total: $4.30

Cook the ramen noodles in slightly salted boiling water until *al dente*, 3–4 minutes, omitting the flavor packets. Drain well and rinse under cold water. Set aside and let cool.

Mix together the pasta, bell pepper, tomatoes, beans, olives and capers in a large bowl. Mix the oil, vinegar, garlic and one flavor packet and pour over the pasta. Toss well just before serving.

SUBSTITUTIONS & OMISSIONS

Add one more package of ramen and reduce the tomatoes by three-quarters. Use green pepper instead of red, canned green beans and lose the white vinegar. Or leave out the beans. Use just a few capers and vegetable oil for olive oil.

4 packages Oriental ramen	.40
1 large tomato, diced	.40
1 green bell pepper, sliced	.25
1 cup black olives	.50
1 teaspoon capers	.30
4 tablespoons vegetable oil	.05
2 cloves garlic, minced	.10
	Total: $2.00

$$$ BIG SPLURGE $$$

Use a variety of good olives—some Greek, Spanish, spiced and Italian. And use spaghetti in place of ramen noodles.

ORANGE AND SPINACH RAMEN SALAD

Serves four

Notes: Fennel seed is a nice addition to this salad—a salad that is becoming commonplace. But the flavor will survive without the fennel, so don't be too concerned. Make sure the oranges are present, however. And enjoy the teaming of fresh spinach and the juicy taste of citrus.

3 packages vegetable ramen	.30
3 cups fresh spinach leaves, torn	1.50
2 medium naval oranges, peeled and sectioned	.40
¼ cup green onions, sliced	.10
½ cup olive oil	.50
½ cup orange juice	.50
¼ teaspoon fennel seed	.10
	Total: $3.40

Prepare ramen by boiling for two to three minutes, then removing from heat. Drain well and set aside.

Combine olive oil, orange juice, fennel seed and one flavor packet. Mix well and set aside.

Place ramen noodles in a medium bowl and add oil, dressing and onion, tossing to coat. Refrigerate, along with the remaining dressing, until chilled.

Just before serving, add the spinach, oranges and onions to the chilled pasta and toss to combine. Serve.

SUBSTITUTIONS & OMISSIONS

Use vegetable oil for olive oil, leave out the fennel and orange juice, use less spinach and bulk up with another package of ramen.

Ingredient	Cost
4 packages vegetable ramen	.40
2 cups fresh spinach leaves, torn	1.00
2 medium naval oranges, peeled and sectioned	.40
¼ cup green onions, sliced	.10
½ cup vegetable oil	.10
	Total: $2.00

$$$ BIG SPLURGE $$$

Use spinach tortellini in place of ramen and use a few teaspoons of triple sec.

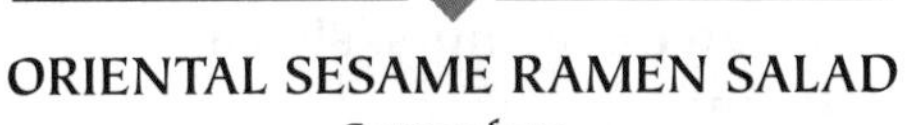

ORIENTAL SESAME RAMEN SALAD

Serves four

Notes: The tofu makes this dish, but if you don't like it (and who the hell really does?), can't find it, or can't afford it, omit it. Or maybe use beef. The lychees add an interesting taste you might not agree with, so eliminate them if necessary. Water chestnuts are keepers, as are the sesame seeds.

Ingredient	Cost
2 packages Oriental ramen	.20
1 small carrot, shredded	.10
6 leaves romaine lettuce, torn into 1-inch pieces	.30
6 leaves red leaf lettuce, torn into 1-inch pieces	.30
1 red bell pepper, diced	1.00
1 yellow bell pepper, diced	1.00
½ package (8 ounce size) fried tofu, sliced	1.00
1 cup water chestnuts, sliced	.75
1 11-ounce can mandarin orange wedges, drained	1.25
1 20-ounce can lychees, drained and cut into quarters	1.75

¼ cup sesame seeds, toasted	.40
½ cup brown sugar	.30
¼ cup sesame oil	.75
½ cup lime juice	.50
6 tablespoons rice vinegar	.40
½ cup sesame oil	.50
	Total: $10.50

Prepare ramen by boiling for two to three minutes, then removing from heat. Drain well and set aside.

Toss noodles with carrots, peppers, tofu, water chestnuts, mandarin oranges, and lychees. Chill until ready to serve.

To make the dressing, combine the sesame seeds, brown sugar, lime juice, one flavor packet, rice vinegar and sesame oil and mix well. Toss into the salad.

SUBSTITUTIONS & OMISSIONS

Use the cheapest lettuce and double up. Use green pepper for red and yellow. Leave out the tofu since it tastes like bathroom caulking, omit the sesame, lychees and vinegar. Use lemon for lime juice and vegetable oil for sesame.

4 packages Oriental ramen	.40
1 small carrot, shredded	.10
2 cups lettuce, torn into 1-inch pieces	.30
1 green bell pepper, sliced	.25
½ 8-ounce can water chestnuts, sliced	.35
2 oranges, sectioned	.50
½ tablespoon sugar	*
¼ cup vegetable oil	.05
3 tablespoons lemon juice	*
	Total: $1.95

$$$ BIG SPLURGE $$$

Use fat Oriental noodles for ramen noodles and lots of sesame oil.

PEANUT RAMEN NOODLE SALAD

Serves four

Notes: This is like a Chinese version of sate without the same level of sweetness of Thai cooking. Again, for a change, twice-cook the noodles (boil once then fry).

3 packages of ramen	.30
½ cup bean sprouts	.50
½ carrot, grated	.10
¼ green or red pepper, diced	.10
½ cucumber, sliced	.15
2 tablespoons peanut butter	.40
1 tablespoon rice vinegar	.10
1 teaspoon sugar	.05
2 tablespoons oil	.05
2 teaspoons soy sauce	.10
¼ teaspoon fresh ginger	.10
1 green onion, chopped	.10
2 teaspoons sesame oil	.20
	Total: $2.25

Boil water in a large pot. Add ramen noodles and return to a boil for one minute, then reduce heat and cook another 2-3 minutes. Mix the noodles with sesame oil and set aside.

Mix peanut butter, rice vinegar, soy sauce and sesame oil with ginger, green onion, pepper and carrot. Toss It all into a small saucepan. Bring to a boil, reduce and add cucumber, sugar and one flavor packet. Mix with noodles, let cool and serve.

SUBSTITUTIONS & OMISSIONS

Use less sesame oil.

3 packages vegetable ramen	.30
½ cup bean sprouts	.50
½ carrot, diced	.10
¼ green or red pepper, diced	.10
½ cucumber, diced	.15
2 tablespoons peanut butter	.40
1 tablespoon rice vinegar	.10
1 teaspoon sugar	*
2 tablespoons oil	.05
2 teaspoons soy sauce	*
1 teaspoon fresh ginger, minced	.10
1 green onion, chopped	.10
1 teaspoons sesame oil	.10
	Total: $2.00

$$$ BIG SPLURGE $$$

Serve on fat Oriental noodles.

LAYERED SOUTHWESTERN RAMEN SALAD

Serves four

Notes: Mexican taste, layered like lasagna. In actuality, it'll feed more than four people—or a couple big dudes for a few days.

3 packages spicy chicken ramen	.30
1 teaspoon oil	.05
1 teaspoon cumin	.10
1 15-ounce can dark red kidney beans, drained and washed	1.00
2 cups corn (canned or frozen is fine)	1.00
½ cup bell peppers, chopped	.15
½ cup onions, diced	.15
¾ cup mayonnaise	.30
½ cup sour cream	.30
½ cup taco sauce	.30
Total:	$3.65

Prepare ramen by boiling two to three minutes. Remove from heat and drain. Do not overcook the ramen. Drain and set aside.

Toss ramen noodles with oil, cumin and one flavor packet. Layer ramen, beans, corn, bell peppers and onions. Place in a casserole or baking dish, but don't cook.

In a mixing bowl, combine mayonnaise, sour cream and taco sauce. Spread mixture evenly over top of pasta, sealing to edge of bowl. Cover tightly and chill overnight.

SUBSTITUTIONS & OMISSIONS

Add ramen noodles and reduce the amount of beans and corn.

5 packages spicy chicken ramen	.50
½ teaspoon oil	.05
½ teaspoon cumin	.10
1 cup dark red kidney beans, drained and washed	.50
½ cup corn	.25
½ cup bell peppers, chopped	.15
½ cup onions, chopped	.15
¾ cup mayonnaise	*
½ cup sour cream	.30
½ cup taco sauce	*
Total:	$2.00

$$$ BIG SPLURGE $$$

Use elbow macaroni or make it a cold lasagna with lasagna noodles.

SWEET AND SOUR CUCUMBER SALAD

Serves four

Notes: The combination of cucumbers and chili—of hot and cool—make this a great dish. Again, the bean sauce can be an improvisation (see pages 33–34).

3 packages chicken ramen	.30
2 cucumbers, halved and sliced	.50
1 teaspoon bean sauce	.30
1 tablespoon sesame oil	.20
2 tablespoons sugar	.05
2 tablespoons rice vinegar	.20
1 teaspoon soy sauce	.10
¼ teaspoon crushed red chilies	.10
	Total: $1.75

Boil water in a large pot. Add ramen noodles and return to a boil for one minute, then reduce heat and cook another 2-3 minutes. Drain and set aside to cool.

Mix the cucumber with one flavor packet, add other seasonings and mix. Refrigerate for about an hour then mix with cold ramen noodles. Serve.

SUBSTITUTIONS & OMISSIONS

Use vegetable oil in place of sesame oil, and make your own bean paste (see pages 33–34).

3 packages Oriental flavor ramen	.30
2 cucumbers, chopped into 1-inch pieces	.50
1 teaspoon bean paste	.30
1 tablespoon sesame oil	.20
2 tablespoons sugar	*
2 tablespoons rice vinegar	.20
1 teaspoon soy sauce	*
¼ teaspoon crushed red chilies	*
	Total: $1.50

$$$ BIG SPLURGE $$$

Use some ziti pasta instead of ramen.

TOMATO AND WATERMELON RAMEN SALAD

Serves four

Notes: Too strange a taste combination? How about salt and pepper on a cantaloupe? No stupider is tomato and watermelon. Try it once. You don't like it, sorry.

2 packages tomato ramen	.20
2 cups tomatoes, diced	1.00
2 cups watermelon, diced	.50
¼ cup spinach, torn into 2-inch pieces	.25
¼ cup basil leaves, chopped	.40
¼ cup wine vinegar	.30
¼ cup olive oil	.30
black pepper to taste	.05
	Total: $3.00

Bring about five quarts of water to boil in a large pot. Drop in ramen noodles, boil for a minute and reduce heat. Cook another 2-3 minutes, or until tender. Remove from heat, drain and set aside.

Mix the tomatoes and watermelon with a tomato ramen flavor packet and pepper to taste in a large bowl then mix with the spinach and basil. Add the vinegar and oil and add the ramen noodles. Toss gently.

SUBSTITUTIONS & OMISSIONS

Reduce the amount of watermelon, spinach and tomato by half, adding two packages of ramen to fill out. Use dried basil for fresh and vegetable oil for olive.

4 packages tomato ramen	.40
¾ cup tomatoes, diced	.65
1 cup watermelon, diced	.25
¼ cup spinach	.25
2 teaspoons dried basil leaves	.10
¼ cup wine vinegar	.30
¼ cup vegetable oil	.05
black pepper	*
	Total: $2.00

$$$ BIG SPLURGE $$$

Use fresh spinach, basil, red peppercorns and spaghetti for ramen noodles.

SALADS WITH MEAT
(AND OTHER NON-VEGETARIAN STUFF)

RAMEN WITH ASPARAGUS SALAD
Serves four

Notes: No way to avoid it—asparagus is out of the budget. But if you lighten up on the proportions and add another package of ramen, you can still do this one on the cheap.

3 packages pork ramen	.30
1 pound asparagus, blanched and cut in 1-inch pieces	1.50
¼ cup olive oil	.40
1 clove garlic, minced	.10
1 cup tuna, flaked	.50
½ cup ham, diced	.75
½ cup black olives, sliced	.50
2 tablespoons lemon juice	.25
	Total: $4.30

Cook the ramen noodles in slightly salted boiling water until *al dente,* 3–4 minutes, omitting the flavor packets. Drain well and rinse under cold water. Set aside.

Cook garlic in olive oil and combine with ramen noodles in large bowl. Add remaining ingredients and toss well. Serve at room temperature or refrigerate until cold if desired.

SUBSTITUTIONS & OMISSIONS

Use half or less (depending on how much it costs when you decide to make this dish) of the asparagus, vegetable oil instead of olive oil and take out the tuna. Use cheap ham—and less of it—and drop the amount of olives to ¼ **cup**. Add another package of ramen to fill it out.

4 packages pork ramen	**.40**
½ pound asparagus, blanched and cut in 1-inch pieces	**.75**
¼ cup vegetable oil	**.15**
1 clove garlic, minced	**.10**
¼ cup ham, diced	**.35**
½ cup black olives, sliced	**.25**
juice of 1 lemon	*
	Total: **$2.00**

$$$ BIG SPLURGE $$$

Try some prosciutto instead of ham. And use penne for ramen noodles.

BLT RAMEN SALAD

Serves four

Notes: The cool of the lettuce and the smoke of the bacon make up this taste. Don't have any bacon? Use bacon bits instead.

3 packages ramen: 1 tomato, 2 chicken	**.30**
10 slices bacon, cooked and crumbled	**1.75**
1 large tomato, diced	**.50**
1 cup mayonnaise	**.40**
¼ cup tomato sauce	**.30**
¼ cup lemon juice	**.40**
2 teaspoons sugar	**.05**
¼ cup green onions, sliced	**.25**
2 cups lettuce, thinly sliced	**1.50**
	Total: **$5.45**

Open both packages of ramen. Cook the noodles without the seasoning packets 3-4 minutes in boiling water. When done, drain and toss with the French dressing. Set aside.

In large bowl, combine mayonnaise, tomato sauce, lemon juice, one flavor packet and sugar. Stir in ramen, tomato and onions.

Cover and chill. Just before serving, stir in lettuce and bacon.

SUBSTITUTIONS & OMISSIONS

Use bacon bits for real bacon. Back off the mayo and the lettuce.

Ingredient	Cost
3 packages ramen: 1 tomato, 2 chicken	.30
2 tablespoons bacon bits	*
1 large tomato, diced	.50
¼ cup mayonnaise	*
¼ cup tomato sauce	.30
¼ cup lemon juice	*
2 teaspoons sugar	*
¼ cup green onions, sliced	.15
2 cups lettuce, thinly sliced	.75
	Total: $2.00

$$$ BIG SPLURGE $$$

Use spaghetti in place of ramen noodles and double the amount of bacon.

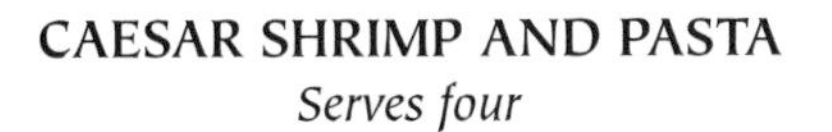

CAESAR SHRIMP AND PASTA

Serves four

Notes: Caesar dressing is a strict formula—which we adhere to pretty well here. Broccoli can be replaced by salad vegetables or by your favorite green veggie.

Ingredient	Cost
3 packages vegetable ramen	.30
2 cups broccoli florets	1.00
3 cloves garlic, minced	.20
¼ cup olive oil	.50
¼ teaspoon Worcestershire sauce	.20
1 teaspoon anchovy paste	.50
¼ cup Romano cheese, grated	.50
1 egg yolk	.10
juice of 2 lemons	.20
	Total: $3.50

Bring water to a boil in a large pot and add ramen noodles and broccoli. Cook approximately four minutes or until tender. Drain and set aside.

Heat olive oil in large skillet over medium-high heat and sauté garlic. When fragrant, add the Worcestershire sauce and the anchovy paste, stirring constantly. Let cool and add lemon juice. Add the egg yolk and continue stirring.

Drain pasta and broccoli. Transfer to a serving bowl. Add Caesar mix with cheese and toss well.

SUBSTITUTIONS & OMISSIONS

Don't worry about the anchovy paste. Instead, use a teaspoon of oil and mix two shrimp ramen flavoring packets into a paste.

3 packages vegetable ramen	**.30**
2 cups broccoli florets	**1.00**
3 cloves garlic, minced	**.10**
¼ cup vegetable oil	**.10**
1 teaspoon Worcestershire sauce	**.20**
¼ cup Romano cheese, grated	*
1 egg yolk	**.10**
juice of 2 lemons	*
	Total: $1.80

$$$ BIG SPLURGE $$$

Use fettuccine for ramen.

MOCK CEVICHE RAMEN SALAD

Serves four

Notes: Lime juice, onion and cilantro makes a can of tuna come alive. Don't like fish? Ease up on the tuna. But don't fret too much about the tuna taste; you won't taste much fish in this anyway. The lime is the most powerful ingredient. Add radishes, onions, or celery to replace the tuna.

3 packages spicy chicken ramen	**.30**
½ cup bell peppers, diced	**.15**
½ cup onions, chopped	**.15**
¼ cup cilantro, chopped	**.15**
2 cans tuna, drained and flaked	**1.00**
½ cup hot sauce	**.50**
½ teaspoon garlic powder	**.10**
juice of 10 limes	**1.00**
black pepper	**.05**
	Total: $3.40

Cook the ramen noodles in boiling, slightly salted water until *al dente*, 3–4 minutes, omitting the flavor packets. Drain well and rinse under cold water.

Set aside.

Add bell peppers, onions and tuna. To prepare dressing, combine lime juice, cilantro, hot sauce, one flavor packet, garlic powder and black pepper in a mixing bowl. Pour over the pasta mixture. Toss lightly. Cover and chill until ready to serve.

SUBSTITUTIONS & OMISSIONS

Lose one can of tuna and add another package ramen noodles. Use a few less limes.

4 packages spicy chicken ramen	.40
½ cup bell peppers, chopped	.15
½ cup onions, chopped	.15
¼ cup cilantro, chopped	.15
½ can tuna in water, drained and flaked	.25
½ cup hot sauce	*
½ teaspoon garlic powder	.10
½ teaspoon black pepper	*
juice of 8 limes	.80
	Total: $2.00

$$$ BIG SPLURGE $$$

Ceviche is typically made without ramen noodles, so leave it out and add more fish.

RAMEN COBB SALAD

Serves four

Notes: Iceberg lettuce is not typically a part of Cobb Salad. So if you're a recipe purist, omit it. But it fills out this dish nicely.

3 packages chicken ramen	.30
¾ cup plain yogurt	.30
¼ cup mayonnaise	.30
1 ½ cups smoked turkey, diced	2.50
2 celery sticks, diced	.25
1 medium Granny Smith apple, diced	.25
1 cup iceberg lettuce, thinly sliced	.90
¼ cup blue cheese, crumbled	.75
	Total: $5.55

In a large pot of boiling water, prepare ramen noodles, cooking 3–4 minutes or until tender. Do not overcook. Drain and set aside.

Add one flavor packet, yogurt and mayonnaise to a bowl, whisking with a fork until smooth. Set aside.

Stir the pasta, smoked turkey, celery, lettuce and apple together. Add the yogurt/mayonnaise sauce and toss until evenly coated. Sprinkle with blue cheese, toss again and serve.

SUBSTITUTIONS & OMISSIONS

Use chicken for turkey and reduce the amount by half. In a pinch you can use blue cheese dressing, but it's a lot better with real cheese.

3 packages chicken ramen	.30
¾ cup plain yogurt	.30
¼ cup mayonnaise	*
½ cup cooked chicken, diced	.50
2 celery sticks, diced	.25
1 medium Granny Smith apple, diced	.25
2 tablespoons blue cheese dressing	*
	Total: $1.60

$$$ BIG SPLURGE $$$

Grill the chicken or turkey first and serve in rotini.

INDIAN CHICKEN SALAD

Serves four

Notes: Raisins and apples make this different; ramen makes it filling. Yes, you have permission to affect an Indian accent while cooking.

3 packages curry chicken ramen	.30
2 cups chicken, cut into ¼-inch strips	1.50
½ cup celery, diced	.25
3 tablespoons butter	.30
1 green apple, peeled and diced	.25
1 onion, thinly sliced	.25
1 tablespoon curry powder	.10
¼ cup raisins	.30
½ teaspoon sugar	.05
3 tablespoons flour	.05

½ cup cream	.50
¼ teaspoon pepper	.05
	Total: $3.90

In a pot of boiling water, cook the chicken for about 10 minutes. Remove chicken and bring broth back to a boil. Drop in ramen noodles and boil for a minute, then reduce heat. Cook another 2-3 minutes, or until tender. Remove from heat, drain (keep chicken broth) and set aside to cool.

In a small saucepan, melt butter and stir in about a cup of the broth. When it comes to a boil, stir in raisins, cream, curry powder and one flavor packet. Let simmer a few more minutes until thick and creamy. Add the cooked chicken and simmer an additional five minutes. Remove from stove and let cool to room temperature, then add the cold celery, onion and apple and mix in the ramen noodles. Serve cool, but not cold.

SUBSTITUTIONS & OMISSIONS

Use chicken thigh meat for breast and use less cream.

3 packages curry chicken ramen	.30
2 cups chicken thigh meat, cut in ¼-inch strips	.50
½ cup celery, sliced	.25
3 tablespoons vegetable oil	.05
1 green apple, peeled and diced	.25
1 onion, thinly sliced	.25
1 tablespoon curry powder	.10
¼ cup raisins	.20
½ teaspoon sugar	*
3 tablespoons flour	.05
3 tablespoons cream, mixed with water	*
¼ teaspoon pepper	*
	Total: $1.95

$$$ BIG SPLURGE $$$

Serve on white rice instead of ramen noodles.

DELI RAMEN SALAD

Serves four

Notes: Get the salami from your grocer's deli section, the olives from any party platter—then improvise on the rest. The olives and salami make this salad.

3 packages tomato ramen	.30
2 medium tomatoes, cut into wedges	1.00
6 ounces hard salami, sliced	1.00
6 ounces provolone cheese, cubed	1.50
¼ cup olives, drained and sliced	.20
1 small red onion, sliced	.75
1 small zucchini, halved and sliced	.25
½ cup green bell pepper, diced	.15
½ cup red bell pepper, diced	.50
¼ cup fresh parsley, chopped	.15
¼ cup Parmesan cheese, grated	.75
½ cup vegetable oil	.40
¼ cup vinegar	.20
1 clove garlic, minced	.10
1 teaspoon dried mustard	.10
1 teaspoon dried basil	.10
1 teaspoon dried oregano	.10
black pepper to taste	.05
	Total: $7.60

Cook the ramen in three quarts of water without using seasoning packages. Rinse in cold water and drain. Set aside.

Combine oil, vinegar, garlic, mustard, basil, oregano, one flavor packet and pepper; stir well. Mix tomatoes with ramen and pour dressing over salad; toss in salami, chili peppers, onions and cheese. Cover and chill.

Substitutions & Omissions

Use Monterey jack cheese for provolone and reduce the amount by half. Add a couple tablespoons Parmesan. Use yellow onion for red and leave out the vinegar. Add two more packages of ramen to fill it out and tomato flavoring to replace the real tomato.

4 packages tomato ramen	.40
1 tablespoon dry salami, chopped	.25
1 cup Monterey jack cheese, cubed	.75
1 small yellow onion, diced	.25
½ small zucchini, halved and sliced	.10
1 cup green bell pepper, chopped	.25
2 tablespoons Parmesan cheese, grated	*
¼ cup mayonnaise	*
1 teaspoon dried oregano	*
black pepper to taste	*
	Total: $2.00

$$$ BIG SPLURGE $$$

Use good San Francisco salami and toss with a pound of penne instead of ramen.

DIJON RAMEN SALAD

Serves four

Notes: Dijon mustard gives this one its post-nasal kick. But you can use Chinese mustard or horseradish instead of Dijon mustard.

3 packages creamy chicken ramen	.30
½ cup oil	.30
2 teaspoons cider vinegar	.20
2 teaspoons Dijon mustard	.20
½ cup mayonnaise	.30
2 stalks celery, sliced	.15
6 slices bacon, cooked and diced	.75
2 eggs, hard-boiled and chopped	.20
2 green onions, chopped	.10
	Total: $2.50

Cook ramen with one of the three seasoning packets in boiling water about 3-4 minutes or until tender. Drain and rinse under cold water and set aside.

In a large bowl, whisk together oil, vinegar, mustard and mayonnaise. Add pasta and all other ingredients to dressing. Mix carefully. Chill thoroughly before serving.

SUBSTITUTIONS & OMISSIONS

Bacon bits will work as well as real bacon, and get rid of the vinegar.

3 packages creamy chicken	.30
½ cup oil	.30
2 teaspoons Dijon mustard	.20
½ cup mayonnaise	.30
2 large celery stalks, chopped	.15
3 tablespoons bacon bits	*
2 eggs, hard-boiled and chopped	.20
2 green onions, chopped	.10
	Total: $1.55

$$$ BIG SPLURGE $$$

Use bow tie pasta for ramen noodles and Sauterne for added taste.

STIR-FRIED PORK SLICES WITH GREEN ONION RAMEN SALAD

Serves four

Notes: This one calls for a good portion of green onions. So use all the green onion, up to about four inches from the very top.

3 packages ramen	.30
½ pound lean boneless pork, cut into ¼-inch slivers	1.50
2 tablespoons sesame oil	.30
1 tablespoon soy sauce	.20
1 cup green onions, chopped	.25
4 tablespoons vegetable oil	.05
	Total: $2.60

Boil water in a large pot. Add ramen noodles and return to a boil for one minute, then reduce heat and cook another 2-3 minutes. Drain and set aside.

Add pork slices to a skillet and stir-fry for 45 seconds, or until brown. Add the soy sauce, one pork ramen flavor packet and stir-fry another 3-5 minutes. Remove and cool.

Throw in another flavor packet into noodles with the sesame oil and toss with chilled pork slices. Mix well. Serve chilled.

SUBSTITUTIONS & OMISSIONS

Back off the pork slightly and add another package ramen to fit the budget.

4 packages ramen	.40
¼ pound lean boneless pork, cut into ¼ inch slivers	1.00
2 tablespoons sesame oil	.30
1 tablespoon soy sauce	*
1 cup green onions, chopped	.25
4 tablespoons vegetable oil	.05
	Total: $2.00

$$$ BIG SPLURGE $$$

Use fat Oriental noodles for ramen and add more pork.

PIZZA RAMEN NOODLES

Serves four

Notes: Pepperoni makes this taste right (dry salami will also work), but you can eliminate it. Just don't lose the bell pepper, too—it won't taste anything like pizza if you do.

3 packages tomato ramen	.30
¾ cup pepperoni, sliced	1.00
1 cup mozzarella cheese, shredded	1.00
1 cup tomatoes, diced	.50
½ cup fresh Parmesan cheese, grated	.75
½ cup Italian salad dressing	.50
1 teaspoon Italian seasoning	.10
1 clove garlic, minced	.10
1 green bell pepper, sliced into rings	.25
	Total: $4.50

In a large pot of boiling water, prepare ramen noodles, cooking 3–4 minutes or until tender. Do not overcook. Drain and set aside to cool.

Cut pepperoni slices into fourths and drop into a bowl with the mozzarella cheese. Add tomatoes, Parmesan cheese, Italian dressing, one packet tomato flavoring, Italian seasoning and garlic.

Add ramen to cheese mixture and toss well. Garnish with green pepper rings.

SUBSTITUTIONS & OMISSIONS

Use less pepperoni and mozzarella and Parmesan cheese. Use onion and one extra ramen package to fill out the dish.

4 packages tomato ramen	.40
¼ cup pepperoni, sliced	.35
¼ cup mozzarella cheese, shredded	.35
½ cup tomatoes, diced	.30
2 tablespoons dried Parmesan cheese, grated	*
½ cup Italian salad dressing	*
1 teaspoon Italian seasoning	.10
1 green bell pepper, sliced into rings	.25
1 onion, diced	.25
	Total: $2.00

$$$ BIG SPLURGE $$$

Use orzo instead of ramen noodles and fresh mozzarella and Parmesan.

SALMON AND AVOCADO RAMEN SALAD

Serves four

Notes: Avocado is the thrust here. But since it's expensive, you'll need to use something less pricey as a substitute. Or just wait until avocados are in season and cheap—or until a crate falls off the back of a delivery truck.

3 packages shrimp ramen	.30
1 can salmon (14¾ ounces), crumbled	1.25
2 tablespoons French dressing	.40
1 red bell pepper, diced	1.00
3 tablespoons cilantro, chopped	.15
¼ cup tomato sauce	.10
½ cup sour cream	.50
½ teaspoon paprika	.10
1 bunch green onions, sliced	.15
2 tablespoons mayonnaise	.10
3 avocados, diced	1.50
juice of 1 lime	.10
	Total: $5.65

Open both packages of ramen. Cook the noodles without the seasoning packets in boiling water, cooking two or three minutes. When done, drain and toss with the French dressing. Set aside to cool.

Drain and crumble the salmon, then mix with green onions, sliced bell pepper and cilantro. Mix in the lime juice and grated rind, the mayonnaise, sour cream, tomato paste and salt and pepper to taste. Mix until thoroughly combined.

Toss with the pasta and chill. Before serving, gently toss the avocados into the salad. Spoon the salad onto a bed of lettuce leaves. Garnish with paprika—if you have it.

SUBSTITUTIONS & OMISSIONS

Reduce the amount of salmon and use cream, lemon and water for sour cream.

4 packages shrimp ramen	.40
¼ can salmon (14¾ ounces)	.35
2 tablespoons French dressing	*
1 green bell pepper, diced	.25
3 tablespoons cilantro, chopped	.15
juice of 1 lime	.10
¼ cup tomato sauce	.10

3 tablespoons cream, mixed with equal parts water and lemon	*
1 bunch green onion, sliced	.15
2 tablespoons mayonnaise	*
1 avocado, diced	.50
	Total: $2.00

$$$ BIG SPLURGE $$$

Use rotini or shells in place of ramen noodles.

CREAMY SEAFOOD RAMEN SALAD

Serves four

Notes: The taste of seafood can be accomplished in a lot of different ways. But a bit of frozen, mixed seafood—available at most stores—is probably the cheapest. It will give you some whitefish, some shellfish, some squid and some crab and perhaps some unidentified fish parts. It's okay. It all tastes like fish, and it probably won't kill you. If not available, use fake crabmeat or tuna.

3 packages shrimp ramen	.30
1 pound mixed seafood, cut into 1-inch pieces	3.00
1 cup red peppers, diced	1.50
1 cup green peppers, diced	.25
¾ cup onions, diced	.25
¾ cup carrots, sliced	.25
½ cup green onion, chopped	.25
1 cup sour cream	1.00
½ cup mayonnaise	.40
2 tablespoons dill weed	.10
2 tablespoons lemon juice	.20
2 tablespoons garlic, minced	.10
2 tablespoons vegetable oil	.10
1 teaspoon Dijon mustard	.20
	Total: $7.90

Open both packages of ramen. Cook the noodles without the seasoning packets for three minutes. When done, drain and set aside.

In a skillet, sauté thawed seafood approximately three minutes in oil. Set aside. Add red and green peppers, onions, carrots and green onions to pasta.

In a small bowl, combine sour cream, mayonnaise, dill, lemon juice, two flavor packets, garlic and mustard. Pour over pasta. Toss and chill.

SUBSTITUTIONS & OMISSIONS

Reduce seafood mix by three-quarters, omit the red pepper and sour cream and use Chinese mustard for Dijon. Reduce amounts of green onion, carrots and onions slightly. Add another package of ramen for filler.

4 packages shrimp ramen	.40
¼ pound mixed seafood, cut into 1-inch pieces	.75
½ cup green pepper, diced	.25
¼ cup onions, diced	.10
¼ cup carrots, thinly sliced	.10
¼ cup green onion, chopped	.10
¼ cup mayonnaise	*
2 tablespoons dill weed	.10
2 tablespoons lemon juice	*
2 cloves garlic, minced	.10
2 tablespoons vegetable oil	.10
1 teaspoon Dijon mustard	*
Total:	**$2.00**

$$$ BIG SPLURGE $$$

Grill the fish, use fresh shrimp, muscles, clams and scallops. And use a pound fettuccine for ramen noodles.

SPICY COLD NOODLES WITH CHICKEN

Serves four

Notes: This is a cheapy dish that gets a lot better if you double cook the noodles (stir-fry after boiling).

3 packages ramen	.30
1 chicken breast (about a third of a pound), diced	.75
2 green onions, chopped	.10
3 eggs	.30
4 tablespoons peanut oil	.20
1 tablespoon soy sauce	.10
1 teaspoon vinegar	.20
1 teaspoon hot chili oil	.20
½ teaspoon dried ginger	.10
1 clove garlic, minced	.10
1 tablespoon sugar	.05
Total:	**$2.40**

Boil water in a large pot. Add ramen noodles and return to a boil for one minute, then reduce heat and cook another 2–3 minutes. Drain and set aside.

Whisk eggs in a small bowl and pour into skillet. Remove when cooked and slice into thin strips.

Slice the green onions. Mix onions with soy, vinegar, chili oil, ginger juice, garlic and sugar. Mix with noodles, cooked egg, chicken and onion. Let cool and serve.

SUBSTITUTIONS & OMISSIONS

Substitute chicken thigh for breast.

3 packages ramen	.30
¼ cup chicken thigh meat, diced	.30
2 green onions, chopped	.10
3 eggs	.30
1 tablespoon soy sauce	*
1 teaspoon vinegar	.20
1 teaspoon hot chili oil	.20
½ teaspoon dried ginger	.10
1 clove garlic, minced	.10
1 tablespoon sugar	.05
2 tablespoons oil	.05
black pepper to taste	*
	Total: $1.70

$$$ BIG SPLURGE $$$

Use grilled or smoked chicken and use fresh rice noodles for ramen noodles.

RAMEN SPINACH SALAD

Serves four

Notes: Blue cheese makes this recipe, so try to keep it. Spinach is a pretty perishable dish, so you'll want to make only as much as you'll need for your guests. Or prepare to pig out.

3 packages chicken flavor ramen	.30
4 cups spinach leaves, torn	1.50
2 cups chicken breast, cooked and diced	1.50
1 cup red or green grapes, halved	.50
1 cup red bell pepper, slivered	1.00
¼ cup almonds, chopped	1.50
¼ cup blue cheese, crumbled	1.00

4 cloves garlic, minced	.10
juice of 1 lemon	.10
¼ cup olive oil	.50
¼ cup mayonnaise	.30
	Total: $8.30

Open both packages of ramen and cook the noodles without the seasoning packets. When done, drain and set aside to cool.

In a small bowl, mix two flavor packets, garlic and lemon juice. Add oil and mayonnaise and blend with fork until smooth.

Mix salad ingredients in a large bowl. Toss with lemon juice mixture thoroughly.

SUBSTITUTIONS & OMISSIONS

Use less chicken—and use thigh meat. Reduce the amount of spinach and use two more ramen noodles packages for bulk. Substitute peanuts for cashews, vegetable oil for olive and blue cheese salad dressing for real blue cheese.

4 packages chicken flavor ramen	.40
2 cups spinach leaves, torn	.75
1 cup turkey or chicken thigh meat, cooked and diced	.50
2 tablespoons peanuts, chopped	*
3 tablespoons blue cheese dressing	*
4 cloves garlic, minced	.10
juice of 1 lemon	*
4 tablespoons mayonnaise	*
	Total: $1.75

$$$ BIG SPLURGE $$$

Use penne instead of ramen noodles and good Danish blue cheese.

CHICKEN AND SPROUTS RAMEN SALAD

Serves four

Notes: This is the way most frugal recipes should be prepared—with meat just for flavoring and heavy on the veggies. This dish is tasty, good for you and will feed a couple fat guys for about a deuce.

3 packages chicken ramen	.30
½ cup cooked chicken, diced	.45
½ cup bean sprouts	.50
¼ cup green onions, sliced	.25
¼ cup red pepper, diced	.30
3 tablespoons peanuts, chopped	.30
2 tablespoons soy sauce	.20
1 clove garlic, minced	.10
¼ teaspoon ginger	.10
¼ teaspoon sesame oil	.20
1 cup lettuce, shredded	.50
	Total: $3.20

Cook the ramen noodles in boiling, slightly salted water until *al dente*, 3–4 minutes, omitting the flavor packets. Drain well and rinse under cold water. Set aside to cool.

In medium mixing bowl, combine ramen noodles, chicken, bean sprouts, green onions, bell pepper and peanuts; set aside.

Combine remaining ingredients—garlic, ginger, oil, two flavor packets and soy sauce (leave out the lettuce)—in a blender and blend at high speed (or beat with a fork). Add to noodle mixture and toss to coat. Cover and refrigerate until chilled.

SUBSTITUTIONS & OMISSIONS

Reduce bean sprouts by half, use green pepper for red and use half the required lettuce. Use an extra package of ramen for bulk.

4 packages chicken ramen	.40
½ cup cooked chicken, diced	.45
½ cup bean sprouts	.25
¼ cup green onions, sliced	.25
¼ cup green pepper, diced	.10
3 tablespoons peanuts, chopped	*
2 tablespoons soy sauce	*
1 clove garlic, minced	.10
¼ teaspoon ginger	.10
¼ teaspoon sesame oil	.10
1 cup lettuce, shredded	.25
	Total: $2.00

$$$ BIG SPLURGE $$$

Use romaine lettuce or endive for iceberg lettuce—and don't shred, but tear into bite-sized pieces. Use bow tie pasta for ramen noodles.

TARRAGON BEEF RAMEN SALAD

Serves four

Notes: Okay, so you can't really have tarragon beef without tarragon. But if you have fresh sage, oregano, thyme, rosemary or bay leaves, you could use them and call this Sage, Oregano, Thyme, Rosemary or Bay Beef Ramen Salad. For the beef part, don't fret over an expensive cut. You're looking for the essence of the beef, not a steak sandwich.

3 packages beef ramen	.30
8 ounces roast beef, cooked, sliced into strips	2.00
1 cup celery, sliced into ¼-inch thick pieces	.30
1 cup cherry tomatoes, halved	1.50
½ cup red onion, diced	.30
1 cup plain yogurt	.50
½ cup mayonnaise	.30
¼ cup fresh parsley, chopped	.10
¼ cup fresh tarragon, chopped	.10
	Total: $5.40

Cook the ramen noodles in boiling, slightly salted water until *al dente*, 3–4 minutes, omitting the flavor packets. Drain well and rinse under cold water. Set aside to cool.

In a large bowl, stir beef, celery, tomatoes and red onions (separated into rings) together. Stir into ramen noodles. Refrigerate at least one hour.

In another bowl, stir together yogurt, mayonnaise, parsley, chives, tarragon, one flavor packet and pepper. Cover and refrigerate at least 1 hour, then mix all together and serve.

SUBSTITUTIONS & OMISSIONS

Use about a quarter of the beef, adding another package of ramen for volume.

4 packages beef ramen	.40
¼ cup roast beef, cooked, sliced in strips	.50
1 cup celery, sliced ¼-inch thick	.30
½ cup tomatoes, diced	.35
½ cup yellow onion, sliced ¼-inch thick	.25
3 tablespoons mayonnaise	*
¼ cup fresh parsley, chopped	.10
2 tablespoons dried tarragon	.10
	Total: $2.00

$$$ BIG SPLURGE $$$

Use good roast beef and a few tablespoons cabernet. Use bow tie pasta for ramen noodles.

VIETNAMESE RAMEN NOODLE SALAD

Serves four

Notes: Vietnamese dishes are lighter than Chinese dishes. Aided by the mint, this is a meal that fills you up, but doesn't make you feel like you ate masonry. You can lighten the load on the meat and still be okay (or use chicken thigh meat, beef or even cooked egg).

3 packages shrimp ramen	.30
2 cloves garlic, minced	.10
2 tablespoons sugar	.05
3 Anaheim or serrano peppers, seeded and thinly sliced	.20
1 lime, peeled and sectioned	.10
1 cup cucumber, diced	.25
2 cups red-leaf lettuce, shredded	.75
¼ cup fresh mint leaves, chopped	.75
¼ cup fresh cilantro, chopped	.15
¼ cup fresh basil, chopped	.75
2 cups fresh bean sprouts	.75
1 cup carrots, shredded	.10
2 cups chicken, cooked and diced	1.50
	Total: $5.75

Boil water in a large pot. Add ramen noodles and return to a boil for one minute, then reduce heat and cook another 2-3 minutes. Drain and set aside to cool.

Mix garlic, sugar, peppers, lime and one shrimp flavor packet in about one quarter cup water. Pour into a small serving bowl and stir in the chili peppers.

Divide the cucumber and lettuce among the bottom of six bowls, then sprinkle on a pinch each of the mint, cilantro and basil. Spoon ramen noodles among the bowls, then top with bean sprouts, carrots and shredded meat and hot pepper. Mix.

SUBSTITUTIONS & OMISSIONS

Get rid of the bean sprouts, and lighten up on the meat, using chicken thigh meat to keep in the budget.

Ingredient	Cost
3 packages shrimp ramen	.30
2 cloves garlic, minced	.10
2 tablespoons sugar	*
1 tablespoon crushed red peppers	*
1 teaspoon lemon	*
1 cup cucumber, diced	.25
1 cup shredded red-leaf or Boston lettuce	.35
2 tablespoons fresh mint leaves	.25
¼ cup fresh cilantro, chopped	.15
1 tablespoon dried basil	.10
1 cup carrots, shredded	.10
¼ cup cooked chicken thigh meat	.40
	Total: $2.00

$$$ BIG SPLURGE $$$

Use Vietnamese rice noodles in place of ramen noodles and ½ pound of shrimp with the chicken breast.

RAMEN WITH ZUCCHINI AND ROAST BEEF SALAD

Serves four

Notes: Mint makes this dish unique, so try to keep it in. Use quality pre-roasted, cold roast beef; something good if possible, but you can settle for any lunch meat in a pinch.

Ingredient	Cost
3 packages beef ramen	.30
2 cups cooked roast beef, cubed	3.00
3 medium ripe tomatoes, diced	1.50
1 cup zucchini, diced	.25
1 cup fresh parsley, chopped	.25
½ cup green onions, finely diced	.25
2 tablespoons fresh mint, minced	.50
3 cloves garlic, minced	.10
½ cup lemon juice	.50
2 tablespoons vegetable oil	.05
	Total: $6.70

In a large pot of boiling water, prepare ramen noodles, cooking 3-4 minutes or until tender. Do not overcook. Drain and set aside to cool.

Combine pasta, beef, tomatoes, zucchini, parsley, onion, one flavor packet and mint in a large mixing bowl. Combine remaining ingredients; mix well.

Toss mixtures with cooked ramen noodles, adding portion of one more flavor packet to taste. Refrigerate two hours prior to serving.

SUBSTITUTIONS & OMISSIONS

Use less beef and put in an onion for volume. Fresh mint is nice, but you can use dried mint if necessary. Add an extra ramen package.

4 packages beef ramen	.40
¼ cup cooked roast beef, cubed	.40
1 medium ripe tomato, diced	.50
½ cup zucchini, diced	.10
¼ cup fresh parsley, chopped	.10
2 tablespoons mint, minced	.10
3 cloves garlic, minced	.10
½ cup lemon juice	*
1 onion, finely chopped	.25
2 tablespoon olive or vegetable oil	.05
	Total: $2.00

$$$ BIG SPLURGE $$$

Use peppered beef, twice the amount of mint, a touch of spearmint schnapps and penne instead of ramen noodles.

Chapter 6

SOUPS AND CHOWDERS

RAMEN CHOWDER

Serves four

Notes: Chowder is chowder, whether it's clam, conch or potato. Chowder—in this case white chowder—just means it's a cream-based white sauce with a pinch of black pepper. It's good, filling and will impress your dates. Improvise at will.

2 packages shrimp ramen	**.20**
3 tablespoons margarine	**.20**
1 small onion, chopped	**.25**
1 clove garlic, minced	**.10**
4 cups milk	**1.25**
2 tablespoons fresh parsley, chopped	**.15**
1 cup Cheddar cheese, shredded	**3.00**
2 6½-ounce cans minced clams, with juice	**3.00**
pepper to taste	**.05**
Total:	**$8.20**

In a large pot of boiling water, prepare ramen noodles, cooking 3–4 minutes or until tender. Do not overcook. Drain and set aside.

While ramen noodles are cooking, sauté onion and garlic in a large saucepan. Cook until tender. Stir in milk, parsley, cheese, clams and one packet of shrimp flavoring. Cook over medium heat, stirring constantly until cheese melts. Do not boil. Stir in ramen noodles, heat through and serve immediately.

SUBSTITUTIONS & OMISSIONS

Lose the milk, clams and a lot of the Cheddar. Use potatoes instead of clams. Add a package of ramen to fill it out.

3 packages shrimp ramen	.30
2 tablespoons oil	.05
1 small onion, chopped	.25
1 clove garlic, minced	.10
½ cup cream, in 3 cups water	*
2 tablespoons fresh, chopped parsley	.15
¾ cup Cheddar cheese, shredded	.85
3 potatoes, diced	.30
pepper to taste	*
	Total: $2.00

$$$ BIG SPLURGE $$$

Use angel hair pasta for ramen noodles.

EGG DROP AND RAMEN NOODLE SOUP

Serves four

Notes: This makes a good dinner for two hungry dudes or about six normal people. It's still soup and that's what ramen is—soup.

3 packages Oriental ramen	.30
2 large eggs	.20
¾ cup Parmesan cheese, grated	.75
1 cup spinach (canned or frozen is fine)	.50
black pepper	.05
	Total: $1.80

Bring water to boil and drop in ramen noodles. Cook with one flavor packet for three or four minutes or until tender, but not overcooked.

Pour some of the warm broth from the ramen into a bowl and beat in eggs until blended. Beat in the Parmesan cheese and pepper. Stir the spinach into the broth and reheat to boiling.

Pour the egg mixture into the soup slowly while stirring constantly with a fork. Cook 30 seconds. Check the seasoning and add one flavor packet. Serve hot.

SUBSTITUTIONS & OMISSIONS

Use dried Parmesan for fresh.

3 packages Oriental flavor ramen	**.30**
2 large eggs	**.20**
2 tablespoons Parmesan cheese, grated	*
1 cup spinach (canned or frozen is fine)	**.50**
black pepper to taste	*
	Total: $1.00

$$$ BIG SPLURGE $$$

Use fat Oriental noodles for ramen noodles.

HOT AND SOUR VEGETABLE SOUP

Serves four

Notes: Tofu, celery and Chinese cabbage make this an all-Chinese dish. Although tofu tastes like crap, it's cheap and good for you.

3 packages vegetable ramen	**.30**
1 cup corn (canned or frozen is fine)	**.30**
1 cup Chinese cabbage, shredded	**.40**
½ cup celery, chopped	**.25**
½ pound tofu, diced	**.50**
2 tablespoons lemon juice	**.20**
2 tablespoons cornstarch, dissolved in 2 tablespoons water	**.10**
2 tablespoons soy sauce	**.20**
black pepper to taste	**.05**
	Total: $2.30

Bring about five quarts of water to boil in a large pot and add vegetables. Reduce heat and simmer about 10 minutes. Increase heat, drop in ramen noodles and boil for a minute, then reduce heat again.

Stir cornstarch paste into soup and continue to cook about three minutes, until soup becomes thicker. Add two ramen flavor packets and set aside for three minutes. Serve hot.

SUBSTITUTIONS & OMISSIONS

Use more celery or cabbage in place of tofu if you aren't a tofu fan (and who is?).

3 packages vegetable ramen	.30
1 cup corn (canned or frozen is fine)	.30
1 cup Chinese cabbage, shredded	.40
½ cup celery, chopped	.25
½ pound tofu, diced	.50
2 tablespoons lemon juice	*
2 tablespoons cornstarch, dissolved in 2 tablespoons water	.10
2 tablespoons soy sauce	*
black pepper to taste	*
	Total: $1.85

$$$ BIG SPLURGE $$$

Add some chicken and use fat Oriental noodles for ramen noodles.

CREAMY MUSHROOM RAMEN SOUP

Serves four

Notes: Don't fret if you only have canned mushrooms, since mushrooms are like flavor sponges—and you have a lot of spices at your disposal to change the flavor.

2 packages chicken mushroom flavor ramen	.20
3 tablespoons butter	.30
3 cloves garlic, minced	.10
½ cup onions, chopped	.25
1 cup mushrooms, sliced	.75
1 cup light cream	1.00
1 tablespoon fresh parsley, chopped	.15
	Total: $2.75

Open both packages of ramen. Cook the noodles and add all three seasoning packets to two quarts water. Stir in cream. Stir in parsley.

Sauté onion and garlic in butter until both are golden brown. Add mushrooms, cook until slightly soft. Add onion, garlic and mushrooms to soup and serve immediately.

SUBSTITUTIONS & OMISSIONS

Use margarine instead of butter.

3 packages mushroom ramen	.30
3 tablespoons margarine	.05
3 cloves garlic, minced	.10
½ cup onions, chopped	.25
1 cup mushrooms, sliced	.75
2 tablespoons cream, mixed with equal amount of water	*
1 tablespoon fresh parsley, chopped	.15
	Total: $1.60

$$$ BIG SPLURGE $$$

Use either portobello or shiitake mushrooms. And serve in penne instead of ramen noodles.

RAMEN SESAME-SATE SOUP

Serves four

Notes: Sate sauce is great with ramen noodles. It's a taste that doesn't cost tons of money to make—even on the toughest of budgets. The key to this one is the peanut butter, so leave it in.

3 packages chicken flavor ramen	.30
2 cups chicken, diced	1.25
1 cup peanut butter	1.00
4 tablespoons rice or wine vinegar	.30
3 tablespoons soy sauce	.30
2 cloves garlic, minced	.10
¼ teaspoon crushed red peppers	.10
3 cups broccoli, cut into bite-sized pieces (frozen is fine)	1.50
1 cup frozen peas (frozen or canned is fine)	.50
1 red bell pepper, cut into thin strips	1.00
2 green onions, thinly sliced	.15
	Total: $6.50

Open all packages of ramen and cook the noodles without seasoning packets for 3–4 minutes on high heat. When done, drain and set aside.

In a small bowl, stir peanut butter, vinegar, soy sauce, garlic, hot pepper and both seasoning packets together until smooth. Set aside.

Sauté chicken in a frying pan six minutes or until tender. Add bell pepper, reduce heat and simmer two more minutes.

Boil broccoli and peas in a quart of water. Cook five minutes. Drain and add ramen noodles and peanut sauce. Serve.

SUBSTITUTIONS & OMISSIONS

Use a lot less peanut butter (although if you can spare it, this is the one ingredient to use more of). Forget the peas and vinegar, easy on the broccoli, and add an extra ramen noodle package and an onion for volume.

4 packages chicken flavor ramen	.40
½ cup chicken thigh meat, diced	.30
3 tablespoons peanut butter	.30
3 tablespoons soy sauce	*
2 cloves garlic, minced	.10
¼ teaspoon crushed red peppers	*
1 green bell pepper, cut into thin strips	.25
2 green onions, thinly sliced	.10
1 yellow onion, quartered	.25
½ cup broccoli, cut into bite-sized pieces (frozen is fine)	.30
	Total: $2.00

$$$ BIG SPLURGE $$$

Add more peanut butter, some sherry and barbecue the chicken on skewers before adding to the noodles. And use wide egg noodles for ramen.

SPICY NOODLE SOUP

Serves four

Notes: Egg whites in hot water create an interesting look and taste. Vegetables give it filler.

3 packages shrimp ramen	.30
4–5 large fresh shrimp	.75
1 egg	.10
1 green onion, sliced	.10

¼ cup celery	.25
¼ cup spinach (frozen or canned is fine)	.25
1 teaspoon soy sauce	.10
2 teaspoons sesame oil	.20
	Total: $2.05

Boil three quarts of water in a large pot. Add ramen noodles and return to a boil for one minute, then reduce heat and cook another 2–3 minutes.

Cut the green onion into one-inch pieces and add them to the soup. Add the ramen noodles, green vegetable and both flavor packets. Break the egg, add the oil, soy sauce and sesame oil. Stir well and serve.

SUBSTITUTIONS & OMISSIONS

Lighten up on the sesame oil.

3 packages shrimp ramen	.30
4–5 fresh shrimp	.75
1 egg	.10
1 green onion, sliced	.10
½ cup mixed vegetables, cut into 1-inch pieces	.50
1 tablespoon oil	.05
1 teaspoon soy sauce	*
1 teaspoon sesame oil	.10
	Total: $1.80

$$$ BIG SPLURGE $$$

Double the amount of shrimp, and use thin Oriental Noodles for ramen.

Chapter 7

MEATLESS MAIN COURSES

RAMEN ALFREDO

Serves four

Notes: Cream and garlic—not Parmesan cheese—are the keys to Alfredo. The Parmesan makes the taste familiar, but you can actually do without it. Or just use a few tablespoons to get similar results.

3 packages ramen, any flavor	.30
1 stick butter	.75
1 cup cream	1.00
1 cup Parmesan cheese, grated	1.50
4 cloves garlic, minced	.10
pepper to taste	.05

Total: **$3.70**

In a large pot of boiling salted water, cook the ramen until tender but still firm, about 4 minutes. Drain well and set aside.

Sauté minced garlic in butter over low heat in a large saucepan. Add cream, one flavor packet and pepper to taste. Continue cooking on low heat. Once mixture is nearly boiling, add Parmesan cheese. The sauce should be very creamy. If not, add more cheese to soak up moisture. Remove from heat.

Add drained ramen noodles to the sauce and mix thoroughly, stirring to completely coat the noodles. Serve immediately.

SUBSTITUTIONS & OMISSIONS

Use cream for milk, margarine for butter and dried cheese for fresh.

Ingredient	Price
3 packages ramen, any flavor	.30
1 stick margarine	.15
3 tablespoons cream, mixed with flour and water	*
3 tablespoons dried grated Parmesan cheese	*
4 cloves garlic, minced	.10
black pepper to taste	*
Total:	$ .55

$$$ BIG SPLURGE $$$

Use fettuccine noodles in place of ramen, lots of cream and lots of butter.

ALOO GOBI MASALA

Serves four

Notes: Think Indian. Think curry. Think bad breath. Indian tastes with the tart of lemon make this special. Try to keep pretty close to the recipe if possible. And bring breath mints.

Ingredient	Price
3 packages chicken ramen	.30
2 large potatoes	.10
1 head cauliflower, cut into 1-inch pieces	1.25
1 tomato, diced	.50
1 onion, thinly sliced	.25
¼ teaspoon cayenne	.10
½ teaspoon turmeric	.10
½ teaspoon basil leaves	.10
1 teaspoon cumin seeds	.10
½ cup lemon juice	.10
1 inch piece ginger, minced	.20
2 cloves garlic, minced	.20
2 tablespoons olive oil	.25
2 tablespoons cilantro, chopped	.10

1 jalapeno, minced	.10
2 green onions, chopped	.10
	Total: $3.85

Boil potatoes in five quarts water for about 20 minutes or until slightly tender. Clean and skin under cold running water. Dice. Put back in the water and add cauliflower florets with one packet ramen flavoring, cayenne, turmeric and canola oil. Cook for approximately 10 minutes.

Meanwhile, bring about five quarts of water to boil in a large pot. Drop in ramen noodles and boil for a minute, then reduce heat. Cook another 2–3 minutes, or until tender. Remove from heat, drain and set aside.

Mix cilantro, green onion and jalapeno with sliced onion. Heat oil and cumin seeds in a skillet and fry until light brown. Add the onions, ginger and garlic and cook for two minutes. Drain the potatoes and cauliflower, then add the diced tomato. Pour the mix over a bed of ramen noodles.

Substitutions & Omissions

Cut back on the tomato, cauliflower and onion. Use vegetable oil for olive and crushed dried chilies for fresh. Add ramen.

4 packages chicken ramen	.40
2 large potatoes	.10
¼ head cauliflower, cut into 1-inch pieces	.30
½ tomato, diced	.25
½ onion, thinly sliced	.10
¼ teaspoon cayenne	.10
½ teaspoon turmeric	.10
½ teaspoon basil leaves	.10
1 teaspoon cumin seeds	.10
¼ cup lemon juice	*
1 teaspoon dried ginger	.10
2 cloves garlic, minced	.20
¼ cup vinegar	.05
2 tablespoons cilantro, chopped	.10
1 teaspoon crushed red chili pepper	*
2 green onions, chopped	.10
	Total: $2.00

$$$ Big Splurge $$$

Throw in some diced, cooked lamb and serve over white steamed basmati rice.

RAMEN NOODLES WITH ASPARAGUS

Serves four

Notes: As always, you can lose the cheese, but don't lose the main ingredient—the asparagus. To save money, just use a hell of a lot less asparagus.

3 packages pork ramen	.30
1 pound asparagus, cut into 1-inch pieces	2.00
1 stick butter	.50
2 cups tomato, diced	1.00
½ cup fresh Parmesan cheese, grated	.50
pepper to taste	.05
	Total: $4.35

In a large pot of boiling salted water, cook the ramen until tender but still firm, about 4 minutes. Drain well and set aside.

Cook the asparagus in a separate pot of boiling salted water until tender, about 3 minutes. Rinse under cold running water to cool; drain well.

Melt 6 tablespoons of the butter over low heat in a large skillet. Add tomatoes, one flavor packet and pepper. Simmer until the sauce is slightly thickened, about 5 minutes, adding the asparagus to the tomato sauce.

Pour the sauce over the ramen noodles, add the remaining 2 tablespoons butter and the Parmesan cheese and toss well. Serve immediately.

SUBSTITUTIONS & OMISSIONS

Use margarine for butter. Also use dried cheese for fresh. Add ramen for bulk.

4 packages pork ramen	.40
¼ pound asparagus, cut into 1-inch pieces	.50
1 stick margarine	.15
1 tomato, diced	.50
½ cup Parmesan cheese, grated	*
pepper to taste	*
	Total: $1.55

$$$ BIG SPLURGE $$$

Use more asparagus and replace ramen with spaghetti or angel hair pasta.

RAMEN NOODLES WITH ASPARAGUS AND GARBANZO BEANS

Serves four

Notes: Garbanzos add bulk and carbs; asparagus and citrus sections add class—at a price. If you leave out the asparagus and just use the citrus juices, you'll still end up with a pretty smoking meal.

3 packages vegetable ramen	.30
1 pound asparagus	3.00
1 cup garbanzo beans	.75
juice of 1 lime	.10
juice of 1 orange	.25
juice of 1 lemon	.10
juice of 1 grapefruit	.25
6 tablespoons olive oil	.35
1 clove garlic, minced	.10
1 teaspoon Dijon mustard	.20
¼ teaspoon thyme	.10
	Total: $5.50

Either boil or steam the asparagus until cooked—but not overcooked. Cut into 1-inch pieces. While cooling, combine the citrus juices in a small saucepan and bring to a boil. Add garlic, oil, thyme and one packet vegetable ramen seasoning. Toss in the asparagus and garbanzos.

Bring about five quarts of water to boil in a large pot, drop in ramen noodles and boil for a minute then reduce heat. Cook another 2–3 minutes, or until tender. Remove from heat, drain and toss the asparagus with the ramen noodles. Serve immediately.

SUBSTITUTIONS & OMISSIONS

Use about three stalks asparagus in place of the pound listed, reduce the garbanzos. Use Chinese hot mustard instead of Dijon and vegetable oil in place of olive oil. Add a package ramen for lost volume.

4 packages vegetable ramen	.40
3 stalks asparagus	.30
½ cup garbanzo beans	.35
1 lime, sectioned	.10
1 orange, sectioned	.25
1 lemon, sectioned	.10
½ grapefruit, sectioned	.10
3 tablespoons olive oil	.05

1 clove garlic, minced	.10
1 teaspoon Chinese mustard	*
¼ teaspoon thyme	.10
	Total: $1.85

$$$ BIG SPLURGE $$$

Use the full amount of asparagus, but toss in some white asparagus as well as green. Also toss in some pine nuts and some artichoke hearts. Plus, use penne instead of ramen noodles.

RAMEN AU GRATIN

Serves four

Notes: Roasted potatoes and a milk-based cheese sauce give this a distinctive taste. Bake it with ramen noodles and you have a nice twist on a traditional dish.

3 packages chicken ramen	.30
4 potatoes, boiled and sliced into ¼-inch slices	.40
1 onion, sliced into rings	.25
3 tablespoons butter	.25
3 tablespoons all-purpose flour	.05
2 cups milk	.50
2 cups Cheddar cheese, shredded	2.00
	Total: $3.75

Bring 3–4 quarts of water to a boil and add ramen noodles. Cook approximately 3 minutes, or until noodles are just slightly tender. Do not overcook. Remove, drain and set aside.

Melt butter in a saucepan. Mix in the flour and one ramen flavor packet. Stir in milk and cook until mixture thickens. Toss in cheese and continue stirring until melted, about 3 minutes.

Preheat oven to 375° and butter a casserole dish. Mix potatoes and ramen in the casserole dish, pour cheese and milk mixture over the ramen and potatoes, and cover the dish with aluminum foil. Bake about 45 minutes, or until top is brown.

SUBSTITUTIONS & OMISSIONS

Use margarine for butter and slightly less onion.

3 packages chicken ramen	.30
4 potatoes, sliced into ¼-inch slices	.40
¾ cup onion, sliced into rings	.20
3 tablespoons butter	.05
3 tablespoons all-purpose flour	.05
½ cup cream, mixed with water	*
1 cups Cheddar cheese, shredded	1.00
	Total: $2.00

$$$ BIG SPLURGE $$$

Use cream rather than milk, Gruyère cheese rather than Cheddar and drop in some leeks. Use fettuccine for ramen.

ITALIAN BEET AND SQUASH RAMEN NOODLES

Serves four

Notes: Squash is sweet. Mixed with the beet, this becomes an interesting dish. Okay, so if you find it too interesting, use zucchini in place of squash, but leave the beet in. It will make you seem mysterious (if not a little stupid) to your dinner guests.

3 packages vegetable ramen	.30
3 cloves garlic, minced	.10
1 cup onions, diced	.25
3 cups butternut squash, diced	1.00
1 cup red beet, diced	.75
2 tablespoons soy sauce	.20
1 tablespoon Italian seasoning	.10
1 tablespoon cornstarch	.20
	Total: $2.90

Bring water to boil and drop in ramen noodles. Cook for three or four minutes or until tender, but not overcooked. Drain and set aside.

Place first six sauce ingredients in a large saucepan. Cook approximately 30 minutes, or until vegetables are soft. Purée in a food processor or blender—or mash with a fork. Return to the pot and add soy sauce and herbs.

In a separate cup, dissolve cornstarch in ½ cup of water. Stir into sauce. Heat again and when sauce begins to bubble, reduce heat.

Pour over ramen noodles and serve. Garnish with dried Parmesan or parsley.

SUBSTITUTIONS & OMISSIONS

Use zucchini for squash.

3 packages ramen	.30
3 cloves garlic, minced	.10
1 cup onions, diced	.25
3 cups zucchini, diced	.75
½ cup red beet, diced	.40
2 tablespoons soy sauce	*
1 tablespoon Italian seasoning	.10
1 tablespoon cornstarch	.10
	Total: $2.00

$$$ BIG SPLURGE $$$

Use fresh oregano and toss in angle hair pasta instead of ramen noodles.

RED BELL PEPPER RAMEN NOODLES

Serves four

Notes: As easy as cooking gets. If you want to get more complicated, roast the peppers first over a gas flame, charring the sides, then bake for about half the time listed below.

3 packages tomato ramen	.30
2 pounds red bell pepper (4 large)	4.00
1 egg	.10
	Total: $4.40

In a large pot of boiling salted water, cook the ramen until tender but still firm, about 4 minutes. Drain well and set aside.

Bake peppers uncovered at 500°, turning each of them until skins are blackened on every side—usually about 40–45 minutes. Remove from heat and let cool five minutes or so, then remove skin, stems, and seeds. Purée 3 of the peppers, 2 flavor packets and the egg in a blender.

In skillet, cook purée over medium heat, stirring constantly for about 10 minutes—or until reduced to about ½ cup. Dice the remaining pepper and mix all with ramen noodles and serve.

SUBSTITUTIONS & OMISSIONS

Use green pepper for red.

3 packages tomato ramen	.30
2 pounds green bell pepper (4 large)	1.00
1 egg	.10
	Total: $1.40

$$$ BIG SPLURGE $$$

Use red peppers with one yellow (the one not puréed) and substitute rigatoni for ramen noodles.

BLACK BEAN RAMEN WITH TOASTED SPICES

Serves four

Notes: The toasted spices make this interesting, and the black beans add a lot of carbs for a filling meal.

3 packages ramen	.30
3 cups black beans, soaked in water	.40
2 jalapeno peppers, minced	.10
1 tablespoon ginger, minced	.10
1 bay leaf	.10
1 cup cilantro, chopped	.25
1 teaspoon cumin seeds	.10
2 tablespoons chili powder	.10
1 teaspoon oregano	.10
½ cup sun-dried tomatoes, chopped	.50
4 cups tomatoes, diced	2.00
½ tablespoon mustard seeds	.10
½ tablespoon fennel seeds	.10
	Total: $4.25

Bring about five quarts of water to a boil in a large pot. Drop in ramen noodles and boil for a minute, then reduce heat. Cook another 2–3 minutes, or until tender. Remove from heat, drain and set aside.

Drop beans and a cup of water into another large pot and bring to a boil. Add peppers, ginger, bay leaf, cilantro and one packet curry ramen flavoring. Stir. Cover and simmer for about a half hour.

Add cumin seeds, chili powder, oregano and tomatoes to a medium pot and heat over high heat until mixture boils. Toss in mustard seeds and fennel seeds. Reduce heat and simmer for a half-hour. Add remaining cilantro and serve over a bed of ramen noodles.

SUBSTITUTIONS & OMISSIONS

No need to use three cups of beans; one is plenty. Although the tomato amount is okay, it costs too much. Just use a half-cup fresh tomatoes and a cup of tomato sauce and you'll be fine. Or use water and a tomato ramen flavor packet. Use crushed dried chilies for fresh and lighten up the cilantro. Add one more ramen noodle package to make up for lost volume.

4 packages ramen: 1 spicy chicken, 1 chili, 2 tomato	.40
1 cup dried black beans, soaked in water	.20
2 teaspoons crushed red chili peppers	*
1 tablespoon ginger, minced	.10
1 bay leaf	.10
¼ cup cilantro, chopped	.10
1 teaspoon cumin seeds	.10
½ tablespoon oregano	.10
1 8-ounce can tomato sauce	.20
½ cup tomatoes, diced	.25
½ tablespoon mustard seeds	.10
½ tablespoon fennel seeds	.10
	Total: $1.75

$$$ BIG SPLURGE $$$

Grill about a ¼ pound sirloin and toss it in. Use fettuccine instead of ramen noodles.

BREAD AND RAMEN NOODLES

Serves four

Notes: Like Thanksgiving stuffing. But it's good, will get rid of your leftover bread and will feed a small army—as long as they don't have to march anytime soon. If you have rye, French, Italian, sourdough, whatever, use it here.

3 packages mushroom ramen	.30
6 large, thick slices of dry, leftover bread	.30
2 cups tomatoes, diced	1.00
3 tablespoons vinegar	.30
¼ cup olive oil	.35
1 teaspoon basil	.10
black pepper to taste	.05
	Total: 2.40

Bring about five quarts of water to boil in a large pot. Drop in ramen noodles and boil for a minute, then reduce heat. Cook another 2–3 minutes, or until tender. Remove from heat, drain and set aside. Toss in bread and mix. Let stand long enough to soak up excess water.

Add tomatoes, vinegar, olive oil, basil, pepper and two packets ramen flavoring and mix together. The extra water from the ramen and the juice from the tomato and oil will be absorbed. Toss again and serve.

SUBSTITUTIONS & OMISSIONS

Ease up on the olive oil and you come in under budget.

3 packages ramen	.30
6 large, thick slices of dry, leftover bread	*
2 cups tomatoes, diced	1.00
3 tablespoons vinegar	.30
¼ cup olive oil	.25
1 teaspoon basil	.10
black pepper to taste	*
	Total: $1.95

$$$ BIG SPLURGE $$$

Use about a fourth of the bread, substituting portobello mushrooms instead. Use spaghetti for ramen noodles.

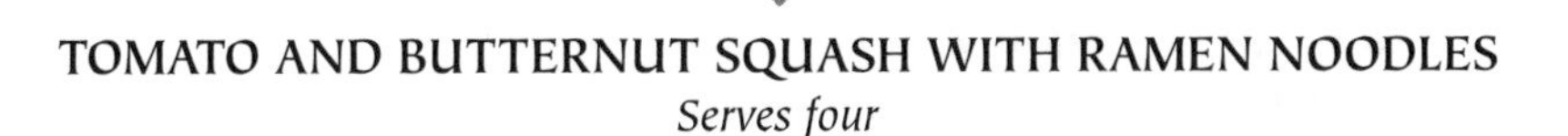

TOMATO AND BUTTERNUT SQUASH WITH RAMEN NOODLES

Serves four

Notes: Butternut squash tastes like it sounds—sweet and nutty. It may not agree with you, and you may not find it in your grocery store either. If not, use two more zucchinis in the butternut's place.

3 packages tomato ramen	.30
1 large onion, diced	.25
3 cloves garlic, minced	.10
3 teaspoons crushed red pepper	.10
1 teaspoon oregano	.10
1 tablespoon butter	.20
¼ cup tomato sauce	.10
2 tomatoes, diced	1.00

½ small butternut squash, cut into small chunks	.75
2 zucchinis, sliced into chunks	.50
2 tablespoons plain yogurt	.20
2 tablespoons parsley, chopped	.10
¼ cup Cheddar cheese, grated	.75
Total:	$4.45

In a large pot of boiling salted water, cook the ramen until tender but still firm, about 4 minutes. Drain well and set aside.

In a saucepan melt the butter with onion, garlic, chilies and oregano. Add tomato, tomato sauce, one packet of tomato ramen seasoning and stir well. Add squash and cook about 25–30 minutes over low heat, stirring frequently. Add the zucchini and simmer another five minutes.

To the cooked ramen noodles, add chopped garlic, parsley, yogurt and butter. Serve the noodles with sauce spooned on top and grated cheese.

SUBSTITUTIONS & OMISSIONS

Use margarine for butter and substitute zucchini for butternut squash. And lose the parsley. Add another packet of Ramen to fill it out.

4 packages tomato ramen	.40
1 large onion, diced	.25
3 cloves garlic, minced	.10
3 teaspoons crushed red peppers	*
1 teaspoon oregano	.10
1 tablespoon margarine	.05
¼ cup tomato sauce	.10
½ 15-ounce can diced or crushed tomatoes	.30
2 zucchinis, sliced into chunks	.50
2 tablespoons plain yogurt	.20
¼ cup Parmesan cheese, grated	*
Total:	$2.00

$$$ BIG SPLURGE $$$

Use linguine instead of ramen noodles.

CHEAPY RAMEN SPAGHETTI

Serves four

Notes: This is the Brother, Can You Spare A Dime? *official mascot recipe. For about ten cents per person you can eat pretty well. Not a balanced meal, for sure. But cheap and one you can return to any time, adding to it when you can.*

4 packages ramen: 2 packages chicken, 2 packages tomato	.40
3 cloves garlic, minced	.10
1 teaspoon crushed red chili peppers	.10
1 teaspoon oregano	.10
	Total: $.70

Boil about six cups of water and toss in the ramen noodles once the water is at a good boil. Cook one minute, then reduce the heat. Cook another 2–3 minutes, drain (setting aside about a quarter-cup of hot noodle water) and set aside.

Put two spicy chicken flavor packets in ¼ cup of water and add the garlic to it. The garlic will heat itself and start to cook in the boiled water. Toss the mixture into the ramen noodles, add the crushed pepper and the oregano and mix. Serve immediately.

SUBSTITUTIONS & OMISSIONS

No Garlic? Don't worry about it.

4 packages ramen: 2 packages chicken, 2 packages tomato	.40
3 cloves garlic, sliced	.10
1 teaspoon crushed red chili peppers	*
1 teaspoon oregano	*
	Total: $.50

$$$ BIG SPLURGE $$$

Use fresh oregano and coat the noodles in good olive oil. Use spaghetti instead of ramen noodles.

RAMEN CHILAQUILES

Serves four

Notes: Chilaquiles is a traditional Mexican breakfast dish that uses up leftover tortillas. You need at least a few old tortillas, but substitute bulk with ramen.

3 packages chicken ramen	.30
6 stale corn tortillas	.20
2 jalapeno peppers, diced	.20
½ cup vegetable oil	.30
1 15-ounce can enchilada sauce	.75

1 tablespoon oregano	.10
½ cup Monterey jack cheese, shredded	.75
½ onion, diced	.10
½ cup sour cream	.50
	Total: $3.20

Bring 3–4 quarts of water to a boil and add ramen noodles. Cook approximately three minutes, or until noodles are just slightly tender. Do not overcook. Remove, drain and set aside.

Cut the tortillas into bite-sized pieces. Fry in oil in a large skillet until crisp and golden. Remove and pat dry on a paper towel. After draining the oil from the skillet, add enchilada sauce, one flavor packet and onions and bring back to a boil. Add the tortilla chips and remove from the heat, then add cheese. Allow it to melt. Mix with ramen noodles then serve topped with sour cream.

SUBSTITUTIONS & OMISSIONS

Use less cheese, substituting Parmesan for jack, and use less sour cream.

3 packages chicken ramen	.30
6 stale corn tortillas	.20
2 jalapeno peppers, diced	.10
½ cup vegetable oil	.30
1 15-ounce can enchilada sauce	.75
1 tablespoon oregano	.10
3 tablespoons Parmesan cheese, grated	*
½ onion, diced	.10
½ cup sour cream	.15
	Total: $2.00

$$$ BIG SPLURGE $$$

Use fresh tomatoes with the enchilada sauce. Leave out the ramen and use more tortillas.

CHIPOTLE CREAM RAMEN

Serves four

Notes: Heavy cream makes the smoky flavor of chipotles seem more complex. Use less cream, water and more peppers if heavy cream is hard to find.

3 packages chicken ramen	.30

1 pint heavy cream	2.00
1 teaspoon Dijon mustard	.10
¼ cup chipotle peppers, boiled and minced	.25
2 cups Monterey jack cheese, grated	3.00
¼ cup sherry	.75
2 tablespoons butter	.20
2 tablespoons flour, mixed in 2 tablespoons water	.05
1 clove garlic, roasted and minced	.10
	Total: $6.75

Bring 3–4 quarts of water to a boil and add ramen noodles. Cook approximately 3 minutes, or until noodles are just slightly tender. Do not overcook. Remove, drain and set aside.

Bring cream to a boil and add sherry, butter and pour in flour/water mixture. When the butter is melted and flour mixture is blended, add pepper and garlic, then the cheese and stir until the cheese is melted.

Mix in ramen noodles and serve.

SUBSTITUTIONS & OMISSIONS

Use less cream, a lot less cheese and drop the sherry. Also, use Chinese mustard instead of Dijon.

3 packages chicken ramen	.30
½ cup cream mixed with water	*
1 teaspoon Chinese mustard	*
¼ cup chipotle peppers, boiled and minced	.25
¾ cup Monterey jack cheese, grated	1.00
2 tablespoons butter	.20
2 tablespoons flour, mixed in 2 tablespoons water	.05
1 clove garlic, roasted and minced	.10
	Total: $1.90

$$$ BIG SPLURGE $$$

Use fettuccine for ramen and add a pound of grilled, sliced chicken breasts. Top with Swiss cheese.

CHINESE CABBAGE AND MUSHROOM

Serves four

Notes: Mushrooms, which can be used canned or fresh (try to use fresh if possible), may be enhanced with the ramen flavor packets.

3 packages mushroom ramen	.30
1 pound Chinese cabbage, chopped	1.25
½ pound mushrooms, chopped	.65
4 tablespoons peanut oil	.20
1 tablespoon cornstarch, dissolved in 1 tablespoon water	.10
	Total: $2.50

Boil water in a large pot. Add ramen noodles and return to a boil for one minute, then reduce heat and cook another 2–3 minutes. Drain and set aside.

Stir-fry the cabbage and mushrooms in peanut oil for about 2–3 minutes. Add one packet mushroom ramen flavoring. Mix in the cornstarch and stir until mix thickens. Pour into a bed of ramen noodles.

SUBSTITUTIONS & OMISSIONS

Lighten up on the cabbage and use vegetable oil for peanut oil.

3 packages ramen	.30
1 pound Chinese cabbage, chopped	.85
½ pound mushrooms, chopped	.65
4 tablespoons vegetable oil	.05
1 tablespoon cornstarch, dissolved in 1 tablespoon water	.10
	Total: $1.95

$$$ BIG SPLURGE $$$

Skiitake mushrooms and smoked chicken over fat Oriental noodles.

CINNAMON-TOMATO RAMEN NOODLES

Serves four

Notes: A bunch of eclectic spices makes this a unique dish. Tomato ramen seasoning gives it a nice salty base flavor.

3 packages tomato ramen	.30

2 cups tomatoes, diced	.75
½ cup onions, diced	.25
3 cloves garlic, minced	.10
½ teaspoon ground cinnamon	.10
½ teaspoon chili powder	.10
½ teaspoon ground cumin	.10
½ teaspoon dry mustard	.10
½ teaspoon ground cloves	.10
½ cup cream	.50
3 tablespoons fresh basil, chopped	.20
¼ cup Parmesan cheese, grated	.40
	Total: $3.00

Boil about six cups of water and toss in the ramen noodles. Cook one minute, then reduce the heat. Cook another 2–3 minutes, drain and set aside.

In a skillet, add tomatoes, onion and garlic, and cook over medium heat for about ten minutes. Add cinnamon, chili powder, cumin, mustard and cloves. Bring to a boil. Reduce heat and cover, cooking another 10 minutes. Stir occasionally.

In a casserole dish, spread half the sauce over the bottom then cover with the ramen noodles. Top with sauce sprinkled with Parmesan cheese. Bake for twenty minutes at 375° and serve immediately.

SUBSTITUTIONS & OMISSIONS

Use half the amount of tomatoes (use tomato flavoring and water to round out the taste).

3 packages tomato ramen	.30
2 cups fresh tomatoes, diced (canned is fine)	.65
½ cup onions, diced	.25
3 cloves garlic, minced	.10
½ teaspoon ground cinnamon	.10
½ teaspoon chili powder	.10
½ teaspoon ground cumin	.10
½ teaspoon dry mustard	.10
½ teaspoon ground cloves	.10
3 tablespoons cream, mixed with water	*
3 tablespoons fresh basil, chopped	.20
3 tablespoons Parmesan cheese, grated	*
	Total: $2.00

$$$ BIG SPLURGE $$$

Use bow tie pasta for ramen noodles and lots of cream.

RAMEN IN MANGO AND COCONUT MILK

Serves four

Notes: There are a couple mango recipes in this book, but this is the simplest—and the least expensive. It's a good and filling dish, hot or leftover cold.

4 packages ramen	**.40**
1 14-ounce can creamy coconut milk	**1.00**
½ cup sugar	**.20**
1 mango, peeled and diced	**.75**
	Total: $2.35

Bring about five quarts of water to a boil in a large pot. Drop in ramen noodles and cook for a minute, then reduce heat. Cook another 2–3 minutes, or until tender. Remove from heat, drain and set aside.

Heat the coconut milk and sugar together in a saucepan and cook until the mixture is well blended and smooth. Add mangoes; cook 10 minutes. Stir well into drained ramen, making sure all the noodles are well coated. Dish the ramen onto individual serving plates, spooning the reserved coconut sauce over each portion.

SUBSTITUTIONS & OMISSIONS

Reduce the amount of coconut milk and add cream.

4 packages ramen	**.40**
½ can (14-ounce) creamy coconut milk	**.65**
2 tablespoons cream, mixed with water	*
½ cup sugar	**.20**
1 mango, peeled and diced	**.75**
	Total: $2.00

$$$ BIG SPLURGE $$$

Omit the ramen and add some apricot brandy for this to become a great crepe-filling recipe (to make crepes, mix 1 cup flour with ½ cup milk, two eggs and a tablespoon sugar; mix well—it should be a runny batter. Pour in a thin stream into a well-buttered or non-stick frying pan. Cook on both sides. When done, drop a portion of the mango coconut mixture and roll up. Serve with whipped cream.

RAMEN, CORN AND BEANS

Serves four

Notes: This is filling, nutritious and cheap. It can also be made very quickly—all in the same pan.

3 packages chicken ramen	.30
1 cup corn (canned or frozen is fine)	.50
1 cup kidney beans (canned is fine)	.50
2 cups spaghetti sauce	1.00
¼ teaspoon chili powder	.10
black pepper to taste	.05
	Total: $2.45

Bring five quarts of water to a boil and toss in the ramen noodles, cooking three or four minutes or until tender but not mushy. Drain and set aside.

Add all the other ingredients—plus one ramen flavor packet—to a small saucepan and cook until everything is thoroughly heated. When done, add the cooled ramen and mix well.

SUBSTITUTIONS & OMISSIONS

Use any beans you can get and use a packet of chili ramen mix for the chili powder. Add a package of ramen for lost volume.

4 packages chicken ramen	.40
1 cup corn (frozen or canned is fine)	.50
1 cup kidney beans (canned is fine)	.50
1 cup tomato sauce	.20
1 teaspoon oregano	.10
1 teaspoon garlic salt	.10
¼ teaspoon chili powder	.10
¼ teaspoon pepper	*
	Total: $1.90

$$$ BIG SPLURGE $$$

Toss in some fresh tarragon and use angel hair pasta for ramen noodles.

CURRIED VEGETABLE RAMEN

Serves four

Notes: Curry livens up vegetables and makes a good nutritious meal. This dish will not keep too long. So if you don't plan on eating all of it within the day, cut the recipe down in size.

3 packages chili ramen	.30
4 tablespoons oil	.05
1 onion, chopped	.25
4 teaspoons curry powder	.20
½ teaspoon fenugreek	.10
2 tomatoes, sliced	1.00
1 clove garlic, minced	.10
1 teaspoon coriander	.10
6 small potatoes, boiled 20 minutes and diced	.50
1 cup spinach (canned or frozen is fine)	.45
1 cup green beans	.45
2 teaspoons crushed red	.10
2 tablespoons cilantro, chopped	.10
¼ cups ginger, sliced	.10
	Total: $3.80

Bring about five quarts of water to boil in a large pot, drop in ramen noodles and boil for a minute, then reduce heat. Cook another 2–3 minutes, or until tender. Remove from heat, drain and set aside.

In a large skillet, heat oil and sauté the onion, fenugreek, tomatoes, garlic, one chili ramen flavor packet and coriander for 3–5 minutes. Add spinach and potatoes. Continue to stir-fry for another five minutes. Add water, cover and simmer for another 15 minutes.

Toss into ramen noodles and serve immediately.

SUBSTITUTIONS & OMISSIONS

Use less onion, tomato, green beans and spinach. Add more potato and another package of ramen for lost volume.

4 packages ramen	.40
4 tablespoons oil	.05
½ onion, chopped	.10
4 teaspoons curry powder	.20
½ teaspoon fenugreek seeds	.10
½ tomato, sliced	.25
1 clove garlic, minced	.10
1 teaspoon coriander	.10

3 small potatoes, boiled and diced	.25
½ cup spinach (canned or frozen is fine)	.25
2 teaspoons crushed red chilies	*
2 tablespoons cilantro, chopped	.10
¼ cups ginger, sliced	.10
	Total: $2.00

$$$ BIG SPLURGE $$$

Add asparagus and serve over fettuccine instead of ramen noodles.

DIRTY RAMEN

Serves four

Notes: A classic Louisiana dish made with a little spare change. Careful, ramen will start to deteriorate if you simmer too long. But you should still get the taste right if you follow the directions.

3 packages spicy chicken ramen	.30
2 tablespoons olive oil	.20
3 cloves garlic, minced	.10
1 cup onion, diced	.25
1 green bell pepper, diced	.25
1 tablespoon chili powder	.10
¼ teaspoon crushed red pepper	.10
1 teaspoon ground cumin	.10
¼ teaspoon ground cinnamon	.10
1 tomato, diced	.50
1 cup corn (canned or frozen is fine)	.35
1 cup black beans, cooked and drained	.35
¼ cup toasted pine nuts	.50
1 red onion, thinly sliced	.35
1 tablespoon fresh lime juice	.10
2 tablespoons fresh cilantro, chopped	.10
1 lime, cut into wedges	.10
black pepper to taste	.10
	Total: $3.95

Sauté garlic and chopped onions in olive oil until brown, about 5 minutes. Mix in the bell pepper, chili powder, ground annatto, chili flakes, cumin, and cinnamon and sauté for another minute or two.

Crumble the uncooked ramen noodles into the saucepan and stir to coat.

Add water and one flavor packet, and bring to a boil over high heat. Cover the pan and turn the heat to low. Simmer for about five minutes then mix in tomatoes, corn, black beans and pine nuts. Stir in pepper and lime juice—and add another flavor packet if desired. When the mixture is heated through, spoon it onto plates and top with sliced red onion and cilantro. Serve with a wedge or two of lime.

SUBSTITUTIONS & OMISSIONS

Use vegetable oil for olive oil, leave out the red onion and use less tomato, onion and bell pepper. Use another package of ramen for lost volume.

4 packages spicy chicken ramen	.40
2 tablespoons vegetable oil	.05
3 cloves garlic, minced	.10
½ cup onion, diced	.15
1 green bell pepper, chopped	.25
1 tablespoon chili powder	.10
¼ teaspoon crushed red pepper	.10
1 teaspoon ground cumin	.10
½ teaspoon ground cinnamon	.10
½ tomato, diced	.25
½ cup corn (canned or frozen is fine)	.20
½ cup black beans, cooked and drained	.10
1 tablespoon lemon juice	*
2 tablespoons chopped fresh cilantro	.10
black pepper to taste	*
	Total: $2.00

$$$ BIG SPLURGE $$$

Forget the ramen. Use rice instead, tossing it in place of the ramen noodles and letting it slow cook to get the full flavor.

RAMEN NOODLES WITH EGGS AND CARAMELIZED ONIONS

Serves four

Notes: Cooking onion brings out its natural sugar. The skin actually caramelizes, giving the onion a different taste from when it's just cooked until tender. This recipe calls for the onion to be boiled then roasted. But you can also fry it until it caramelizes (just set the onion in a very small amount of oil and keep it in the pan until it browns).

3 packages chicken ramen	.30

3 medium onions	.75
1 tablespoon shallots, minced	.20
1 tablespoon vinegar	.20
1 teaspoon sugar	.05
¼ cup olive oil	.25
1 cup lettuce, shredded	.50
2 eggs, hardboiled and deviled	.20
	Total: $2.45

Boil onions in a medium saucepan in enough water to completely cover them for about 20 minutes. Once they're tender (check by piercing with a fork) rinse in cold water and halve each onion. Put a little oil in a roasting pan. Roast about a half-hour, or until the edges take on a crust.

Bring about five quarts of water to boil in a large pot, drop in ramen noodles and boil for a minute, then reduce heat. Cook another 2–3 minutes, or until tender. Remove from heat, drain and toss with the onion/egg mixture.

Meanwhile, mix the shallots with the vinegar, sugar and one ramen flavor packet in olive oil. Toss in lettuce and deviled eggs. At the last minute, add the onions and ramen noodles. Mix. The onions will come apart as you mix (and the salad will wilt immediately; so be prepared to eat as soon as you mix it).

Substitutions & Omissions

Use vegetable oil for olive oil, green onions for shallots and a half lemon for the vinegar.

3 packages ramen	.30
3 medium onions	.75
1 teaspoon lemon juice	*
1 tablespoon vinegar	.20
½ teaspoon sugar	*
¼ cup vegetable oil	.05
1 cup lettuce, shredded	.50
2 eggs, hardboiled and deviled	.20
	Total: $2.00

$$$ Big Splurge $$$

Use rotini for ramen noodles and add some dry sherry.

RAMEN EGG FOO YUNG

Serves four

Notes: Staple of Asian cuisine, this dish is filled with great tastes. You could eliminate a few. But for the price, why not keep it all?

3 package shrimp flavor ramen	.30
3 tablespoons oil	.05
1 cup celery, diced	.25
1 cup green onions, diced	.25
1 cup small shrimp, chopped	1.25
3 tablespoons soy sauce	.30
½ teaspoon dried ginger	.10
3 medium eggs	.30
1 package brown gravy	.50
	Total: $3.30

Open both packages of ramen. Cook the noodles without the seasoning packets two or three minutes. When done, drain and set aside.

Sauté celery, onions and shrimp in oil, adding the soy sauce and ginger. Let cool. Add sautéed mixture, with liquid, to noodles. Mix, and add the beaten egg.

Spoon a quarter of the mixture into a hot frying pan. Fry until golden brown. Repeat.

Serve with brown gravy made from one beef flavored ramen flavoring packet, a teaspoon of flour and ¼ cup water. Garnish with fresh parsley.

SUBSTITUTIONS & OMISSIONS

Reduce the amount of shrimp and add an extra egg.

3 packages shrimp flavor ramen	.30
3 tablespoons vegetable oil	.05
1 cup celery, finely chopped	.25
1 cup green onions, finely chopped	.25
¼ cup shrimp, finely chopped	.65
3 tablespoons soy sauce	*
¼ teaspoon ginger	.10
4 medium eggs	.40
	Total: $2.00

$$$ BIG SPLURGE $$$

Substitute rice noodles for ramen noodles.

ITALIAN EGGPLANT AND CHEESE RAMEN NOODLES

Serves eight

Notes: Besides being weird-looking, eggplant is filling and nutritious—and if you can find it cheap, it will feed for more than one meal and last for several days in the refrigerator.

5 packages chicken ramen	.50
1 medium eggplant, peeled and cut into strips	1.25
2 teaspoons olive oil	.20
2 teaspoons dried basil	.10
2 tablespoons Parmesan cheese, grated	.20
2 8-ounce cans tomato sauce	.50
½ teaspoon Italian seasoning	.10
1 15-ounce container ricotta cheese	1.75
1 cup mozzarella cheese, shredded	2.00
¼ cup fresh parsley, chopped	.25
	Total: **$6.85**

Heat about six cups of water and toss in the ramen noodles when the water is at a good boil. Cook one minute, then reduce the heat. Cook another 2–3 minutes, drain and set aside.

Broil eggplant in an oven at approximately 375° for about ten minutes. When the upside is brown, turn over and brown the other side. Remove and set aside.

Mix tomato sauce with Italian seasoning and one flavor packet. Set aside.

Spread the ramen noodles in the bottom of a casserole dish and add tomato sauce, eggplant, Parmesan, mozzarella cheese, and ricotta, and begin the process again. Bake about 45 minutes at 375°.

SUBSTITUTIONS & OMISSIONS

Use about half the mozzarella cheese, cottage cheese instead of ricotta and use half the required amount. Lose the parsley and use vegetable oil for olive. Add another package of ramen for volume.

6 packages chicken ramen	.60
1 medium eggplant, peeled and cut into strips	1.25
2 teaspoons vegetable oil	.05
2 teaspoons dried basil	.10
2 tablespoons grated Parmesan cheese	*
2 8-ounce cans tomato sauce	.40
½ teaspoon Italian seasoning	.10
1 cup cottage cheese	.50
1 cup shredded mozzarella cheese	1.00
	Total: **$4.00**

$$$ BIG SPLURGE $$$

Use smoked buffalo mozzarella and extra virgin olive oil. And use lasagna or manicotti instead of ramen noodles.

FRAGRANT RAMEN NOODLES

Serves four

Notes: Lots of things to say about the word 'fragrant' when it concerns student kitchens, but we won't take easy the shots here. Lots of spices and garlic make this a great dish for the senses. It's filling and good for you at the same time. And it keeps you in line with even the tightest budget.

3 packages ramen	.30
½ cup shallots, minced	.50
¼ teaspoon crushed red pepper	.10
3 cloves garlic, minced	.10
4 red bell peppers, roasted over open stove burner and cut into strips	4.00
3 cups spinach, rinsed and chopped	1.50
2 teaspoons vegetable or olive oil	.05
½ teaspoon dried basil	.10
¼ cup parsley, chopped	.15
	Total: $6.80

Heat oil in a large frying pan. Sauté shallots, crushed red pepper flakes and garlic about 2 minutes.

Add roasted red peppers and simmer five minutes on medium heat. Add spinach, basil, parsley and sauté for 2 minutes.

Bring water to boil and drop in ramen noodles. Cook for three or four minutes or until tender. Do not overcook. Drain and toss with the sauce. Serve immediately.

SUBSTITUTIONS & OMISSIONS

Use green peppers for red, green onions for shallots and ease off the spinach, using half an onion and an extra package of ramen for bulk.

4 packages ramen	.40
½ cup green onions, minced	.15
¼ teaspoon crushed red pepper	*
3 cloves garlic, minced	.10

2 green bell peppers, roasted and cut into strips	.50
½ cup spinach, rinsed and chopped	.50
2 teaspoons vegetable oil	.05
½ teaspoon dried basil	.10
¼ cup parsley, minced	.15
	Total: $1.95

$$$ BIG SPLURGE $$$

Use tortellini or cheese ravioli for ramen noodles. And keep the extra-virgin olive oil.

INDIAN-STYLE NUTS AND DRIED FRUITS IN RAMEN NOODLES

Serves four

Notes: This is a tough one to do on a budget. Even the smallest portion of dried fruit tends to be expensive. If worse comes to worse, you can pick and choose just a few of the ingredients, no matter how small an amount, and you can still use them to spice up the ramen.

3 packages curry flavor ramen	.30
2 tablespoons oil	.05
1 onion, thinly sliced	.25
1 tablespoon ginger, minced	.10
2 cloves garlic, minced	.10
2 jalapeno peppers, chopped	.10
½ teaspoon curry powder	.10
¼ cup dried apricots, diced	.50
¼ cup walnuts, chopped and toasted	.50
¼ cup cashews, toasted	.50
¼ cup raisins	.50
2 tablespoons green onion, chopped	.10
2 tablespoons coconut, toasted and grated	.20
¼ cup orange marmalade	.50
	Total: $3.80

Bring about five quarts of water to boil in a large pot. Drop in ramen noodles and boil for a minute, then reduce heat. Cook another 2–3 minutes, or until tender. Remove from heat, drain and set aside.

Add oil to a heavy skillet and sauté onion until it is lightly browned. Add ginger, garlic, chilies, one packet chili ramen flavoring and pepper. Cook, stirring constantly. Add a ¼ cup of water or so, another flavor packet and bring to a boil.

Toss with ramen noodles and pour into a serving bowl. Sprinkle the apricots, nuts, prunes, green onions and coconut over the ramen mixture. Serve with the marmalade on the side.

SUBSTITUTIONS & OMISSIONS

Reduce all fruit and nuts significantly. Add a fourth package of ramen for volume lost.

4 packages curry ramen	.40
2 tablespoons oil	.05
1 onion, thinly sliced	.25
1 tablespoon ginger, minced	.10
2 cloves garlic, minced	.10
2 jalapeno peppers, chopped	.10
½ teaspoon curry powder	.10
2 dried apricots, diced	.10
1 tablespoon walnuts, toasted and chopped	.10
1 tablespoon cashews, toasted	.10
1 tablespoon raisins	.10
2 tablespoons green onion, chopped	.10
2 tablespoons coconut, chopped and toasted	.20
½ orange peel	.10
Total:	$1.90

$$$ BIG SPLURGE $$$

Use white rice instead of ramen noodles.

RAMEN FRITATTA

Serves four

Notes: In terms of price, there's not a lot of difference between leftover ramen and fresh ramen. Eggs make this filling and cheap.

3 packages Oriental ramen	.30
8 eggs	.80
1 cup milk	.30
1 cup Cheddar cheese, shredded	1.00
1 4-ounce can green chilies, chopped	.35
½ cup green onions, sliced	.15
½ teaspoon cumin	.10
Total:	$3.00

Cook the ramen noodles in boiling, slightly salted water until *al dente*, 3–4 minutes, omitting the flavor packets. Drain well and rinse under cold water. Set aside.

Crack eggs and whip with a fork until bubbles appear. Combine raw eggs with ramen and milk, cheese, chilies, onions, cumin and one packet chicken ramen flavoring (if using leftover ramen, you'll have one flavor packet leftover from somewhere, we'd bet).

Oil a skillet and heat over medium flame. Pour pasta-egg mixture into the pan until it covers the bottom and cover. Cook 4 to 5 minutes until set and lightly golden. Turn over (this is difficult; the best way is to slide it out onto a plate, invert the skillet over the frittata, and flip it back into the skillet). Cook another 3 minutes.

Remove to a serving dish and keep warm. Repeat with remaining mixture twice. Top each frittata with whatever sauce you have available and serve.

SUBSTITUTIONS & OMISSIONS

Lighten up on the cheese. Add ramen.

4 packages vegetable ramen	.40
8 eggs	.80
2 tablespoons cream, mixed with 2 tablespoons water	*
¼ cup Cheddar cheese, shredded	.30
1 jalapeno, chopped	.10
1 cup green onions, sliced	.25
½ teaspoon cumin	.10
Total:	$1.95

$$$ BIG SPLURGE $$$

Use elbow macaroni for ramen noodles. And use some Glouster cheese, some shallots and a touch of dry sherry or white wine to taste.

RAMEN CON FUNGHI E PINOLI

Serves four

Notes: Funghi e Pinoli—it tastes a lot better than it sounds. The key to this is the skiitake mushrooms and prosciutto, which of course on a budget must go. Use ham and good old-fashioned white mushrooms—or even canned if that's what you can afford.

3 packages tomato ramen	.30
½ cup olive oil	.40

2 tablespoons red wine vinegar	**.30**
¼ teaspoon crushed red pepper	**.10**
3 cloves garlic, minced	**.10**
8 ounces shiitake mushrooms, sliced	**1.50**
¼ cup shallots, finely chopped	**.40**
½ cup prosciutto, finely chopped	**3.00**
15 sun-dried tomatoes, minced	**2.00**
1 cup black olives, diced	**.50**
½ cup dry white wine	**1.00**
½ cup Italian parsley, finely chopped	**.10**
1 cup pine nuts, toasted lightly and chopped	**.50**
2 tablespoons Parmesan cheese, grated	**.30**
black pepper to taste	**.05**
	Total: $10.55

Cook the ramen noodles in boiling, slightly salted water until *al dente*, 3–4 minutes, omitting the flavor packets. Drain well and rinse under cold water. Set aside.

In a bowl, mix together olive oil (all but 2 tablespoons), vinegar, red pepper, garlic, black pepper and one flavor packet. Add the shiitake mushrooms and toss to coat them.

In a large skillet, heat two tablespoons of oil over low heat and sauté the garlic, shallots and prosciutto until the heavy smell of garlic is present (but don't brown the garlic). Add the mushroom mixture, sun-dried tomatoes and olives and cook over moderate heat for five minutes. Add the wine and another ramen flavoring packet along with a half-cup of water; bring to boil for 3 minutes. Add parsley and simmer, covered, for 10 minutes.

Toss the ramen with the mushroom sauce, pine nuts and the Parmesan in a large bowl.

SUBSTITUTIONS & OMISSIONS

Instead of 15 sun-dried tomatoes use only one (Really? Yes, really. Just mince very well. The flavor is intense and all you need is a hint), get rid of the vinegar, the skiitake mushrooms, the white wine, the pine nuts and the prosciutto (if you'd like, throw in a few white mushrooms and a small bit of refried ham). Use green onions for shallots, vegetable oil for olive and reduce by half. Add another package of ramen for lost volume. Simple.

4 packages tomato ramen	**.40**
¼ cup oil	**.10**
2 white mushrooms, sliced	**.10**
2 tablespoons fried ham, diced	**.25**
¼ teaspoon crushed red pepper	**.10**

3 cloves garlic, minced	.10
¼ cup green onions, finely chopped	.15
1 sun-dried tomato, minced	.20
1 cup black olives, diced	.50
½ cup Italian parsley, finely chopped	.10
Parmesan cheese, grated	*
	Total: $2.00

$$$ BIG SPLURGE $$$

Use penne for ramen noodles.

GARLIC RAMEN

Serves four

Notes: A true Brother-Can-You-Spare-a-Dime classic. For about 20¢ you can eat like a movie star. Just don't eat it before a hot date. The garlic is deadly.

4 packages chicken ramen	.40
8 cloves garlic, minced	.30
3 tablespoons olive oil	.30
½ cup heavy cream	.50
black pepper to taste	.05
1 tablespoon Parmesan cheese, grated	.25
	Total: $1.55

Bring 4 quarts water to boil. Add ramen noodles and cook until tender, about 3–4 minutes.

Mince the garlic and sauté in the olive oil. Add the cream, pepper and a packet of vegetable ramen flavoring. Simmer and then toss with the hot pasta. Add cheese and serve.

SUBSTITUTIONS & OMISSIONS

Use vegetable oil for olive and a couple tablespoons cream mixed with water.

4 packages chicken ramen	.40
8 cloves garlic, minced	.30
3 tablespoons oil	.05
2 tablespoons cream, mixed with 2 tablespoons water	*
½ teaspoon black pepper	*
1 tablespoon Parmesan cheese, grated	*
	Total: $.75

$$$ BIG SPLURGE $$$

Use elephant garlic, more cream and butter, add a couple tablespoons of brandy and use tagliatelle for ramen noodles.

ROASTED POTATOES WITH GARLIC, HERBS AND RAMEN

Serves four

Notes: Potatoes give a bigger portion and will tend to fill you up. You can cook the potatoes right in the frying pan, but it isn't as efficient as boiling them first.

3 packages spicy chicken ramen	.30
1 pound potatoes	.50
¼ cup olive oil	.50
6 cloves garlic, minced	.20
¼ teaspoon rosemary	.10
¼ teaspoon thyme	.10
¼ teaspoon sage	.10
¼ teaspoon oregano	.10
	Total: $1.90

Bring about five quarts of water to boil in a large pot. Drop in ramen noodles and boil for a minute, then reduce heat. Cook another 2–3 minutes, or until tender. Remove from heat, drain and set aside.

In the same water, boil the potatoes for approximately 45 minutes or until tender. Check tenderness by piercing with a fork. Once finished, rinse potatoes in cold water and remove skin with your fingers.

Halve the potatoes and arrange in the bottom of a baking dish in a bit of oil with the ground herbs. Sprinkle with two packages of spicy chicken ramen flavoring. Roast for about 45 minutes, until crusts begin to form on the edges of the potatoes.

Serve either over a bed of ramen or toss the noodles with the potatoes and olive oil and serve.

SUBSTITUTIONS & OMISSIONS

Use vegetable oil for olive oil.

3 packages spicy chicken ramen	.30
1 pound potatoes	.50
¼ cup vegetable oil	.05
6 cloves garlic, minced	.20
¼ teaspoon rosemary	.10

¼ teaspoon thyme	.10
¼ teaspoon sage	.10
¼ teaspoon oregano	.10
	Total: $1.45

$$$ BIG SPLURGE $$$

Use fresh herbs, extra-virgin olive oil and serve in penne instead of ramen noodles.

CRISP RAMEN CAKES WITH HERBED GOAT CHEESE

Serves four

Notes: The taste of goat cheese is essential in this, but almost everything else can be substituted. Goat cheese—either feta or French goat cheese—is available at most stores and is sharp and salty. It will be the overpowering ingredient, so if you don't like it, skip the recipe.

3 packages mushroom ramen	.30
½ cup vegetable oil	.10
4 ounces goat cheese	1.50
2 tablespoons cream cheese	.20
2 tablespoons sour cream	.20
1 tablespoon chives, chopped	.20
1 tablespoon fresh parsley, chopped	.05
1 teaspoon fresh thyme leaves, chopped	.10
1 clove garlic, minced	.10
1 teaspoon shallots, chopped	.10
2 tablespoons Dijon mustard	.20
1 teaspoon red wine vinegar	.10
2 tablespoons olive oil	.40
1 head lettuce, chopped	1.00
½ head radicchio	.75
black pepper to taste	.05
	Total: $5.35

Boil ramen 2–3 minutes, drain and cool. Heat a skillet with oil (do not allow oil to smoke). Shape cooled noodles into thin patties then fry until crisp, about 15 seconds per side. Set aside.

Thoroughly mix the goat cheese, cream cheese, sour cream, chives, parsley, thyme, garlic, and shallots in a small bowl. Season to taste with freshly-ground pepper and one flavor packet. Set aside.

On each deep-fried ramen patty, spread some of the cheese mixture. Top with lettuce and remaining ingredients. Serve warm.

SUBSTITUTIONS & OMISSIONS

Use sour cream for cream cheese. Chives and shallots can be replaced by green onions. Thyme is nice, and so is endive, but not essential.

3 packages mushroom ramen	.30
3 tablespoons vegetable oil	.05
2 tablespoons goat cheese	.35
1 tablespoon green onions, chopped	.05
1 tablespoon fresh parsley, chopped	.05
2 tablespoons Chinese mustard	*
2 teaspoons lemon	*
2 cloves garlic, minced	.10
1 head lettuce	1.00
black pepper to taste	*
	Total: $1.90

$$$ BIG SPLURGE $$$

Use fresh thyme, shred a Belgian endive or two and make sure you keep the shallots. Use fettuccine or linguine for ramen noodles.

RAMEN NOODLES WITH GREEN BEANS AND MUSHROOMS

Serves four

Notes: Try to use fresh green beans if possible—or use snow peas—to keep this dish true to taste.

3 packages mushroom ramen	.30
1 ½ pounds fresh green beans, cleaned, cut into 1-inch pieces	1.50
½ pound fresh mushrooms, sliced	1.00
1 onion, sliced	.25
8 cloves garlic, minced	.15
½ cup red wine	.50
2 cups tomatoes, diced	1.00
2 teaspoons dried basil	.10
1 teaspoon dried marjoram	.10
black pepper to taste	.05
	Total: $4.95

Bring five quarts of water to a boil and toss in the ramen noodles. Cook three or four minutes or until tender but not mushy. Drain and set aside.

Pour wine into a large skillet and add all veggies and herbs, plus one flavor packet. Add tomatoes, then let simmer 10 minutes. Let simmer on low heat another 20 more minutes then pour over bed of ramen noodles.

SUBSTITUTIONS & OMISSIONS

If you have to, use canned green beans and back off the stated amount. Wine is nice, but can be eliminated. Take out the marjoram, use canned mushrooms and beans for fresh. Add another package of ramen.

4 packages mushroom ramen	.40
¾ can green beans, cut into 1-inch pieces	.40
1 6-ounce can mushrooms, sliced	.50
1 onion, sliced	.25
8 cloves garlic, minced	.15
1 8-ounce can tomato sauce	.20
2 teaspoons dried basil	.10
black pepper to taste	*
	Total: $2.00

$$$ BIG SPLURGE $$$

Use a combination of portobello, porcini and skiitake mushrooms, and substitute tagliatelle for ramen noodles.

GREEN BELL PEPPERS STUFFED RAMEN NOODLES

Serves four

Notes: Green peppers serve as the casserole dish; ramen and ground beef are the casserole ingredients.

3 packages vegetable ramen	.30
1 onion, diced	.25
1 clove garlic, minced	.10
½ cup tomatoes, diced	.50
1 tablespoon oil	.05
¼ teaspoon thyme	.10
½ pound ground beef, browned and crumbled	.50
2 tablespoons parsley, chopped	.10

4 green peppers, sliced in half, lengthwise	1.00
black pepper to taste	.05
	Total: $2.95

Boil about six cups of water and toss in the ramen noodles. Cook one minute, then reduce the heat. Cook another 2–3 minutes, drain and set aside.

In a large skillet, sauté garlic, onion, parsley, and cook about two minutes, until tender. Add ground beef and a packet of beef ramen flavoring. Cook well.

Add all to the noodles, and mix well, cutting smaller pieces of noodles off if they become unruly. Stuff the eight half-pieces of pepper.

Place all eight half bell peppers on a baking sheet and bake for 40 minutes in a 350° oven. Serve immediately.

SUBSTITUTIONS & OMISSIONS

Reduce the amount of beef, lose the tomato and drop the amount of onion. Add a package of ramen to bulk it back up.

4 packages vegetable ramen	.40
5 green onions, sliced	.10
1 tablespoon oil	.05
¼ teaspoon thyme	.10
¼ pound ground beef, browned and crumbled	.25
2 tablespoons parsley, chopped	.10
4 green peppers, sliced in half	1.00
black pepper to taste	*
	Total: $2.00

$$$ BIG SPLURGE $$$

Use red, yellow or orange peppers and use ground lamb instead of beef.

GRILLED PASTA TOSS

Serves four

Notes: Good, easy and nutritious. What else do you want?

3 packages ramen: one tomato, one spicy chicken	.30
4 zucchini or small yellow squash, sliced	1.00
1 red onion, cut into large chunks	1.00
1 red pepper	.75
juice of two lemons	.20
	Total: $3.25

Prepare ramen by boiling two to three minutes, then removing from heat and draining. You do not want the ramen overcooked. Drain and set aside.

On broiler pan, arrange zucchini and onion. Combine both flavor packages with juice of two lemons. Add three tablespoons water and ¼ cup oil. Mix. Brush the zucchini and onions and grill about fifteen minutes on a baking sheet.

Toss cooked ramen, vegetables, peppers and vinegar together. Serve.

SUBSTITUTIONS & OMISSIONS

Use green peppers for red and yellow onion for red. Add another package of ramen.

4 packages ramen: one tomato, one spicy chicken	.40
3 zucchini and/or yellow squash, sliced	.75
1 red onion, cut into large chunks	.50
¾ cup diced roasted green peppers	.25
juice of two lemons	*
	Total: $1.90

$$$ BIG SPLURGE $$$

Use a little white Zinfandel in the marinade and serve over penne instead of ramen.

HADES' BOLD RAMEN NOODLES

Serves four

Notes: "Bold" is not quite the word. If you stick to the recipe and use habaneros, you'll need a tongue transplant. Habaneros are nature's natural paint remover. The bananas make this interesting but do not mask the heat—which is substantial.

3 packages spicy chicken ramen	.30
2 tablespoons olive oil	.20
1 yellow onion, diced	.25
1 red bell pepper, diced	1.00
2 bananas, sliced	.20
¼ cup pineapple juice	.30
juice of 3 oranges	.50
¼ cup cilantro, chopped	.25
4 tablespoons lime juice	.40
4 tablespoons habaneros, finely chopped, or 6 tablespoons inner beauty peppers, chopped	.35

¼ cup grated Monterey jack	.50
2 teaspoons unsalted butter	.20
Total:	$4.45

Bring five quarts of water to a boil and toss in the ramen noodles, cooking three or four minutes or until tender but not mushy. Drain and set aside.

Heat oil and sauté onion and red pepper about four minutes. Add bananas, pineapple and orange juices and one flavor packet. Simmer five minutes over medium heat. Add lime juice, cilantro, peppers and cheese. Mix well.

Add mixture to ramen noodles and mix thoroughly. God be with you.

SUBSTITUTIONS & OMISSIONS

Use vegetable oil for olive, green pepper for red, the pineapple juice can be eliminated, and use margarine for butter.

3 packages spicy chicken ramen	.30
2 vegetable oil	.05
1 yellow onion, diced	.25
1 green bell pepper, diced	.25
1 banana, sliced	.10
juice of 1 orange	.15
¼ cup chopped cilantro	.25
4 tablespoons lemon juice	*
4 tablespoons finely chopped habaneros or 6 tablespoons inner beauty peppers, chopped	.35
¼ cup grated Monterey jack	.50
2 teaspoons margarine	.05
Total:	$2.25

$$$ BIG SPLURGE $$$

Use some triple sec and some Rose's lime juice to add to the flavor. And use bow tie pasta for ramen noodles.

JAMBALAYA RAMEN

Serves four

Notes: Beans and rice are the main ingredients typically. This time, you can omit either or both and still have something pretty close—and a heck of a lot cheaper.

3 packages spicy chicken ramen	.30
1 teaspoon vegetable oil	.05
1 cup onions, diced	.25

½ cup celery, diced	**.10**
½ cup green peppers, diced	**.10**
2 cloves garlic, minced	**.10**
1 cup salsa	**.60**
1 cup tomato sauce	**.20**
1 cup rice	**.50**
½ teaspoon dried thyme	**.10**
¼ teaspoon ground pepper	**.10**
½ 19-ounce can pinto beans, drained	**.30**
1 cup corn (frozen or canned is fine)	**.35**
	Total: $3.05

In a large pot, boil 4 quarts of water and drop in the ramen. Cook 2–3 minutes until tender. Drain and set aside.

Sauté onions, celery, green peppers and garlic in oil, stirring frequently for 4 to 5 minutes or until just tender. Stir in the salsa, tomato sauce, rice, thyme, red pepper and a flavor packet. Bring to a boil for three minutes.

Reduce the heat to low. Stir in the beans and corn, then simmer for 10 to 20 minutes longer, or until the rice is cooked. Stir in the ramen, mixing to coat, cook for another three minutes until hot and serve.

SUBSTITUTIONS & OMISSIONS

Leave out the rice, use only a portion of the beans and lose the salsa. Add a teaspoon of Louisiana hot sauce instead of salsa and bring the bulk up by adding a fourth package of ramen.

4 packages spicy chicken ramen	**.40**
1 teaspoon vegetable oil	**.05**
2 teaspoons hot sauce	*
1 cup onions, diced	**.25**
½ cup celery, diced	**.10**
½ cup green peppers, diced	**.10**
2 cloves garlic, minced	**.10**
1 cup tomato sauce	**.20**
½ teaspoon dried thyme	**.10**
¼ teaspoon ground red pepper	**.10**
¼ cup pinto beans, drained	**.10**
1 cup corn (frozen or canned is fine)	**.35**
	Total: $1.85

$$$ BIG SPLURGE $$$

Tough to change a down-home dish into something it isn't. But if you must, double the amount of beans, use bulgur for rice and leave out the ramen.

JAPANESE-STYLE RAMEN NOODLES
Serves four

Notes: Use canned shrimp for this one if you don't have fresh shrimp in the budget. And if you don't have skiitake mushrooms, don't fret; use white instead.

3 packages shrimp flavored ramen	.30
½ cup carrots, julienned	.25
1 cup spinach leaves, torn into 1-inch pieces	.40
¼ cup shiitake mushrooms, chopped	1.00
1 cup tamago (Japanese fried omelet, below), julienned	.60
¼ cup green onions, slivered	.15
	Total: $2.70

In a large pot of boiling salted water, cook the ramen until tender but still firm, about 4 minutes. Drain well and mix with sesame oil.

Tomago is essentially a cut-up omelet added as a main ingredient. To make it, beat eggs and cook a thin omelet in an oiled frying pan, then slice into long strips.

Afterward, in the same frying pan, heat the carrots, mushroom and green onions, and cook for approximately four minutes on medium heat. Add spinach and cook another minute, stirring constantly.

Combine ramen noodles with the tomago and shrimp and serve.

SUBSTITUTIONS & OMISSIONS

Forget the skiitake mushrooms; use white mushrooms instead, or use canned mushrooms.

3 packages shrimp flavored ramen	.30
½ cup carrots, julienned	.25
1 cup spinach leaves, torn into 1-inch pieces	.40
¼ cup white mushrooms, chopped	.40
½ cup tamago (Japanese fried omelet), julienned	.40
¼ cup green onions, slivered	.15
	Total: $1.90

$$$ BIG SPLURGE $$$

Use fat Oriental noodles instead of ramen noodles.

JICAMA AND RAMEN

Serves four

Notes: Jicama is nutritious and versatile—albeit a little weird tasting (like a cross between a raw potato and a radish). But it will fill you up, and it doesn't cost a fortune. Use it in this recipe—either hot or cold.

3 packages spicy chicken ramen	.30
2 jicamas, peeled and julienned	.75
1 red bell pepper, julienned	1.00
½ jalapeno, minced	.10
4 mint leaves, chopped	.10
½ cup mushrooms, canned	.40
1 tablespoon butter or olive oil	.20
	Total: $2.85

Bring about five quarts of water to boil in a large pot. Drop in ramen noodles and boil for a minute, then reduce heat. Cook another 2–3 minutes, or until tender. Remove from heat, drain and set aside.

Mix all raw vegetables together and pour into ramen noodles. Add the mint leaves, mushrooms, one spicy chicken flavor packet and olive oil. Toss well and serve.

SUBSTITUTIONS & OMISSIONS

Use green pepper for red, vegetable oil or margarine for butter or olive oil.

3 packages spicy chicken ramen	.30
2 jicamas, peeled and julienned	.75
1 green bell pepper, julienned	.25
½ jalapeno, minced	.10
4 mint leaves	.10
½ cup mushrooms	.40
1 tablespoon margarine	.05
	Total: $1.95

$$$ BIG SPLURGE $$$

Use more butter, add different color bell peppers, and use rigatoni for ramen noodles.

HOME-STYLE RAMEN MAC AND CHEESE

Serves four

Notes: Frankly, if what you're after here is a cheap meal, skip it and buy a box of macaroni and cheese from the store. This is too extravagant. However, if you find yourself with a block of cheese and not too much else, give it a try.

3 packages ramen, any flavor	.30
1 ½ cups milk	.60
1 teaspoon powdered mustard	.10
1 teaspoon Worcestershire sauce	.10
½ stick butter	.30
1 egg, beaten	.10
3 cups grated sharp Cheddar cheese (about 1 pound)	3.00
½ cup fresh bread crumbs	.50
½ teaspoon paprika	.10
	Total: $5.10

Cook the ramen until tender but still firm in a large pot of boiling salted water, about 4 minutes. Drain well.

Meanwhile, bring the milk to a boil in a small saucepan. Reduce and stir in the powdered mustard, Worcestershire sauce, one flavor packet and hot pepper sauce. Blend a few seconds then set aside.

Toss the ramen in a bowl and add the butter and egg and mix well. Stir in the Cheddar cheese then spread the ramen in a baking dish. Pour the milk/cheese mixture over the ramen noodles, stir in the bread crumbs and top with paprika.

Bake for 30 minutes at 375°, or until bubbly and brown.

SUBSTITUTIONS & OMISSIONS

Use a couple tablespoons cream mixed with water for the milk, margarine for butter and use your own old bread for bread crumbs. Also, ease up on the cheese and add another package ramen noodles.

4 packages ramen, any flavor	.40
2 tablespoons cream, mixed with water	*
1 teaspoon powdered mustard	.10
1 teaspoon Worcestershire sauce	.10
3 tablespoons margarine	.05
1 egg, beaten	.10
1 ½ cups grated sharp Cheddar cheese (about a third-pound)	1.00
½ cup fresh bread crumbs	*
½ teaspoon paprika	.10
	Total: $1.85

$$$ BIG SPLURGE $$$

Use elbow macaroni for ramen. And use all the cheese, plus some Stilton or some English double Glouster.

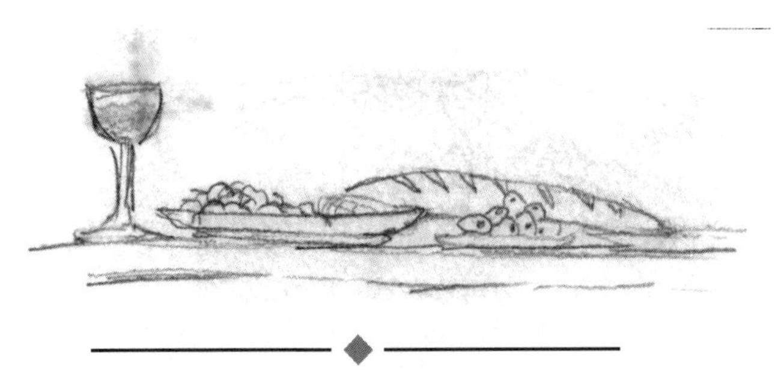

RAMEN MARINARA

Serves four

Notes: Easy and inexpensive. Add herbs to your liking, or leave as is for a filling and inexpensive meal.

3 packages tomato ramen	.30
2 cups tomatoes, diced (canned is fine)	1.00
¼ cup olive oil	.50
½ cup red wine	.50
1 large onion, chopped	.25
1 teaspoon dried basil	.10
3 cloves garlic, minced	.10
½ teaspoon oregano	.10
	Total: $2.85

Bring 4 quarts water to boil. Add ramen noodles and cook until tender, about 4 minutes. Drain and set aside.

Sauté garlic and onion in oil until lightly browned. Add one flavor packet and all the other ingredients. Simmer about 20 minutes, stirring often to prevent sticking. Pour over ramen and serve.

SUBSTITUTIONS & OMISSIONS

If you have no wine—or can't afford the wine—just leave it out. And use vegetable oil for olive oil.

3 packages tomato ramen	.30
2 cups tomatoes, diced (canned is fine)	1.00
¼ cup vegetable oil	.10

1 large onion, chopped	.25
1 teaspoon dried basil	.10
3 cloves garlic, minced	.10
½ teaspoon oregano	.10
	Total: $1.95

$$$ BIG SPLURGE $$$

Use spaghetti in place of ramen noodles.

RAMEN WITH TOMATOES, MARJORAM AND BLUE CHEESE

Serves four

Notes: Blue cheese is the key here. You can use blue cheese dressing in a pinch, but you'll get the flavor of a lot of other undesirable things. Omit the basil rather than the blue cheese.

3 packages tomato ramen	.30
4 tomatoes, quartered	1.50
½ cup fresh basil leaves	.75
2 tablespoons blue cheese, crumbled	.75
2 tablespoons olive oil	.30
2 tablespoons wine vinegar	.20
pepper to taste	.05
	Total: $3.85

Toss basil, cheese, oil and vinegar in a serving bowl. Add tomatoes, part of one ramen flavor packet and pepper to taste. Refrigerate and let marinate at least one hour.

Bring water to a boil in a large pot and add ramen noodles. Cook for approximately four minutes, or until tender. Drain.

In a serving bowl, toss everything (tomatoes will warm up immediately). Serve hot.

SUBSTITUTIONS & OMISSIONS

Use canned, diced tomatoes for fresh. Change the basil for parsley.

3 packages tomato ramen	.30
2 cups tomatoes, diced (canned is okay)	1.00
¼ cup fresh marjoram	.10
2 tablespoons blue cheese dressing	*
2 tablespoons olive or vegetable oil	.05
pepper to taste	*
	Total: $1.45

$$$ BIG SPLURGE $$$

Use fresh cheese and use linguine for ramen noodles.

RAMEN NOODLES IN FRESH TOMATO, MINT AND GARLIC SAUCE

Serves four

Notes: Another cheap dish. Mint adds a zest different from any you'll taste. With the tomatoes and the garlic, it creates a fresh tasting meal.

3 packages tomato or vegetable ramen	.30
4 cloves garlic, minced	.10
3 tablespoons olive oil	.30
2 pounds tomatoes, diced	2.00
1 tablespoon fresh mint leaves, chopped	.20
black pepper to taste	.05
	Total: $2.95

Bring water to boil and drop in ramen noodles. Cook three or four minutes or until tender, but not overcooked. Drain and set aside.

Sauté garlic in olive oil over low heat about 2 minutes. Add one flavor packet to a half-cup of water and pour it in. Add the tomatoes and cook over high heat, stirring occasionally until the sauce is thick but chunky, about 10 minutes. Reduce the heat and add one more tomato ramen flavor packet, then the mint.

Toss with ramen noodles and serve immediately.

SUBSTITUTIONS & OMISSIONS

Use vegetable oil for olive oil. Add ramen for bulk.

4 packages tomato or vegetable ramen	.40
4 cloves garlic, minced	.10
2 tablespoons vegetable oil	.05
3 tomatoes, diced	1.25
1 tablespoon fresh mint, chopped leaves	.20
black pepper to taste	*
	Total: $2.00

$$$ BIG SPLURGE $$$

Grill a piece of swordfish and use linguine for ramen noodles.

RAMEN NOODLES IN MUSHROOM SAUCE

Serves four

Notes: Porcini mushrooms add a nice flavor, but they also add a bigger price tag. Don't worry if you have to use regular white mushrooms.

3 packages mushroom ramen	.30
½ onion, diced	.15
½ cup porcini mushrooms, sliced	1.00
1 cup white mushrooms, sliced	1.00
½ cup cream	.50
2 tablespoons butter	.20
¼ cup tomato paste	.25
	Total: $3.40

Sauté onion in a frying pan until translucent. Reduce heat and add mushrooms. Add cream and simmer until sauce begins to thicken. Add one mushroom flavor packet. Simmer another two minutes then add the tomato paste.

Place ramen on each individual plate and pour mushroom sauce over. Serve immediately.

SUBSTITUTIONS & OMISSIONS

Use white mushrooms for porcini, vegetable oil for olive.

3 packages mushroom ramen	.30
½ onion, diced	.15
1 ¼ cup regular white mushrooms, sliced	1.25
2 tablespoons cream (added to same amount of water)	*
2 tablespoons vegetable oil	.05
¼ cup tomato paste	.25
	Total: $2.00

$$$ BIG SPLURGE $$$

Add portobello mushrooms with the porcini, and use penne for ramen noodles.

OKRA AND TOMATO RAMEN NOODLES

Serves four

Notes: Prickly and rough on the outside and booger-like inside, if you're from the South, this okra-based main course is right up your alley. If not, try it. You may like it. Then again, you may not.

3 packages pork ramen	**.30**
2 cups okra, cooked and sliced (canned or frozen is fine)	**1.00**
3 cups tomato sauce	**.60**
1 teaspoon basil	**.10**
1 teaspoon thyme	**.10**
2 bay leaves	**.10**
1 tomato, diced	**.50**
	Total: $2.70

Cook the ramen noodles in slightly salted boiling water until *al dente*, 3–4 minutes, omitting the flavor packets. Drain well and set aside. Cook the okra in the same pot for about 5–8 minutes.

Pour the tomato sauce in a medium saucepan and add spices and one flavor packet. Bring to a boil and drop in the pre-cooked okra. Cook until hot then toss with ramen noodles.

SUBSTITUTIONS & OMISSIONS

Forget the okra altogether. Because if you've never tasted okra or acquired a taste for it, you'll hate the whole recipe. Or try this—lose the tomato, the basil and a portion of the okra and you come in at under $2.

4 packages pork ramen	**.40**
1 cup okra, cooked and sliced (canned or frozen is fine)	**.50**
3 cups tomato sauce	**.60**
1 teaspoon thyme	**.10**
2 bay leaves	**.10**
	Total: $1.70

$$$ BIG SPLURGE $$$

With okra? You might as well try to make something extravagant with tofu.

RAMEN NOODLES WITH ORIENTAL SEASONING

Serves four

Notes: Cheap and great tasting. What else do you want? This one gives you the essence of Asian food, and can be made on the shortest of shoestring budgets.

3 packages Oriental flavor ramen	**.30**
¼ pound snow peas	**.50**

2 tablespoons soy sauce	.10
1 teaspoon vinegar	.10
1 teaspoon sugar	.05
1 teaspoon cornstarch, mixed in 1 teaspoon water	.10
1 tablespoon vegetable oil	.05
2 green onions, thinly sliced	.15
1 clove garlic, minced	.10
½ teaspoon dried ginger	.10
	Total: $1.55

Stir water, soy sauce, vinegar, sugar, one flavor packet and cornstarch together in a small bowl until the sugar and cornstarch are dissolved. Set aside.

In a frying pan, heat vegetable oil and sauté the green onions, garlic and ginger and stir until the garlic and ginger are fragrant, about 1 minute. Add the cornstarch mixture and bring to a boil then add snow peas. Toss just until the peas begin to change color to bright green, about another minute.

Meanwhile, bring water to boil and drop in ramen noodles. Cook for three or four minutes or until tender, but not overcooked. Drain.

Add together peas, sauce and the noodles and coat evenly. Serve immediately.

SUBSTITUTIONS & OMISSIONS

Omit vinegar.

3 packages ramen	.30
¼ pound snow peas, trimmed	.50
2 tablespoons soy sauce	.10
1 teaspoon sugar	.05
1 teaspoon cornstarch, mixed in 1 teaspoon water	.10
1 tablespoon vegetable oil	.05
2 green onions, thinly sliced	.15
1 clove garlic, minced	.10
½ teaspoon dried ginger	.10
	Total: $1.45

$$$ BIG SPLURGE $$$

Use fat Oriental noodles for ramen noodles.

RAMEN PEANUT STIR-FRY

Serves four

Notes: This is a rendition of sate noodles. This, however, is more sedate than some other versions. But it's still chic and exotic—not to mention cheap. The cucumber takes the place of chicken or meat.

3 packages sesame ramen	.30
1 teaspoon vegetable oil	.05
4 medium carrots, cut julienne	.25
½ teaspoon crushed red peppers	.10
1 bunch green onions, sliced	.25
1 large cucumber, peeled, julienned	.25
3 tablespoons smooth peanut butter	.35
¼ cup lime juice	.50
¼ cup soy sauce	.20
black pepper to taste	.05
	Total: $2.30

Bring water to boil and drop in ramen noodles. Cook for three or four minutes or until tender, but not overcooked. Set aside.

Sauté carrots in vegetable oil for 2 to 3 minutes, or until tender. Add the red pepper flakes, cucumbers and green onions and sauté another 2 minutes.

Add a few teaspoons of water, one flavor packet and all other ingredients—except the cucumbers—to the skillet. Season with pepper to taste. Bring to a boil. At the last minute, drop in the cucumbers. Drain and toss with the sauce. Serve immediately.

SUBSTITUTIONS & OMISSIONS

Substitute lemon juice for lime juice.

3 packages ramen	.30
1 teaspoon vegetable oil	.05
4 medium carrots, sliced julienne	.25
½ teaspoon crushed red peppers	*
1 bunch green onions, sliced	.25
1 large cucumber, sliced	.25
3 tablespoons smooth peanut butter	.35
¼ cup lemon juice	*
¼ cup soy sauce	*
black pepper to taste	*
	Total: $1.45

$$$ BIG SPLURGE $$$

Serve on white rice.

PEARS IN VINEGAR AND RAMEN NOODLES

Serves four

Notes: Pears make it sweet, balsamic vinegar gives it a savory taste. Together they make this a nice little ditty that costs little.

3 packages teriyaki ramen	**.30**
½ cup fresh orange juice	**.10**
4 tablespoons balsamic vinegar	**.20**
2 tablespoons fresh lemon juice	**.20**
1 garlic clove, minced	**.10**
1 tablespoon orange zest	**.10**
1 tablespoon vegetable or olive oil	**.05**
1 bunch spinach, chopped	**1.00**
4 pears (red, green or mixed), cored and sliced	**1.00**
½ cup raisins	**.50**
¼ cup walnut pieces, chopped	**.50**
	Total: $4.05

Heat about six cups of water and toss in ramen noodles once the water is at a good boil. Cook one minute, then reduce heat. Cook another 2–3 minutes, drain and set aside.

Mix the orange juice, balsamic vinegar, lemon juice, garlic, orange zest, oil and one flavor packet in bowl. In another bowl, combine pears, raisins and walnuts. When thoroughly mixed, combine the contents of the two bowls together.

In a large skillet, sauté spinach in oil a couple minutes, then add all ingredients to the ramen. Toss once more and serve immediately.

SUBSTITUTIONS & OMISSIONS

Reduce the spinach and the pears by half and add another package ramen to keep same portions. Lose the raisins and the orange zest, and use fewer walnuts.

4 packages teriyaki ramen	**.40**
4 tablespoons balsamic vinegar	**.20**

2 tablespoons lemon juice	*
1 garlic clove, minced	.10
1 tablespoon vegetable oil	.05
1 bunch spinach, cleaned and chopped	.50
2 pears (red or green, or mixed), cored and sliced	.50
2 tablespoons walnuts, chopped	.20
	Total: $1.95

$$$ BIG SPLURGE $$$

Use orzo for ramen noodles.

RAMEN PESTO

Serves four

Notes: Potatoes and green beans round this dish out and make the pesto last longer. Use fresh basil only. If none available, try another recipe.

3 packages vegetable ramen	.30
1 cup fresh basil leaves	1.50
2 tablespoons pine nuts	.40
3 cloves garlic, minced	.10
¼ cup tablespoon Parmesan cheese, grated	.50
½ cup olive oil	.50
2 medium potatoes, boiled, peeled and diced	.30
1 pound green beans	1.50
	Total: $5.10

Bring water to boil and drop in ramen noodles. Cook for three or four minutes or until tender, but not overcooked. Drain and set aside.

Combine pine nuts, garlic, basil, one flavor packet and cheeses in a blender and purée (or mix well with a fork if you don't own a blender). Pour the basil mixture into a small bowl and stir in the olive oil. Do not blend or it will turn the pesto into something resembling transmission lubricant.

Toss noodles with the pesto and serve.

SUBSTITUTIONS & OMISSIONS

Use walnuts or hazelnuts for pine nuts, vegetable oil for olive oil, and two tablespoons dried grated cheese for fresh. Lose the green beans if you don't have them. Add another potato or two for volume.

3 vegetable ramen packages	.30
1 cup fresh basil leaves	1.00

2 tablespoons nuts	*
3 cloves garlic, minced	.10
3 tablespoons dried Parmesan cheese	*
½ cup olive oil	.05
4 medium potatoes, boiled peeled and diced	.30
Total:	$1.75

$$$ BIG SPLURGE $$$

Use fresh Parmesan, and use fettuccine for ramen noodles. If you have some roasted chicken, yeah; that'll make it.

PASTA WITH PIMENTO AND BROCCOLI

Serves four

Notes: Pimentos have a different taste from bell peppers and should be used here. But you can reduce the amount by more than half, replacing it with onion, and still get the essence of this dish.

3 packages vegetable ramen	.30
2 tablespoons vegetable oil	.30
½ teaspoon crushed red pepper	.10
4 cups broccoli florets	1.50
2 whole pimientos, diced	3.00
¼ cup Parmesan cheese, grated	.75
Total:	$5.95

In a large pot of boiling water prepare ramen noodles, cooking 3–4 minutes or until tender. Do not overcook. Drain and set aside.

While ramen is cooking, sauté the broccoli and red pepper flakes for about three minutes. Then add about a half-cup water and one vegetable flavor package to the broccoli and cover. Cook another three minutes or so.

Toss the ramen noodles with diced peppers. Season with pepper and another flavor packet to taste. Pour the broccoli over pasta, sprinkle with Parmesan cheese, toss and serve.

SUBSTITUTIONS & OMISSIONS

Use two tablespoons dried Parmesan cheese in place of fresh.

4 packages vegetable ramen	.40
2 tablespoons vegetable oil	.05

½ teaspoon crushed red pepper	*
2¾ cups broccoli florets	1.00
½ pimiento, diced	.40
3 tablespoons Parmesan cheese, grated	*
	Total: $1.85

$$$ BIG SPLURGE $$$

Use fresh Parmesan for dried and asparagus in place of broccoli. Serve on angel hair pasta instead of ramen noodles.

RAMEN PUTTANESCA

Serves four

Notes: Bay leaves, with their pungent flavor, and capers, with their sour and earthy taste, give this dish a unique flavor. Leave out the olives and cheese if you must; the rest will still stand without a problem.

3 packages vegetable ramen	.30
4 cloves garlic, minced	.20
1 cup fresh basil leaves, coarsely chopped	.50
2 cups tomatoes, diced	1.00
½ cup olive oil	.75
1 tablespoon crushed red pepper	.10
¼ cup capers, rinsed, drained	.50
½ cup pitted Kalamata olives	.75
2 tablespoons parsley, chopped	.10
¼ cup Parmesan cheese, grated	.75
black pepper to taste	.05
	Total: $5.00

In a large pot of boiling salted water, cook the ramen until tender but still firm, about 4 minutes. Drain well and set aside.

Combine the garlic and basil in a food processor or mash with a fork. Add one flavor packet of ramen, black pepper to taste and mix together. Stir into the tomatoes and set aside.

Heat olive oil in a large skillet, then add the garlic, parsley, capers, olives and crushed red pepper. Cook about a minute. Stir in the tomato sauce and simmer five more minutes. Add the Parmesan to the ramen noodles and pour over the sauce. Stir well and serve.

SUBSTITUTIONS & OMISSIONS

Use vegetable oil for olive, dried basil for fresh and dried Parmesan for fresh. Add ramen to fill out.

4 packages vegetable ramen	.40
4 cloves garlic, minced	.10
1 tablespoon dried basil	.10
1 cup tomatoes, diced	.50
¼ cup vegetable oil	.05
1 tablespoon crushed red pepper	*
2 teaspoons capers, rinsed, drained	.20
¼ cup pitted Kalamata olives	.50
2 tablespoons parsley, chopped	.10
¼ cup Parmesan cheese, grated	*
black pepper to taste	*
	Total: $1.95

$$$ BIG SPLURGE $$$

Use penne for ramen noodles and fresh Pecorino cheese for Parmesan.

GREEN BEAN RAGOUT

Serves four

Notes: Beans and onions are the mediums; flavor packets add punch. Plus, this dish is both cheap and easy to prepare. Just what you'd expect from us, right?

3 packages vegetable ramen	.30
1 pound green beans, cut into 1-inch pieces	1.25
1 medium onion, diced	.25
2 cloves garlic, minced	.10
1 teaspoon fresh sage	.30
2 tablespoons olive oil	.30
	Total: $2.50

Bring about five quarts of water to boil in a large pot. Drop in ramen noodles and boil for a minute, then reduce heat. Cook another 2–3 minutes, or until tender. Remove from heat, drain and set aside.

Cook the green beans in just enough water to cover them by an inch, boiling them for a few seconds, then turning down to a slow simmer. Add one flavor packet and a bit of olive oil. Cook until tender, about 20–30 minutes.

Set aside.

Sauté the onions and garlic in olive oil in a skillet and pour into the green beans. Toss with ramen noodles and serve immediately.

SUBSTITUTIONS & OMISSIONS

Use less green beans and substitute dried sage for fresh. And use vegetable oil instead of olive oil.

3 packages ramen	.30
1 pound green beans, cut into 1-inch pieces	1.20
1 medium onion, diced	.25
2 cloves garlic, minced	.10
1 teaspoon dried sage	.10
2 tablespoons vegetable oil	.05
	Total: **$2.00**

$$$ BIG SPLURGE $$$

Use shallots for onions and rigatoni for ramen noodles.

RATATOUILLE RAMEN NOODLES

Serves four

Notes: You'll need a good bit of eggplant and zucchini for this one. If you don't like either, skip the recipe. If you decide to try it, it's a nutritious, filling meal. And if you find squash and eggplant in season, it will also be inexpensive.

3 packages vegetable ramen	.30
4 cloves garlic, minced	.10
2 tablespoons olive oil	.20
1 onion, diced	.25
2 small eggplant, diced into ½-inch pieces	2.00
2 small zucchinis, diced into ½-inch pieces	.50
2 cups fresh tomatoes, diced	1.00
2 teaspoons dried basil	.20
2 tablespoons Parmesan, grated	.30
pepper to taste	.05
	Total: **$4.90**

Bring water to a boil in a large pot. Add ramen noodles. Cook for approximately four minutes, or until tender. Drain and set aside.

In a large skillet, add minced garlic and onion and sauté 1 minute. Add eggplant and zucchini to onion mixture. Over medium heat, sauté vegetables until tender, about 5–10 minutes, stirring often. Remove from skillet and reserve.

In same skillet, heat tomatoes over high heat for 5 minutes until liquid is reduced by about half. Add basil. Cook one more minute. Add eggplant and ramen, and toss. Sprinkle with grated cheese.

SUBSTITUTIONS & OMISSIONS

Eliminate the eggplant if necessary, substituting with zucchini, other squash or onion. Add ramen for bulk.

4 packages vegetable ramen	.40
4 cloves garlic, minced	.10
2 tablespoons vegetable oil	.05
2 medium yellow onions, diced	.25
4 small zucchinis, diced into ½-inch pieces	.50
2 cups tomatoes, diced (canned is fine)	.50
2 teaspoons dried basil	.20
2 tablespoons grated Parmesan	*
pepper to taste	*

Total: $2.00

$$$ BIG SPLURGE $$$

Before dicing eggplant, grill it on the barbecue then marinate it in extra-virgin olive oil. Serve it in penne instead of ramen noodles.

RAMEN NOODLES ROMANOFF

Serves four

Notes: Cottage cheese is easy to find, filling and—if you use low-fat cottage cheese—not fattening. You can also use ricotta if you have it.

3 packages Oriental ramen	.30
2 tablespoons margarine, melted	.05
1 cup flour	.10
¼ cup milk	.10
1 onion, diced	.25
1 teaspoon garlic powder	.10
½ tablespoon Parmesan cheese, grated	.10
½ cup cottage cheese	.25

½ cup sour cream	.25
1 teaspoon paprika	.10
1 cup American cheese, diced	1.50
	Total: $3.10

Boil about six cups of water and toss in the ramen noodles. Cook one minute, then reduce the heat. Cook another 2–3 minutes, drain and set aside.

Sauté onions in butter or margarine and toss in all spices, cheese, sour cream, cottage cheese and milk. Bring to a boil and reduce, simmering for about three minutes. Add the ramen noodles, one flavor packet and the diced American cheese and mix well. Pour the entire mixture into a casserole dish. Bake at 350° for 35 minutes.

SUBSTITUTIONS & OMISSIONS

Use less cheese, more ramen.

4 packages Oriental ramen	.40
2 tablespoons margarine, melted	.05
¼ cup flour	.10
¼ cup milk	*
1 onion, diced	.25
1 teaspoon garlic powder	.10
½ tablespoon Parmesan cheese	*
½ cup cottage cheese	.25
3 tablespoons cream, mixed with 3 tablespoons water	*
1 teaspoon lemon juice	*
1 teaspoon paprika	.10
½ cup American cheese, chopped	.75
	Total: $2.00

$$$ BIG SPLURGE $$$

Toss in some good Romano or Pecorino cheese and use fettuccine for ramen noodles.

SAFFRON RAMEN NOODLES

Serves four

Notes: Good quality saffron is like gold, about twelve dollars for a smidgen. But for this all you need is the cheap stuff, which is available at most grocery stores in the Mexican section.

4 packages vegetable ramen	.40
1 teaspoon olive oil	.10
2 shallots, minced	.75
1 clove garlic, minced	.10
2 teaspoons crushed saffron threads	.10
2 teaspoons currants	.30
1 teaspoon fresh parsley, chopped	.10
black pepper to taste	.05
	Total: $1.90

Sauté shallots and garlic in a large skillet over medium heat about 2 minutes. Add a half-cup water, saffron and one chicken ramen flavor packet stock. Bring to a boil, then reduce heat and toss in currants, parsley and pepper. Simmer about three minutes.

Boil about six cups of water and toss in the ramen noodles. Cook another 2–3 minutes, drain and mix with the saffron sauce. Serve.

SUBSTITUTIONS & OMISSIONS

Substitute green onions for shallots and vegetable oil for olive.

4 packages vegetable ramen	.40
1 teaspoon olive oil	.10
2 shallots or small onions, minced	.20
1 clove garlic, minced	.10
¼ teaspoon crushed saffron threads	.10
2 teaspoons currants	.30
1 teaspoon chopped fresh parsley	.10
1 teaspoon pepper	*
	Total: $1.30

$$$ BIG SPLURGE $$$

Toss in some diced pork tenderloin, some chicken breast, or maybe some fresh halibut. And use fettuccine for ramen noodles.

MEXICAN RAMEN SALSA

Serves four

Notes: This is simple and light, with a nice taste from the tomatillos and the limes. If you want a different touch, roast the jalapenos.

4 packages spicy chicken ramen	.40

6 tomatillos, diced	.30
2 jalapeno chilies, diced	.10
1 tablespoon cilantro, chopped	.10
2 tablespoons vegetable oil	.05
juice of two limes	.20
zest from one lime peel	.10
	Total: $1.25

Prepare ramen by boiling two to three minutes. Remove from heat and drain. Do not overcook the ramen. Set aside.

In a small saucepan, mix the ramen noodles, tomatillos, chilies and cilantro. Mix in the two flavor packets with the lime and lime zest. Toss. Serve immediately.

SUBSTITUTIONS & OMISSIONS

You can use lemon if lime is unavailable.

4 packages spicy chicken ramen	.40
6 tomatillos, diced	.30
2 jalapeno chilies, diced	.10
1 tablespoon cilantro, chopped	.10
2 tablespoons vegetable oil	.05
juice of two limes	.20
zest from one lime peel	.10
	Total: $1.25

$$$ BIG SPLURGE $$$

Roast the chilies first and serve over saffron rice or angel hair pasta. Sprinkle with crumbled *queso fresco*.

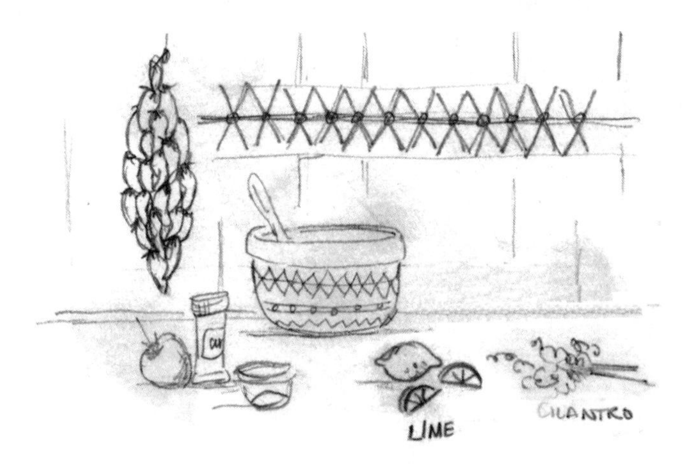

SAN FRANCISCO STYLE RAMEN AND RICE

Serves four

Notes: Fried, chopped ramen and rice make this a San Francisco treat (according to that other stuff sold out of a box). Ours is as filling and a lot cheaper.

3 packages chicken ramen	.30
1 onion, minced	.25
1 red bell pepper, minced	1.00
¼ cup green onions, chopped	.10
3 tablespoons butter	.25
2 cups white rice	.75
	Total: $2.65

Bring 3–4 quarts of water to a boil and add ramen noodles. Cook approximately 3 minutes, or until noodles are just slightly tender. Do not overcook. Remove and drain.

Chop the cooked ramen into small pieces and fry the pieces in butter until just golden brown. Remove and set aside.

Boil four cups of water and add rice. Simmer covered about 30 minutes, or until rice is fluffy, but still slightly watery. Add vegetables and noodles, cover again and simmer on low heat another ten minutes, until rice is done. Serve immediately.

SUBSTITUTIONS & OMISSIONS

Use green pepper in place of red.

3 packages chicken ramen	.30
1 onion, minced	.25
1 green bell pepper, minced	.25
¼ cup green onions, chopped	.10
3 tablespoons butter	.25
2 cups white rice	.75
	Total: $1.90

$$$ BIG SPLURGE $$$

Add some shrimp or some crab and use shallots instead of green onions.

SESAME SAUCE RAMEN NOODLES

Serves four

Notes: Tahini is available in a lot of stores, but you may not have access to it. In its place use a couple of tablespoons of sesame seeds.

3 packages ramen	.30
2 cloves garlic, minced	.10
1 tablespoon ginger, minced	.20
½ cup Oriental sesame paste (tahini)	1.00
¾ cup Oriental sesame oil	.50
2 tablespoons soy sauce	.10
2 tablespoons vinegar	.20
2 green onions, minced	.10
2 teaspoons Szechuan peppercorns	.10
2 teaspoons sugar	.05
2 tablespoons chili sauce	.10
	Total: $2.75

In a large pot of boiling salted water, cook the ramen until tender but still firm, about 4 minutes. Drain well and mix with sesame oil.

Mix the garlic and ginger in water, adding one flavor packet. Stir in the sesame paste until the texture is even. Combine paste, oil, soy, vinegar and pepper to taste and mix well. Add chili sauce and mix well.

Place the noodles on a platter, then top with the sauce and serve.

SUBSTITUTIONS & OMISSIONS

Omit the tahini and the vinegar and use hot sauce in place of chili sauce.

3 packages ramen	.30
2 cloves garlic, minced	.10
1 tablespoon ginger, minced	.20
¼ cup tahini	.70
¾ cup Oriental sesame oil	.50
2 tablespoons soy sauce	.10
2 green onions, minced	.10
2 teaspoons crushed red chilies	*
2 teaspoons sugar	*
2 tablespoons hot sauce	*
	Total: $2.00

$$$ BIG SPLURGE $$$

Toss in some crab meat and use fat Oriental noodles for ramen noodles.

RAMEN IN SPINACH SAUCE

Serves four

Notes: Popeye couldn't have asked for more. This is a nutritious dish that costs pennies. And you can make it even cheaper by following the directions below. The feta is a great taste, but may not fit the budget or the palate. Try it with or without.

3 packages vegetable ramen	.30
1 cup spinach, chopped	.50
2 tablespoons olive oil	.30
½ cup plain yogurt	.50
2 cloves garlic, minced	.10
1 teaspoon basil	.10
¼ cup parsley, chopped	.10
2 tablespoons feta cheese, crumbled	.50
juice of one lemon	.10
	Total: $2.50

Bring water to boil and drop in ramen noodles. Cook for three or four minutes or until tender, but not overcooked. Drain and set aside.

In a blender, mix spinach, yogurt, garlic, basil, parsley and lemon juice and blend on low speed until chunky-smooth. Add warm water if you need to thin the mix. Do not add the oil to the blender. Instead, remove the mixture from the blender and add the oil and feta cheese separately.

Toss with ramen noodles and serve immediately.

SUBSTITUTIONS & OMISSIONS

Substitute Parmesan for feta, vegetable oil for olive oil.

3 packages ramen	.30
1 cup spinach, chopped	.50
2 tablespoons vegetable oil	.05
½ cup plain yogurt	.50
2 cloves garlic, minced	.10
1 teaspoon basil	.10
¼ cup fresh parsley, chopped	.10
2 tablespoons Parmesan cheese	*

juice of one lemon	*
	Total: $1.65

$$$ BIG SPLURGE $$$

Use linguine instead of ramen noodles, and use fresh Parmesan or Romano cheese.

SWISS CHARD, PARMESAN AND RAMEN NOODLES

Serves four

Notes: Use both stalks and stems of the Swiss chard for this one.

3 packages pork ramen	.30
1 bunch Swiss chard, washed	1.50
6 cloves garlic, minced	.10
¼ cup olive oil	.45
½ cup Parmesan cheese, diced	1.50
black pepper to taste	.05
	Total: $3.90

Cook the ramen noodles in slightly salted boiling water until *al dente,* 3–4 minutes. Drain well and set aside.

Tear one-inch pieces of leaf from the chard stalks and place in a bowl. Chop stalks into ½ inch slices and place in bowl as well.

Sauté the garlic in a bit of oil until brown and dump the oil/garlic mixture into the chard. Add the rest of the oil and one flavor packet. Mix well. Add the ramen noodles and cheese and refrigerate. Serve chilled.

SUBSTITUTIONS & OMISSIONS

Use half the amount of Swiss chard, use dried grated Parmesan for fresh and add one more package ramen.

4 packages pork ramen	.40
½ bunch Swiss chard, washed	.75
6 cloves garlic, minced	.10
¼ cup olive oil	.45
½ cup Parmesan cheese	*
black pepper to taste	*
	Total: $1.70

$$$ BIG SPLURGE $$$

Use fusilli instead of ramen.

THREE PEPPER RAMEN NOODLES

Serves four

Notes: For color, you need all three types of bell peppers; for budget, you just need green ones. Fresh basil is great, but you can use dried here.

3 packages chicken ramen	.30
¼ cup olive oil	.40
3 cloves garlic, minced	.10
½ cup fresh basil, torn into 1-inch pieces	.75
½ cup green bell pepper, cut into strips	.15
½ cup red bell pepper, cut into strips	.50
½ cup yellow bell pepper, cut into strips	.50
¼ cup Parmesan cheese, grated	1.00
	Total: $3.70

Bring water to boil and drop in ramen noodles. Cook three or four minutes, adding one chicken flavor packet until tender but not overcooked. Drain and set aside.

Sauté garlic and cook strips of pepper in olive oil over low heat in a medium skillet. Cook for approximately three minutes, stirring constantly. Add one more packet of chicken flavoring to the peppers and stir until mixed. Add the basil and cook another minutes. Toss with ramen noodles, sprinkle with Parmesan cheese and serve.

SUBSTITUTIONS & OMISSIONS

Use green pepper for yellow and red, dried basil for fresh, vegetable oil for olive and dried grated cheese for fresh. Add a package of ramen to fill out.

4 packages chicken ramen	.40
¼ cup vegetable oil	.10
3 cloves garlic, minced	.10
1 tablespoon dried basil	.10
1 ½ cups green bell pepper, cut in strips	.15
2 tablespoons dried Parmesan cheese	*
	Total: $ .85

$$$ BIG SPLURGE $$$

Use good extra-virgin olive oil and gnocchi for ramen noodles.

SNOW PEAS AND TOFU

Serves four

Notes: This is a good, cheap vegetarian recipe—complete with the tofu. Sure, tofu doesn't taste any better than when it came out three decades ago, but at least you can get it at most grocery stores now. Funny how in three decades they can't make it taste any less like molded rubber bands, huh?

3 packages chicken ramen	.30
1 package (12 ounces) of firm tofu	1.50
½ pound snow peas	.75
1 green onion, chopped	.10
3 tablespoons oil	.20
1 teaspoon sesame oil	.20
1 teaspoon soy sauce	.10
1 tablespoon cornstarch, dissolved in 1 tablespoon water	.10
	Total: $3.25

Boil water in a large pot. Add ramen noodles and return to a boil for one minute. Reduce heat and cook another 2–3 minutes. Drain and set aside.

Cut the tofu into one-inch pieces and mix with green onions that have been cut into thin one-inch strips. Drop both into a heated skillet or wok with oil. Add the snow peas and stir-fry for about a minute.

Add the soy sauce, one flavor packet, sesame oil and two tablespoons of water. Cover the wok for 2 minutes; serve over a bed of ramen noodles.

SUBSTITUTIONS & OMISSIONS

Cut tofu amount in half, use a quarter cup of snow peas instead of a ½ cup, and add another package ramen noodles for volume.

4 packages chicken ramen	.40
½ package (6 ounces) of firm tofu	.75
¼ pound snow peas	.75
1 green onion, chopped	.10
3 tablespoons oil	.20
1 teaspoon sesame oil	.20

1 teaspoon soy sauce	*
1 tablespoon cornstarch, dissolved in 1 tablespoon water	.10
	Total: $2.50

$$$ BIG SPLURGE $$$

Use fat Oriental noodles for ramen noodles ... and get rid of the tofu and use something that tastes good.

TOMATO CREAM RAMEN NOODLES

Serves four

Notes: The essence of tomato cream is very inexpensive and can be accomplished with little or no extra money. It's the added ingredients, however, that make this meal more expensive. If you're light on cash, ease up on everything else but the tomato and the cream.

3 packages tomato ramen	.30
2 teaspoons vegetable oil	.05
¾ cup red pepper, diced	.75
¼ cup onion, diced	.10
1 clove garlic, minced	.10
2 cups tomatoes, diced	.75
1 teaspoon sugar	.05
½ teaspoon dried basil	.10
2 teaspoons all-purpose flour, mixed in 2 teaspoons water	.05
¼ cup milk	.20
black pepper to taste	.05
	Total: $2.50

Heat about six cups of water and toss in the ramen noodles once the water is at a good boil. Cook one minute, then reduce the heat. Cook another 2–3 minutes, drain and set aside.

In a large skillet, sauté the garlic in a bit of oil until light brown, then add the bell pepper and onion. Cook about three minutes, stirring constantly. Add the milk or cream, one flavor packet and the tomato sauce and cook another five or so minutes.

Add ramen noodles to the pan and coat well. Serve immediately.

SUBSTITUTIONS & OMISSIONS

Forget the red pepper; use green instead. Use tomato sauce instead of tomatoes, and use free cream for milk.

3 packages tomato ramen	.30
2 teaspoons vegetable oil	.05
¾ cup green pepper, chopped	.15
¼ cup onion, chopped	.10
1 clove garlic, minced	.10
1 8-ounce can tomato sauce	.25
1 teaspoon sugar	.05
½ teaspoon dried basil	.10
¼ teaspoon pepper	*
2 teaspoons all-purpose flour, mixed with 2 teaspoons water	.05
3 tablespoons cream, mixed with water	*
	Total: $1.15

$$$ BIG SPLURGE $$$

Cream for milk served over linguine instead of ramen noodles.

RAMEN TOSTADAS

Serves four

Notes: No tortillas needed for this traditional Mexican dish.

4 packages chicken ramen	.40
1 cup vegetable oil	.30
1 can refried beans	.40
2 cups lettuce, shredded	.50
¼ cup cilantro, chopped	.10
¼ cup Monterey jack cheese, shredded	.75
½ cup sour cream	.50
¼ cup hot sauce	.30
	Total: $3.25

Bring 3–4 quarts of water to a boil and add ramen noodles. Cook approximately 3 minutes, or until noodles are just slightly tender. Do not overcook. Remove, drain and set aside.

Form thin, 6-inch flat pancake-style patties of the noodles and set aside. Heat a skillet with oil until hot and fry the patties until crisp. Drain on paper towels.

While fried ramen is cooling, spread a thin layer of beans on the ramen circles then top with lettuce, cilantro and cheese. Top with hot sauce to taste and serve.

SUBSTITUTIONS & OMISSIONS

Use Parmesan for jack and less lettuce.

4 packages chicken ramen	.40
1 cup vegetable oil	.30
1 can refried beans	.40
2 cups lettuce, shredded	.50
¼ cup cilantro, chopped	.10
¼ cup Parmesan cheese, grated	*
1 cup sour cream	.30
¼ cup hot sauce	*
	Total: $2.00

$$$ BIG SPLURGE $$$

Just use real crisp-fried tortillas and get it over with. Use good Oaxaca or *queso fresco*.

RAMEN WITH VEGETABLES AND LEMON

Serves four

Notes: Hot pepper adds to the heat, but omit it and you'll still be fine. Filled with nutritious ingredients, you can skimp on a couple and still be okay.

3 packages vegetable ramen	.30
1 teaspoon olive oil	.30
1 carrot, thinly sliced	.10
¼ cup onion, chopped	.25
2 cups broccoli, cut into bite-size pieces	1.25
1 cup sliced zucchini, sliced	.50
1 teaspoon ginger, freshly grated	.30
1 lemon grass stalk, finely chopped	.75
¼ teaspoon crushed hot pepper	.10
	Total: $3.85

In large skillet, sauté carrot and onion in olive oil until onion has softened, about two minutes. Add broccoli, zucchini, ½ cup water mixed with one chicken ramen flavoring packet. Cover and simmer.

Cook ramen for 4–6 minutes until tender, but not overdone. Drain and set aside.

Combine another flavor packet with a few teaspoons water and add to vegetables. Stir in ginger, lemon grass and hot pepper flakes, if desired. Cook about three minutes. Serve immediately over ramen noodles.

SUBSTITUTIONS & OMISSIONS

Reduce the zucchini down to only one, use powdered ginger and lose the lemon grass. Add ramen for lost volume.

4 packages vegetable ramen	.40
1 teaspoon vegetable oil	.05
1 carrot, thinly sliced	.10
¼ cup onion, chopped	.10
1 cup broccoli, cut into bite-size pieces	.75
1 zucchini, sliced	.50
1 teaspoon powdered ginger	.10
¼ teaspoon crushed hot pepper	*
	Total: $2.00

$$$ BIG SPLURGE $$$

Use Chinese eggplant for half the zucchini and double the amount of ginger. Use tagliatelle for ramen noodles.

WATERCRESS WITH EGG RAMEN NOODLES

Serves four

Notes: Watercress gives a cool flavor sensation similar to cilantro or Italian parsley without the overpowering taste. What you'll taste most in this dish is the egg and the vinegar.

3 packages vegetable ramen	.30
2 hard-boiled eggs, chopped	.20
1 cup watercress, lightly chopped	.40
¼ cup olive oil	.50
½ cup onions, diced	.25
2 tablespoons red wine vinegar	.30
	Total: $1.95

Bring about five quarts of water to boil in a large pot. Drop in ramen noodles and boil for a minute, then reduce heat. Cook another 2–3 minutes, or until tender. Remove from heat, drain and set aside.

Chop the watercress, discarding most of the stems. Combine watercress with the eggs and add onions, black pepper, vinegar and one vegetable ramen flavor packet. In a small saucepan, heat olive oil and very, very quickly (maybe 20 seconds or so), scald the watercress mixture in oil, mixing constantly.

Toss and serve immediately with noodles.

SUBSTITUTIONS & OMISSIONS

Use vegetable oil for olive oil and lemon for vinegar, if needed.

3 packages vegetable ramen	.30
2 hard-boiled eggs, chopped	.20
1 cup watercress, chopped	.40
¼ cup vegetable oil	.10
½ cup onions, diced	.25
2 tablespoons lemon juice	*
	Total: $1.25

$$$ BIG SPLURGE $$$

Use spaghetti for ramen noodles and extra-virgin olive oil.

Chapter 8

POULTRY MAIN COURSES

ALMOND RAMEN CHICKEN

Serves four

Notes: An Oriental-flavored dish with a cornucopia of ingredients to hide any single particular taste flaw. With this one, you can easily drop one or two things and still end up with a good meal.

Ingredient	Cost
1 pound chicken breast, diced	2.50
1 cup vegetable oil	.40
¼ cup fresh ginger root, sliced	.40
3 green onions, chopped	.15
1 green pepper, chopped	.25
½ cup bamboo shoots	.75
¼ cup almonds, slivered	.50
2 teaspoons cornstarch	.20
1 tablespoon soy sauce	.10
1 egg white	.10
1 tablespoon rice vinegar	.20
1 tablespoon dry sherry	.50
1 teaspoon sugar	.05
black pepper to taste	.05
	Total: $6.15

Boil water in a large pot. Add ramen noodles and return to a boil for one minute, then reduce heat and cook another 2-3 minutes. Drain and set aside.

Combine soy sauce, egg white, rice vinegar, sherry, sugar, two flavor packets and cornstarch. Add chicken and mix well. Let stand a few minutes.

In a skillet or wok, heat oil and add chicken and marinade when hot. Stir-fry until browned. Remove when done. Stir-fry ginger, onion, pepper and bamboo chutes for about 3 minutes in the same pan. Remove. Add almonds, mix well and serve immediately.

SUBSTITUTIONS & OMISSIONS

Use thigh meat instead of breast meat, lighten the vegetable oil amount, use dried powdered ginger in place of fresh, use fewer almonds than called for, and reduce the amount of bamboo shoots. It's probably okay as is, but if you're really hungry, add an extra package of ramen.

4 packages ramen	.40
¼ pound chicken thigh meat, diced	.30
¼ cup vegetable oil	.10
2 teaspoons dried ginger	.10
3 green onions, chopped into 1-inch pieces	.15
1 green pepper, chopped	.25
¼ cup diced bamboo chutes	.35
2 tablespoons peanuts	.25
2 teaspoons cornstarch	.10
1 tablespoon soy sauce	*
1 teaspoon sugar	*
black pepper to taste	*
Total:	$2.00

$$$ BIG SPLURGE $$$

Use ¼ cup amaretto, ¼ cup sherry, and fettuccine in place of ramen.

AMARETTO CHICKEN

Serves four

Notes: Amaretto, or a sweet almond-flavored liquor, makes this dish. But hey, Amaretto is expensive. So if you can't steal some from your parents' liquor cabinet, you can always use some almond flavoring and sugar instead.

3 packages chicken ramen	.30
1 pound boneless chicken breasts	2.50
1 teaspoon paprika	.10
1 tablespoon butter	.10
3 tablespoons flour	.10
2 tablespoons vegetable oil	.05
1 tablespoon Dijon mustard	.10
¼ cup Amaretto	.50
2 cloves garlic, minced	.10
black pepper to taste	.05
	Total: $3.90

Heat about six cups of water and toss in ramen noodles once the water is at a good boil. Cook one minute, then reduce the heat. Cook another 2-3 minutes, drain and set aside.

Cut chicken into strips and combine flour, pepper, paprika, garlic and two flavor packets. Coat chicken, then sauté chicken until cooked through, adding butter if it sticks. Add mustard, orange juice and Amaretto to the skillet and increase heat until the mix boils, stirring until thick. Pour sauce over chicken, toss into noodles and serve.

SUBSTITUTIONS & OMISSIONS

Use chicken thigh meat for chicken breast meat, and reduce the amount. Fill it out with another package of ramen.

4 packages chicken ramen	.40
½ pound chicken thigh meat	.50
1 teaspoon paprika	.10
1 tablespoon butter	.10
3 tablespoons flour	.10
2 tablespoons vegetable oil	.05
1 tablespoon Dijon mustard	.10
2 teaspoons almond flavoring	.50
2 cloves garlic, minced	.10
	Total: $1.95

$$$ BIG SPLURGE $$$

Use lots of amaretto and a half-cup slivered, blanched almonds. And use fettuccine in place of ramen noodles.

ASIAN EGG AND CHICKEN STIR-FRIED RAMEN NOODLE

Serves four

Notes: Eggs fill this dish out, and broccoli and jalapenos give it flavor. For more or less heat, change the amount of jalapenos.

3 packages chicken ramen	.30
½ pound chicken, cut into 1-inch chunks	1.25
2 teaspoons soy sauce	.20
4 cups broccoli, cut into bite-sized pieces	1.25
3 tablespoons peanut oil	.30
6 cloves garlic, minced	.20
3 teaspoons sugar	.05
3 large eggs	.30
1 tablespoon jalapeno peppers, diced	.10
black pepper to taste	.05
Total:	$4.00

Bring about five quarts of water to boil in a large pot. Drop in ramen noodles and boil for a minute, then reduce heat. Cook another 2-3 minutes, or until tender. Remove from heat, drain and set aside.

In a large bowl, add pepper and mix with soy sauce and one packet of ramen seasoning. Coat chicken pieces evenly and set aside. In a medium skillet, sauté garlic in oil a few moments, then add the chicken. Stir-fry until the chicken turns white. Toss in the noodles along with a bit more soy sauce and stir-fry another minute.

Add broccoli, eggs and jalapenos and stir-fry again until eggs are cooked and dispersed throughout. Serve immediately.

SUBSTITUTIONS & OMISSIONS

Use less chicken and use thigh meat for breast; use only about two-thirds a cup of broccoli and vegetable oil for peanut oil. Add another package of ramen.

4 packages chicken ramen	.40
½ cup chicken thigh meat, cut into ½-inch chunks	.40
2 teaspoons soy sauce	*
¼ cup broccoli, cut into bite-sized pieces	.30
3 tablespoons vegetable oil	.05
2 cloves garlic, minced	.10
2 teaspoons sugar	*
3 large eggs	.30

1 tablespoon jalapeno peppers, diced	.10
black pepper to taste	.05
	Total: $1.70

$$$ BIG SPLURGE $$$

Grill the chicken; use white pepper for black, Thai chilies and spaghetti for ramen noodles.

BLACKENED CHICKEN RAMEN NOODLES

Serves four

Notes: Blackening a piece of chicken is actually a lot more complicated than this recipe describes (it needs an extremely hot frying pan that can't be achieved on a domestic stove). But this will do okay in a pinch.

3 packages spicy chicken ramen	.30
2 red bell peppers, roasted over an open stove burner	2.00
½ cup shallots, chopped	.40
1 clove garlic, minced	.10
1 tablespoon lemon	.10
1 tablespoon dried basil	.10
1 pound chicken tenders	2.50
4 tablespoons blackening seasoning	.10
1 tablespoon paprika	.10
1 teaspoon dried thyme	.10
2 tablespoons cream	.20
	Total: $6.00

After peppers are cooked over the open burner, remove, let cool for a few minutes and remove the seeds and inner membranes (the white stuff). Add to a blender with shallots, garlic, vinegar and a packet of shrimp flavor ramen noodles (mash well with a fork if you don't have a food processor or blender). Return to a small saucepan, add cream and let simmer 10 minutes.

Heat about six cups of water and toss in the ramen noodles once the water is at a good boil. Cook one minute, then reduce the heat. Cook another 2-3 minutes, drain and set aside.

Coat the tenders in blackening spice and add paprika and thyme. In a large skillet on high, sear the chicken tenders for about 2 minutes on each side, then reduce the heat to low and cook approximately five minutes, until the chicken is done all the way through.

Serve over a bed of ramen noodles, with the blackened chicken on top and the pepper sauce poured over. Serve immediately.

SUBSTITUTIONS & OMISSIONS

Reduce the amount of chicken; use green peppers for red and green onions for shallots. Add another package of ramen.

4 packages spicy chicken ramen	.40
2 green bell peppers, roasted over an open burner	.50
¼ cup green onions, chopped	.10
1 clove garlic, minced	.10
1 tablespoon lemon	*
¼ cup chicken tenders	.55
2 tablespoons blackening seasoning	.10
½ tablespoon paprika	.10
½ teaspoon dried thyme	.10
	Total: $1.95

$$$ BIG SPLURGE $$$

Serve on red beans and rice instead of ramen noodles.

BUFFALO CHICKEN RAMEN NOODLES

Serves four

Notes: Buffalo wings give this dish its name. All that means is that you really need Louisiana hot sauce, butter, celery and blue cheese. In you're in a bind, just use blue cheese dressing instead of real cheese. This is one place where hot is expected. Have at it.

3 packages spicy chicken ramen	.30
1 pound chicken breasts, diced	2.50
2 teaspoons vegetable oil	.05
1 tablespoon hot sauce	.10
1 cup celery, sliced	.15
½ cup red onion, chopped	.25
1 cup mayonnaise	.30
½ cup blue cheese salad dressing	.50
¾ cup skim milk	.50

2 tablespoons blue cheese, crumbled	.50
1 teaspoon paprika	.10
½ teaspoon garlic powder	.10
black pepper to taste	.05
	Total: $5.40

In a large pot of boiling water, prepare ramen noodles, cooking 3-4 minutes or until tender. Do not overcook. Drain and set aside.

While ramen noodles are cooking, combine paprika, salt, garlic powder, one flavor packet and pepper, then sprinkle over chicken.

Sauté chicken in 1 teaspoon oil in a large skillet over medium-high heat, about five minutes. Add hot sauce and cook another minute, then remove from pan.

In the same pan, add remaining oil, celery and onion and cook about two minutes.

In a small bowl, combine dressing with the vegetables. Pour into the skillet, stir and add chicken again. Cook over medium-low heat and stir constantly for about three minutes.

Place ramen noodles in a large serving bowl with all cooked ingredients and sprinkle with cheese. Mix and serve immediately.

SUBSTITUTIONS & OMISSIONS

Use a half-pound of chicken—and use thighs instead of breasts. Try extra celery in place of the chicken. Yellow onion is fine, and use dressing instead of real cheese. Add another package of ramen.

4 packages spicy chicken ramen	.40
½ pound chicken thigh meat, diced	.50
2 teaspoons vegetable oil	.05
1 tablespoon hot sauce	*
1 cup celery, sliced	.25
½ cup onions, chopped	.25
1 cup mayonnaise	*
½ cup blue cheese salad dressing	*
3 tablespoons cream, mixed with 3 tablespoons water	*
1 teaspoon paprika	.10
½ teaspoon garlic powder	.10
black pepper to taste	*
	Total: $1.65

$$$ BIG SPLURGE $$$

Use bow-tie pasta instead of ramen and buy some good blue cheese.

CAJUN CHICKEN RAMEN NOODLES

Serves four

Notes: Heavy on the butter and chili pepper makes it Cajun. Ramen makes it filling.

3 packages chicken ramen	.30
2 boneless chicken breasts, cut into thin strips	1.25
2 tablespoons butter	.05
¼ cup green bell peppers, diced	.10
¼ cup red bell peppers, diced	.25
½ cup mushrooms, sliced	.50
½ cup green onion, sliced	.10
1 cup heavy cream	1.00
¼ teaspoon basil	.10
1 teaspoon crushed red peppers	.10
¼ teaspoon lemon pepper	.10
¼ teaspoon garlic powder	.10
black pepper to taste	.05
Total:	$4.00

Heat about six cups of water and toss in the ramen noodles once the water is at a good boil. Cook one minute, then reduce the heat. Cook another 2-3 minutes, drain and set aside.

Put chicken, oregano and Cajun seasoning in a bowl and toss to coat. Sauté chicken in butter over medium heat until chicken is tender, about 5-7 minutes.

Add green and red bell peppers, sliced mushrooms and onions and cook for 2-3 minutes. Reduce heat. Add heavy cream, basil, lemon pepper, salt, garlic powder, one flavor packet and pepper, then heat through.

In a large bowl, toss ramen with sauce. Sprinkle with grated Parmesan cheese if desired.

SUBSTITUTIONS & OMISSIONS

Use thigh meat for breast meat and canned mushrooms for fresh. Reduce the amount of cream and add one package of ramen noodles or volume.

4 packages chicken ramen	.40
1 cup boneless thigh meat, cut into thin strips	.50
2 tablespoons margarine	.05
¼ cup green bell peppers, diced	.10
¼ cup red bell peppers, diced	.25
1 6-ounce can mushrooms, sliced	.25

2 green onions, sliced	.10
3 tablespoons cream, mixed with water	*
¼ teaspoon dried basil	.10
1 teaspoon crushed red pepper	*
¼ teaspoon lemon pepper	.10
¼ teaspoon garlic powder	.10
black pepper to taste	*
	Total: $1.95

$$$ BIG SPLURGE $$$

Marinate the chicken breasts in white wine and black pepper before pan-frying over high heat. Use fettuccine for ramen noodles.

RAMEN WITH TERIYAKI SAUCE

Serves four

Notes: Teriyaki sauce makes this dish. You can find teriyaki sauce at most stores, but if you feel up to it, you can make a version of your own. See below for more details. Either way, this is an inexpensive and familiar joint you'll come back to time after time.

3 packages spicy chicken ramen	.30
1 pound boneless, skinless chicken breasts	2.50
1 cup peas (frozen or canned is fine)	.60
1 red bell pepper, chopped into 1-inch pieces	1.00
3 stalks celery, diced	.15
1 medium onion, quartered	.25
1 2-inch piece fresh ginger, chopped	.25
½ cup teriyaki sauce	.70
1 teaspoon dried thyme	.10
¼ cup brown sugar	.30
	Total: $6.15

Make your own teriyaki sauce by combining two teaspoons brown sugar with three tablespoons soy sauce, a pinch of ginger and garlic powder—all the same ingredients you're using here anyway—and save money.

In a large pot of boiling water prepare ramen noodles, cooking 3-4 minutes or until tender. Do not overcook. Drain and set aside.

While ramen is cooking, preheat oven to 450°. Purée together ginger, teriyaki sauce, dried thyme, brown sugar and one flavor packet with a fork.

Put the chicken in a casserole or baking dish and pour half the sauce over it. Bake 30-40 minutes, or until chicken is cooked through, turning halfway into cooking. Remove the chicken from the oven and slice it into strips.

In a large serving bowl, toss the ramen with the peas, red pepper, celery, chicken flavor packet, 3-4 tablespoons water and remaining sauce. Arrange the chicken slices on top and serve.

SUBSTITUTIONS & OMISSIONS

You can use half the chicken, substituting thigh meat for breast; and halve the peas, adding more celery. Use green pepper for red and dried ginger for fresh. Take out the thyme altogether. Add a fourth package of ramen.

4 packages spicy chicken ramen	.40
½ pound chicken thigh meat	.50
1 green bell pepper, chopped into 1-inch pieces	.25
1 ½ cups celery, diced	.45
1 medium onion, quartered	.25
1 tablespoon powdered ginger	.10
1 tablespoon soy sauce	*
	Total: $1.95

$$$ BIG SPLURGE $$$

Grill breasts and serve over white steamed rice.

CHICKEN RAMEN CASSEROLE

Serves eight

Notes: This is a tough one to skimp on. But if you modify just a few things and store it properly, you can live on this dish a week.

5 packages ramen, any flavor	.50
2 cups chicken, cooked and diced	2.00
2 tablespoons butter	.30
1 medium onion, chopped	.25
¼ pound mushrooms, sliced	.60
2 cups tomatoes, diced	1.00
½ teaspoon basil	.10
½ teaspoon oregano	.10
3 tablespoons flour	.05
½ cup half-and-half	.40
1 cup mozzarella cheese, grated	1.00

½ cup ricotta cheese 1.00
¼ cup Parmesan cheese, grated .75
pepper to taste .05
Total: $8.10

In a large pot of boiling salted water, cook the ramen until tender but still firm, about 4 minutes. Drain well.

Melt butter in skillet. Sauté onions. Add mushrooms, basil, oregano, one flavor packet and pepper. Blend tomatoes in blender or processor (or mash well with a fork) and add to mushrooms. Simmer while making cream sauce, adding more tomatoes if needed. Stir in chicken.

Make cream sauce by melting butter in a saucepan and stirring in flour. Add one flavor packet, some water and bring to a boil. Stir in half-and-half and cook until thickened.

Spoon a small amount of cream sauce into a casserole dish. Spread approximately a half-inch of cooked ramen noodles in dish. Add one-third of the meat mixture and one-third of the cream sauce. Sprinkle each layer with cheese. Repeat with remaining noodles and sauces. Sprinkle top with Parmesan cheese. Bake at 350° for 30 to 45 minutes. Serve hot.

SUBSTITUTIONS & OMISSIONS

Use half the required amount of chicken (and use thigh meat), margarine for butter, a few tablespoons of cream and water for the half-and-half, go easy on the mozzarella and use dried Parmesan for fresh. Also use cottage cheese for ricotta.

5 packages ramen, any flavor .50
½ cup chicken thigh meat, cooked and diced .50
2 tablespoons margarine .05
½ medium onion, chopped .10
¼ pound mushrooms, sliced .60
1 16-ounce can tomatoes 1.00
½ teaspoon basil .10
½ teaspoon oregano .10
3 tablespoons all-purpose flour .05
½ cup cream, mixed with water *
½ cup shredded mozzarella cheese .50
½ cup cottage cheese .50
¼ cup Parmesan cheese *
Total: $4.00

$$$ BIG SPLURGE $$$

Use lasagna noodles and make it creamy lasagna.

CREAMY CHICKEN AND MUSHROOM RAMEN

Serves four

Notes: Using mushroom or cream of mushroom ramen makes this easy. As usual, use thigh meat if breast meat is out of the budget.

3 packages mushroom ramen	**.30**
1 cup chicken breast meat, diced	**1.00**
1 cup mushrooms, sliced	**1.00**
½ cup red bell pepper, diced	**.50**
1 cup mayonnaise	**.30**
2 tablespoons butter	**.30**
¾ cup milk	**.30**
¼ cup Parmesan cheese, grated	**.50**
1 teaspoon dried basil	**.10**
½ teaspoon paprika	**.10**
black pepper to taste	**.05**
Total:	**$4.45**

In a large pot of boiling water, prepare ramen noodles, cooking 3-4 minutes or until tender. Do not overcook. Drain and set aside.

While ramen noodles are cooking, sauté chicken in butter over medium-high heat, stirring frequently, about three minutes. Drop in mushrooms and red pepper. Cook until tender, about 3 minutes.

Combine the mayonnaise, milk, cheese, basil, pepper and paprika in a small bowl. Add to the vegetables in the skillet.

Combine the contents of the skillet with the ramen noodles and mix well. Serve immediately.

SUBSTITUTIONS & OMISSIONS

Use thighs for breasts, canned mushrooms for fresh and green bell pepper instead of red. Add ramen.

4 packages mushroom ramen	**.40**
1 cup cooked chicken thighs, boneless, diced	**.50**
1 8-ounce can mushrooms, sliced	**.50**
½ cup green bell pepper, diced	**.15**
1 cup mayonnaise	*
2 tablespoons cream, mixed with water	*
2 tablespoons Parmesan cheese	*
1 teaspoon dried basil	**.10**
1 teaspoon black pepper	*
½ teaspoon paprika	**.10**
Total:	**$1.75**

$$$ BIG SPLURGE $$$

Add cream for milk and serve penne instead of ramen noodles. Grate some Stilton and sprinkle on top.

CHICKEN CREOLE

Serves four

Notes: Celery, onion and parsley—with some chili heat—makes it Creole. Ramen makes it filling and inexpensive.

3 packages spicy chicken ramen	.30
1 pound boneless chicken breasts, cut in strips	2.50
1 cup tomatoes, diced	.50
1 cup hot sauce	.50
1 cup green pepper, chopped	.25
½ cup celery, chopped	.25
¼ cup onion, diced	.10
2 cloves garlic, minced	.10
1 tablespoon fresh basil, chopped	.10
1 tablespoon fresh parsley, chopped	.10
¼ teaspoon crushed red pepper	.10
	Total: $4.80

Heat about six cups of water and toss in the ramen noodles once the water is at a good boil. Cook one minute, then reduce the heat. Cook another 2-3 minutes, drain and set aside.

In a bit of oil, sauté chicken strips until golden brown. Remove and set aside.

Sauté onion and celery in the same pan until tender, three minutes or so. Add a half cup water, tomatoes, a bit of your favorite hot sauce, green pepper, basil, parsley, crushed red pepper and one packet spicy chicken ramen flavoring. Boil, then reduce heat. Add chicken again and simmer for about five more minutes. Pour over a bed of ramen noodles and serve.

SUBSTITUTIONS & OMISSIONS

Lose some of the chicken. Add a couple more teaspoons of hot sauce and another packet of ramen for filler.

4 packages spicy chicken ramen	.40
½ pound chicken thigh meat, cut in strips	.35
2 tablespoons hot sauce	*
1 cup tomatoes, diced	.50
1 cup green pepper, chopped	.25
¼ cup celery, chopped	.10
¼ cup onion, chopped	.10
2 cloves garlic, minced	.10
1 tablespoon fresh basil, chopped	.10
1 tablespoon fresh parsley, chopped	.10
¼ teaspoon crushed red pepper	*
	Total: $2.00

$$$ BIG SPLURGE $$$

Use breast meat, shallots, white wine and bow tie pasta.

CURRIED RAMEN WITH FRUIT AND CHICKEN

Serves four

Notes: The blend of curry and fruit—or sweet and savory—makes this dish kick. Try it on a hot day. Or, if you crank up the chili mix, it will heat up a cold day.

3 packages curry ramen	.30
¾ pound chicken, boned and diced into ½-inch pieces	2.00
1 cup seedless red grapes	.75
1 cup orange, sectioned	.25
1 cup green apple, diced	.30
1 20-ounce can pineapple chunks, drained	1.50
½ cup mayonnaise	.30
2 tablespoons lemon juice	.20
¼ cup frozen orange juice concentrate	.25
1 tablespoon curry powder	.20
1 bunch green onions, sliced	.25
	Total: $6.30

In a large pot of boiling water, prepare ramen noodles, cooking 3-4 minutes or until tender. Do not overcook. Drain and set aside.

While pasta is cooking, stir together mayonnaise, lemon juice, orange juice concentrate and curry powder in a small bowl. Set aside.

In a large bowl, toss chicken, grapes, oranges, apples and pineapple together. Stir ramen noodles into fruit mixture, then mix in dressing. Toss green onions over top and serve.

SUBSTITUTIONS & OMISSIONS

You can ease out of almost any of the ingredients, but specifically reduce the chicken, grapes and the pineapple. You can eliminate the pineapple completely, substituting an extra orange; and you can lose the OJ and the curry powder, using two ramen curry flavor packets and a pinch of sugar instead.

4 packages curry ramen	.40
½ cup cooked chicken or turkey, cut into ½-inch pieces	.50
2 cups orange, sectioned and sliced	.50
1 cup green apple, diced	.30
½ cup mayonnaise	*
2 tablespoons lemon juice	*
¼ cup green onions, sliced	.10
	Total: $1.80

$$$ BIG SPLURGE $$$

Use elbow macaroni for ramen noodles.

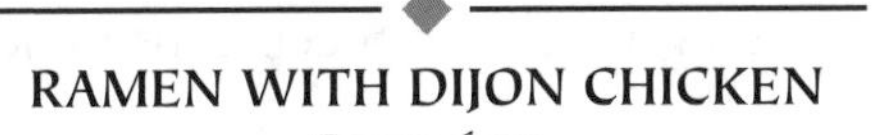

RAMEN WITH DIJON CHICKEN

Serves four

Notes: The zest in this recipe comes from the Dijon mustard. But you can use Chinese hot mustard just as easily. Or try horseradish.

3 packages spicy chicken ramen	.30
1½ cups chicken, cooked and chopped	2.00
1 tablespoon butter or margarine	.20
1 medium onion, diced	.25
1 tablespoon Dijon mustard	.25
2 tablespoons all-purpose flour	.05
¼ cup lemon juice	.30
2 cups peas (frozen or canned is fine)	1.00
¼ cup fresh parsley, chopped	.25
	Total: $4.60

In a large pot of boiling water, prepare ramen noodles, cooking 3-4 minutes or until tender, Do not overcook. Drain and set aside.

While pasta is cooking, sauté onion in butter about three minutes. Stir in the Dijon mustard and flour. Add one flavor packet to a cup of warm water, then whisk into the mustard and onion mixture. Bring it to a boil and stir in the lemon juice, peas and parsley. Wait for half the liquid to cook off.

Mix ramen and cooked chicken, then toss with sauce, season with one flavor packet and serve.

SUBSTITUTIONS & OMISSIONS

Take out parsley, reduce amount of lemon, add an onion and reduce the amount of chicken, substituting thigh meat for breast meat. Use vegetable oil for butter. Add ramen.

4 packages chicken ramen	**.40**
½ cup chicken thigh meat, cooked and chopped	**.50**
1 tablespoon vegetable oil	**.05**
2 medium onions, chopped	**.50**
1 tablespoon Dijon mustard	*
2 tablespoons all-purpose flour	**.05**
juice of one lemon	*
1 cup peas (frozen or canned is fine)	**.50**
Total:	**$2.00**

$$$ BIG SPLURGE $$$

Marinate the chicken in lemon, oregano and 2 packets chicken ramen flavoring for 24 hours then grill. Use fettuccine for ramen noodles.

FAJITA RAMEN

Serves four

Notes: No tortillas for your fajitas? Try this one. It'll fill you up. And it uses only a marginal amount of fajita meat.

3 packages spicy chicken ramen	**.30**
1 tablespoon vegetable oil	**.05**
½ pound chicken breast meat (or steak)	**1.25**
1 cup onion, sliced	**.25**
1 cup red bell pepper, sliced	**1.00**
1 cup yellow bell pepper, sliced	**1.00**
1 cup whole green chilies	**.50**

1 teaspoon oregano	.10
¼ cup chopped fresh cilantro	.10
black pepper to taste	.05
	Total: $4.60

Boil about six cups of water and toss in the ramen noodles. Cook one minute, then reduce the heat. Cook another 2-3 minutes, drain and set aside.

Boil the chicken breasts for about three minutes or until white. Remove and cut into strips about a half-inch long. Sauté the onion and peppers in a large skillet in vegetable oil until tender; then re-add the chicken strips, cooking until they are browned on all sides. Add the chilies and the spices.

Stir in the chicken fajita ingredients and the cilantro with the ramen noodles and serve immediately.

SUBSTITUTIONS & OMISSIONS

Use green bell pepper for red and yellow and back off the amount of chicken. Add ramen.

4 packages spicy chicken ramen	.40
1 tablespoon vegetable oil	.05
¼ pound boneless, skinless chicken breast	.70
1 cup onion, sliced	.25
1 cup green bell pepper, sliced	.25
1 teaspoon black pepper	*
¼ teaspoon oregano	*
½ cup green chilies, diced	.25
¼ cup fresh cilantro, chopped	.10
	Total: $2.00

$$$ BIG SPLURGE $$$

Use this with shell pasta—or better yet, forget the pasta and use tortillas, grilled onion, sour cream, guacamole and salsa.

CHICKEN AND FETA CASSEROLE

Serves four

Notes: As usual, feta becomes the dominant ingredient. So if you find it too sharp, ease up on the proportions; or just eliminate it altogether. But it adds a richness that's hard to beat.

3 packages chicken ramen	.30

2 cups chicken breast meat, cooked and cubed	1.50
2 eggs	.20
1 cup cream	1.00
1 cup plain yogurt	.50
¼ cup feta cheese, crumbled	.75
¼ pound Swiss cheese, shredded	1.50
¼ cup fresh parsley, chopped	.25
1 teaspoon dried basil	.10
1 teaspoon dried oregano	.10
4 cloves garlic, minced	.10
1 tomato, diced	.35
½ onion, diced	.15
2 serrano chilies, diced	.20
3 tablespoons hot sauce	.20
1 pound chicken, diced	2.50
½ pound mozzarella cheese, shredded	2.00
	Total: $11.70

Bring a medium saucepan of salted water to a boil. Add ramen and cook until *al dente,* about four minutes. Drain, set aside.

Blend eggs, milk, yogurt, feta, Swiss and mozzarella cheeses (saving half the mozzarella for later), parsley, basil, oregano, garlic and cooked chicken cubes. Spread half the ramen noodles over bottom of a baking dish. Follow with a layer of the chicken-cheese mixture.

Make a salsa of the chilies, tomatoes, onions, hot sauce and cilantro. Cover the chicken mixture with salsa. Spread remaining ramen over layers. Top with remaining mozzarella cheese. Bake 30 minutes at 375° and serve.

Substitutions & Omissions

Use a couple tablespoons of cream mixed with water, halve the chicken amount and use thighs in place of breasts, and get rid of the Swiss and mozzarella cheese and use hot sauce for salsa. Add another package of ramen.

4 packages chicken ramen	.40
2 large eggs	.20
3 tablespoons cream, mixed with equal parts water	*
¼ cup feta cheese, crumbled	.50
¼ cup fresh parsley, chopped	.25
1 teaspoon dried basil	.10
1 teaspoon dried oregano	*
4 cloves garlic, minced	.10
3 tablespoons hot sauce	*

½ pound chicken thigh meat, diced	.45
½ pound mozzarella cheese, shredded	2.00
	Total: $4.00

$$$ BIG SPLURGE $$$

Macaroni noodles for ramen and add some Greek Metaxa brandy.

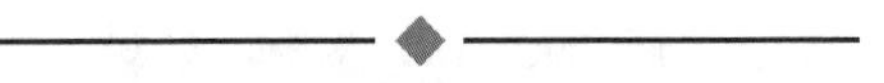

GENERAL'S CHICKEN RAMEN

Serves four

Notes: General's Chicken, also known as General Tsao's Chicken (among other things), is a popular dish at Chinese restaurants. It is not typically served with noodles. But, hey, there are a lot of things in this cookbook that aren't typical.

3 packages chicken ramen	.30
1 pound boneless chicken, cubed	1.25
3 eggs, beaten	.30
½ cup cornstarch, mixed in ½ cup water	.10
2 teaspoons crushed red pepper	.10
2 tablespoons rice vinegar	.10
2 tablespoons rice wine	.30
3 tablespoons sugar	.05
3 tablespoons soy sauce	.10
	Total: $2.60

Heat about six cups of water and toss in the ramen noodles once the water is at a good boil. Cook one minute, then reduce the heat. Cook another 2-3 minutes, drain and set aside.

Combine wine, vinegar, sugar, one flavor packet and soy sauce in small bowl. Set aside. Mix dissolved cornstarch, eggs and the chicken in another small bowl, coating well.

Fry the chicken in oil about five minutes, until brown. Add crushed red peppers to the chicken and stir. Add the vinegar mixture to the chicken and cook until the cornstarch causes the sauce to glaze. Toss with the ramen and serve immediately.

SUBSTITUTIONS & OMISSIONS

Use half the amount of chicken. Add ramen for volume.

4 packages chicken ramen	.40

½ pound boneless chicken, cubed	.65
3 eggs, beaten	.30
½ cup cornstarch, mixed in ½ cup water	.10
2 teaspoons crushed red pepper	*
1 tablespoon rice vinegar	.10
2 tablespoons rice wine	.30
3 tablespoons sugar	*
3 tablespoons soy sauce	*
	Total: $1.85

$$$ BIG SPLURGE $$$

Double the amount of chicken and serve over white rice.

RAMEN NOODLES WITH GRILLED CHICKEN

Serves four

Notes: Save your expensive chicken cuts for good occasions. This easy-to-make dish is fine with thigh meat. Buried in sauce, nobody will even know the difference between white and brown meat.

3 packages ramen: 1 vegetable, 1 chicken, 1 tomato	.30
2 pounds boneless, skinless chicken breasts	2.50
4 tablespoons olive oil	.30
2 cloves garlic, minced	.10
2 teaspoons lemon juice	.20
1 teaspoon sesame oil	.30
1 tablespoon fresh oregano	.10
1 teaspoon basil	.10
	Total: $3.90

Cook ramen for 4-6 minutes until tender, but not overdone. Drain and set aside.

Take one tomato flavoring packet, one chicken flavor packet and add one tablespoon olive oil and the juice of one lemon. Mix together. Then combine all ingredients but the chicken.

Fry the chicken two minutes on each side on high heat. Lower temperature and cook until thickest part of chicken shows no pink and juices run clear. Slice thinly before adding to sauce. Mix with noodles and serve.

SUBSTITUTIONS & OMISSIONS

Substitute vegetable oil for olive, lose the sesame oil and use half the chicken, substituting thigh meat for breast. Add a fourth ramen noodle package for volume.

4 packages ramen: 2 vegetable, 1 chicken, 1 tomato	.40
1 cup chicken thigh meat	.50
3 tablespoons vegetable oil	.05
2 cloves garlic, minced	.10
2 teaspoons lemon juice	*
½ teaspoon sesame oil	.30
1 tablespoon oregano	.10
1 teaspoon basil	.10
	Total: $1.55

$$$ BIG SPLURGE $$$

Use fresh oregano and basil, smoke the chicken and serve over fresh gnocchi.

JERK CHICKEN RAMEN

Serves four

Notes: Jamaican Jerk Chicken is usually accomplished with a whole chicken—something you can do if you have more cash (triple the amount of ingredients and stuff the cavity of a whole chicken with the spices above, coating the outside as well). So this recipe uses most of the right ingredients, just the wrong chicken. Try it anyway.

3 packages spicy chicken ramen	.30
2 pounds chicken fryer parts (assorted wings, breasts, drumsticks, etc.)	2.00
1 cup green onion, chopped	.25
2 tablespoons fresh thyme leaves, chopped	.10
2 tablespoons vegetable oil	.05
1 tablespoon ground coriander seeds	.10
1 tablespoon ginger, grated	.10
1 tablespoon lime juice	.10
1 teaspoon allspice	.10
1 teaspoon nutmeg	.10
1 teaspoon cinnamon	.10
5 cloves garlic, minced	.10
1 bay leaf	.10
1 habanero pepper, halved, seeded and minced	.10
black pepper to taste	.05
	Total: $3.65

Blend all the spices—including 2 flavor packets—in a blender or a food processor until the result is a paste-like substance. Marinate the raw chicken in about half the paste for at least four hours.

Pour the second half of the jerk marinade into a small saucepan and bring to a boil. Reduce heat and simmer about five minutes.

Bake the chicken for approximately 45 minutes at 400°. Cut chicken into strips.

Heat about six cups of water and toss in the ramen noodles once the water is at a good boil. Cook one minute, then reduce the heat. Cook another 2-3 minutes, drain and toss the cooked chicken into the ramen noodles. Mix in the cooked marinade and serve immediately.

SUBSTITUTIONS & OMISSIONS

Use thigh meat for breast meat and lemon juice for lime juice.

3 packages spicy chicken ramen	.30
1 cup chicken thigh meat	.50
1 cup green onion, chopped	.25
2 tablespoons fresh thyme leaves, chopped	.10
2 tablespoons vegetable oil	.05
1 tablespoon coriander seeds	.10
1 tablespoon ginger, grated	.10
1 tablespoon lemon juice	*
1 teaspoon allspice	.10
1 teaspoon nutmeg	.10
1 teaspoon cinnamon	.10
5 cloves garlic, peeled and halved	.10
1 bay leaf	.10
1 habanero pepper, halved and seeded	.10
black pepper to taste	*
	Total: $2.00

$$$ BIG SPLURGE $$$

Use more chicken breasts, add some fresh ground pepper and use rigatoni in place of ramen noodles.

CHINESE LEMON CHICKEN IN RAMEN NOODLES

Serves four

Notes: You can use pre-made lemon sauce in a jar (bought in a Chinese grocery). But why spend the cash? Prepare your own, below.

3 packages chicken ramen	.30
1 pound chicken breasts, cut into 2-inch pieces	1.25
¼ cup flour	.10
2 tablespoons vegetable oil	.05
¼ cup lemon juice	.50
2 tablespoons cornstarch, mixed with lemon juice	.10
1 tablespoon sugar	.10
black pepper to taste	.05
	Total: $2.45

Boil about six cups of water and toss in the ramen noodles. Cook one minute, then reduce the heat. Cook another 2-3 minutes, drain and set aside.

Roll the chicken pieces in flour and fry in a large skillet until brown on all sides. Remove chicken. Pour a cup and a half of water into the skillet and stir to deglaze the pan (in other words, to get the baked-on juices off the pan and into the gravy).

Add lemon juice, lemon zest, one flavor packet and sugar to the skillet. Before the sauce starts to thicken, remove it from the heat.

Mix the chicken into the noodles, then mix in the lemon sauce. Coat all thoroughly and serve immediately.

SUBSTITUTIONS & OMISSIONS

Use thigh meat for breast meat and ease up on the amount.

4 packages chicken ramen	.40
¾ pound chicken, cut into strips	.90
¼ cup flour	.10
2 tablespoons cooking oil.	.05
¼ cup lemon juice	.40
1 tablespoon cornstarch, mixed with lemon juice	.10
1 tablespoon sugar	*
black pepper to taste	.05
	Total: $1.95

$$$ BIG SPLURGE $$$

Use double the amount of chicken breast meat, and serve over rice instead of mixing with ramen noodles.

MANGO CHICKEN WITH MADEIRA AND ORANGES

Serves four

*Notes: If you're reading this cookbook, Madeira is definitely not in your liquor cabinet (in fact, other than the bottle of triple sec you stole from your parents years ago, you don't **have** a liquor cabinet). You can use any sweet wine, using port or cream sherry or a sauterne or something as equally expensive. Or you can use a cheap wine, add a little fruit juice and some more sugar and pretend you have an extensive liquor cabinet.*

3 packages chicken ramen	.30
1 cup mango, cut into 1-inch chunks	.75
2 chicken breasts, cut into half-inch strips	1.25
2 oranges, sectioned and cubed	.50
3 tablespoons olive oil	.25
1 cup Madeira wine	2.00
1 onion, diced	.25
1 teaspoon butter	.20
pepper to taste	.05
	Total: $5.55

Bring about five quarts of water to boil in a large pot. Drop in ramen noodles and boil for a minute, then reduce heat. Cook another 2-3 minutes, or until tender. Remove from heat, drain and set aside.

Sauté chicken in butter in a skillet until slightly brown, but not fully cooked. Add mango and oranges and mix with pepper, onion and one flavor packet.

Reduce heat and simmer for about 15 minutes until the fruit and onion mix begins bubble and thicken. Add port wine, simmer another three minutes and then remove. Pour over ramen noodles, mix and serve immediately.

SUBSTITUTIONS & OMISSIONS

Lose most of the wine, adding a little sugar to a few teaspoons of cheap white or red wine. Use chicken thigh meat for breast, margarine for butter and ease up on the oranges. Add ramen.

4 packages ramen	.40
1 cup mango, cut into 1-inch chunks	.75
½ cup chicken thigh meat, diced	.40
½ orange, sectioned and chopped	.15
3 tablespoons vegetable oil	.05
½ onion, diced	.15
1 teaspoon margarine	.05

1 tablespoon sugar	*
pepper to taste	*
	Total: $1.95

$$$ BIG SPLURGE $$$

Use shallots instead of onion, extra-virgin olive oil and double the amount of butter and chicken breasts. Use fettuccine instead of ramen noodles.

RAMEN GARAM MASALA

Serves four

Notes: Try to leave this one in tact. Garam Masala is actually a curry combination, so you can use it in other cooking. This recipe calls for twice the needed amount so you can use half later.

3 packages curry ramen	.30
1 cup chicken breast, cut into ½-inch strips	.75
1 cup onions, quartered and separated	.25
½ cup cream	.50
1 tablespoon cardamom seeds	.10
2 cinnamon sticks, crushed	.10
2 teaspoons cloves	.10
1 teaspoon pepper	.05
3 tablespoons cumin seeds	.10
3 tablespoons coriander seeds	.10
	Total: $2.35

Roast spices in a skillet about five minutes. Set aside and let cool. After ten minutes, grind the spices and two packets of curry ramen flavoring to a fine powder in a coffee grinder or with a pestle and mortar. Save half for later.

Bring about five quarts of water to boil in a large pot. Drop in ramen noodles and boil for a minute, then reduce heat. Cook another 2-3 minutes, or until tender. Remove from heat, drain and set aside.

In the skillet in which you roasted the spices, put in chicken strips and cook until browned, stirring constantly. Add cream, a few tablespoons water, the spices and simmer ten minutes.

Serve over a bed of ramen, or toss in ramen noodles and serve immediately.

SUBSTITUTIONS & OMISSIONS

Use less cream combined with water.

3 packages curry ramen	.30
1 cup chicken breast, cut into ½-inch strips	.75
1 cup onions, quartered and separated	.25
4 tablespoons cream, mixed with water	*
1 tablespoon cardamom seeds	.10
2 teaspoons cinnamon	.10
2 teaspoons cloves	.10
1 teaspoon pepper	.05
3 tablespoons cumin seeds	.10
3 tablespoons coriander seeds	.10
	Total: $1.85

$$$ BIG SPLURGE $$$

Use steamed, herbed white rice in place of ramen noodles.

RAMEN MOLE

Serves four

Notes: This traditional Mexican dish is a great flavor combination—even without the chicken. If you can't find good Mexican chocolate, use cocoa or a touch of bittersweet chocolate.

3 packages chicken ramen	.30
2 pounds chicken, cut into pieces	2.00
2 tablespoons butter	.20
1 onion, minced	.25
1 clove garlic, minced	.10
1 bay leaf	.10
½ teaspoon ground cloves	.10
1 cup tomato sauce	.20
¼ teaspoon anise seed	.10
½ teaspoon cinnamon	.10
1 teaspoon sugar	.05
2 tablespoons crushed red chili pepper	.10
2 tablespoons sesame seeds	.20
½ cup almonds, slivered	.50
½ cup sliced bread crumbs	.20
2 ounces Mexican chocolate, grated	.50
	Total: $5.00

Bring 3-4 quarts of water to a boil and add ramen noodles. Cook approximately three minutes, or until noodles are just slightly tender. Do not overcook. Remove, drain and set aside.

Sauté onion and garlic in butter about 3-5 minutes, or until onion is wilted. Mix in the bay leaf, cloves, tomato sauce, anise seeds, cinnamon, sugar, crushed red pepper flakes, sesame seeds, almonds and bread crumbs. Stir in two chicken flavor packets and pepper to taste. Then stir in chocolate until melted. Pour the cooked mix into a casserole dish. Add chicken pieces, coating each piece with mole sauce. Add the noodles, coating them with the mole sauce.

Cover and bake for about one hour at 375°, or until the chicken is done (check it by taking one of the center pieces of chicken out and cutting through it). It should be very heavy with thick sauce when you serve it.

SUBSTITUTIONS & OMISSIONS

Substitute chicken thigh meat for whole chicken, and use a lot less. Use butter for margarine, lose the almonds, use your own dry bread crumbs, half the amount of tomato sauce and sesame seeds, and lose the bay leaf. Fill it out with two more packages ramen.

5 packages chicken ramen	.50
½ cup chicken thigh meat, cut into 1-inch pieces	.25
2 tablespoons margarine	.05
½ onion, minced	.10
1 clove garlic, minced	.10
½ teaspoon ground cloves	.10
½ cup tomato sauce	.10
¼ teaspoon anise seed	.10
½ teaspoon cinnamon	.10
1 teaspoon sugar	*
2 tablespoons crushed red chili pepper	*
2 tablespoons sesame seeds	.10
½ cup sliced bread crumbs	*
2 ounces Mexican chocolate, grated	.50
Total:	$2.00

$$$ BIG SPLURGE $$$

Use 4 pounds boneless, skinless chicken breasts, use more Mexican chocolate and leave out the ramen completely. Top with crumbled Cojita cheese.

CHICKEN PEPPERONI RAMEN NOODLES

Serves four

Notes: Pepperoni makes this a filling meal with a lot of oily baggage. For a less fatty meal, use less pepperoni and improvise on the spices to create your own taste.

3 packages spicy chicken ramen	.30
½ pound pepperoni, sliced and quartered	1.50
¼ cup flour	.30
1 pound boneless chicken breast	2.50
1 16-ounce can tomato sauce	.50
½ teaspoon oregano	.10
½ teaspoon basil	.10
½ teaspoon tarragon	.10
½ teaspoon garlic powder	.10
½ teaspoon onion powder	.10
black pepper to taste	.05
Total:	$5.65

Dice pepperoni into ¼-inch cubes. Cook over medium heat until mostly degreased. Remove from pan and pat dry with paper towels to eliminate remaining grease. Set aside. Cut chicken into bite-sized pieces then fry in same pan. Set aside.

Cook ramen for 4-6 minutes until tender, but not overdone.

Stir tomato sauce, chicken and pepperoni together in same pan. Add about a half-cup water, stir in the remainder of the ingredients, plus one packet of spicy chicken flavoring. Allow to simmer 20–35 minutes or until chicken is tender. Serve over a bed of ramen noodles.

SUBSTITUTIONS & OMISSIONS

Reduce the amount of pepperoni, as well as the amount of chicken, using thigh meat for breast. Use one can tomato sauce (enhance by using a packet of tomato ramen and water) instead of two, and combine the oregano, basil and tarragon into just one teaspoon Italian spice.

4 packages spicy chicken ramen	.40
3 tablespoons pepperoni, chopped	.25
¼ cup flour	.30
1 cup boneless chicken thigh meat, diced	.50
1 8-ounce can tomato sauce	.25
1 teaspoon Italian seasoning	.10
½ teaspoon garlic powder	.10

½ teaspoon onion powder	.10
black pepper to taste	*
	Total: $2.00

$$$ BIG SPLURGE $$$

Use more pepperoni if you need to, and use rotini or bow tie pasta for ramen noodles.

PACIFIC PESTO PASTA

Serves four

Notes: If you don't have basil, don't try this one. Other than that, this is a pretty straightforward recipe that will keep in the refrigerator a few days.

3 packages vegetable ramen	.30
1 tablespoon olive oil	.20
¾ pounds chicken breasts, cut into 1-inch pieces	2.00
2 cloves garlic, minced	.10
1 red onion, diced	.50
1 yellow bell pepper, diced	1.00
1 red bell pepper, diced	1.00
1 green bell pepper, diced	1.00
1 zucchini, diced	.30
1 tomato, diced	.50
2 tablespoons sun-dried tomato paste	.30
½ cup basil	.30
2 tablespoons olive oil	.20
1 teaspoon pine nuts	.30
1 tablespoon Parmesan cheese, grated	.30
pepper to taste	.05
	Total: $8.35

Bring water to a boil in a large pot, and add ramen noodles. Cook for approximately four minutes, or until tender. Drain and set aside.

While ramen is cooking, sauté chicken strips in a skillet over medium-high heat for about six minutes. Add garlic and vegetables, and continue cooking until soft, approximately five minutes. Add tomato paste, one flavor packet and basil. Mix well.

Add ramen noodles to vegetable mixture and toss. Season with one more flavor packet and pepper to taste. Serve immediately.

SUBSTITUTIONS & OMISSIONS

Use green onion and tomato sauce for sun-dried tomatoes. Use thighs for breasts and vegetable oil for olive oil. Also, you can reduce the amount of chicken down to a half cup. Add ramen for volume.

4 packages vegetable ramen	.40
1 tablespoon vegetable oil	.05
½ cup pounds chicken, any meat, cut into 1-inch strips	.50
2 cloves garlic, minced	.10
2 green onions, diced	.05
1 zucchini, diced	.25
½ cup tomato sauce	.10
¼ cup basil	.30
1 teaspoon pine nuts	.20
1 tablespoon Parmesan cheese, grated	*
pepper to taste	*
	Total: $1.95

$$$ BIG SPLURGE $$$

Substitute grilled chicken, more basil, extra virgin olive oil and use penne in place of ramen noodles.

RAMEN NOODLES AND SMOKED CHICKEN IN GARLIC SAUCE

Serves four

Notes: We're not sophisticated enough to go into how to smoke chicken, so you'll have to find your own pre-smoked chicken. Or use smoked salmon, smoked sausage, bacon or something else (as long as it isn't smoked cigarettes) to get the same flavor.

3 packages chicken ramen	.30
3 tablespoons shallots, minced	.50
2 cloves garlic, minced	.10
3 cups heavy cream	3.00
2 cups smoked chicken meat, diced	2.00
3 tablespoons sun-dried tomatoes	.50
2 tablespoons dried Parmesan cheese	.20
2 tablespoons oil	.05
	Total: $6.65

Bring five quarts of water to a boil and toss in the ramen noodles, cooking three or four minutes or until tender but not mushy. Drain and set aside.

Sauté shallots in oil and add garlic, cream, pepper and one chicken ramen flavor packet. Bring to boil, simmer until thick. Cut chicken into large thin slices and drop into mix.

Put ramen noodles on individual plate and spoon sauce over. Top with freshly grated cheese.

SUBSTITUTIONS & OMISSIONS

Use less cream, mixing with margarine, water and flour. Forget the smoked chicken if it doesn't fit the budget. Although sun-dried tomatoes are nice, eliminate them. And use green onions for shallots. Add ramen.

4 packages chicken ramen	.40
3 tablespoons green onions, minced	.10
2 cloves garlic, minced	.10
1 cup heavy cream	*
2 tablespoons flour	.10
1 cup smoked chicken	1.00
2 tablespoons dried Parmesan cheese	*
2 tablespoons oil	.05
	Total: $1.75

$$$ BIG SPLURGE $$$

Use smoked oysters instead of chicken and use fettuccine instead of ramen.

TANDOORI RAMEN CHICKEN

Serves four

Notes: Strictly speaking, Tandoori Chicken is supposed to be a dish of chicken drumsticks marinated and baked, then served over rice. If you notice, there are no drumsticks—and hardly anywhere in the book will you find rice. That's to keep it in the ramen realm and to make it cheaper. When you're rich, you'll make it correctly. In the meantime, try it our way.

3 packages spicy ramen	.30
1 ½ cups chicken, cut into strips	.65
1 teaspoon mustard powder	.10
3 tablespoons ginger, minced	.25
½ teaspoon cumin seeds	.10

½ teaspoon ground dried coriander	.10
½ teaspoon turmeric	.10
¼ teaspoon chili powder	.10
2 teaspoons tomato paste	.10
¼ cup vegetable oil	.20
1 cup plain yogurt	.50
juice of 1 lemon	.10
	Total: $2.60

Bring about five quarts of water to boil in a large pot. Drop in ramen noodles and boil for a minute, then reduce heat. Cook another 2–3 minutes, or until tender. Remove from heat, drain and set aside.

In a small bowl, mix mustard, ginger, cumin, coriander, turmeric, lemon juice and one packet chili ramen. Add tomato paste, oil and a half cup water, mixing well to form a smooth paste. Add yogurt and blend.

In a large saucepan, pour in oil and stir-fry the chicken pieces until just slightly seared. Pour marinade over the chicken, reduce heat, cover and cook 30–35 minutes, adding water if the mixture begins to dry out. Serve over a bed of ramen noodles.

SUBSTITUTIONS & OMISSIONS

Use less turkey or chicken. Cut back to half a cup of yogurt (or use one lemon, some cream and water). And add ramen.

4 packages ramen	.40
1 cup chicken thigh meat, cut into strips	.45
1 teaspoon mustard powder	.10
3 tablespoons ginger, minced	.25
½ teaspoon cumin seeds	.10
½ teaspoon ground dried coriander	.10
½ teaspoon turmeric	.10
¼ teaspoon chili powder	.10
2 teaspoons tomato paste	.10
2 tablespoons vegetable oil	.05
½ cup plain yogurt	.25
1 teaspoon lemon juice	*
	Total: $2.00

$$$ BIG SPLURGE $$$

Use chicken drumsticks and serve over white rice, like you were supposed to.

TAMARIND RAMEN CHICKEN

Serves four

Notes: Tamarind is one of the most underrated ingredients in cooking. Its tangy-sour taste has more flavor than lemon and less bite. It is cheap and it will last forever in a dry cupboard. Give it a try.

3 packages chicken ramen	.30
1 pound boneless chicken breasts	2.50
½ cup tamarind pulp	1.00
3 tablespoons ground coriander	.10
2 tablespoons soy sauce	.10
5 tablespoons sugar	.05
4 tablespoons peanut oil	.05
	Total: $4.10

Heat about six cups of water and toss in the ramen noodles once the water is at a good boil. Cook one minute, then reduce the heat. Cook another 2–3 minutes, drain and set aside.

Soak tamarind in about a cup of warm water and discard seeds; allow the tamarind to completely dissolve. Heat the tamarind water until is darkens in color, then add the soy, sugar, and a packet of spicy chicken ramen seasoning. Remove.

Sauté chicken in a skillet with oil and onions, cooking until brown. Add the tamarind mixture to the pan and cook until bubbly. Toss everything into the ramen noodles. Mix well. Serve immediately.

SUBSTITUTIONS & OMISSIONS

Use less chicken meat and use thigh meat instead of breast.

3 packages chicken ramen	.30
1 cup chicken thigh meat	.50
½ cup tamarind pulp	1.00
3 tablespoons ground coriander	.10
2 tablespoons sweet soy sauce	*
5 tablespoons sugar	*
4 tablespoons peanut oil	.05
	Total: $1.95

$$$ BIG SPLURGE $$$

Serve over thin Oriental noodles.

THAI BASIL AND CHICKEN RAMEN

Serves four

Notes: Sweet basil is a very Thai flavor. This dish, mixed with lime and jalapenos, may not be a typical Thai recipe, but it is a typical Thai taste.

3 packages chicken ramen	.30
½ pound boneless chicken, cooked and diced	.40
6 cloves garlic, chopped	.10
3 shallots, thinly sliced	.30
3 cups broccoli, cut into 1-inch pieces	.75
2 jalapeno peppers, minced	.10
3 tablespoons peanut oil	.20
2 teaspoons soy sauce	.20
1 cup basil leaves	.75
1 lime, cut into wedges	.10
Total:	$3.20

Bring about five quarts of water to boil in a large pot. Drop in ramen noodles and boil for a minute, then reduce heat. Cook another 2–3 minutes, or until tender. Remove from heat, drain and set aside.

In a large skillet, heat oil and add chopped garlic and chicken. Sauté until the chicken turns white and toss in the shallots and chilies.

Stir-fry about a minute and add cooked ramen noodles. Add soy sauce, broccoli and basil, cooking approximately three minutes. Toss in ramen noodles and one flavor packet and mix; serve immediately.

SUBSTITUTIONS & OMISSIONS

Use green onions for shallots, less broccoli and vegetable oil for sesame oil.

4 packages chicken ramen	.40
½ pound boneless chicken, cut into small bite-sized pieces	.40
6 cloves garlic, chopped	.10
3-4 green onions, thinly sliced	.10
½ cup broccoli	.30
2 jalapeno peppers, minced	.10
3 tablespoons vegetable oil	.05
2 teaspoons soy sauce	*
½ cup basil leaves	.40
1 lime, cut into four wedges	.10
Total:	$1.95

$$$ BIG SPLURGE $$$

Serve with fat Oriental noodles instead of ramen noodles.

RAMEN CHICKEN TIKKA

Serves four

Notes: A big portion of ginger makes this different from a lot of Indian dishes. Try it for a change—or if you have a butt-load of ginger around the house.

3 packages chili ramen	.30
1 pound chicken breast, diced	2.50
1 teaspoon coriander	.10
2 tablespoons lime juice	.20
2 cloves garlic, minced	.10
1 teaspoon ginger, minced	.10
2 tablespoons oil	.05
1 cup yogurt	.50
	Total: $3.85

Bring about five quarts of water to boil in a large pot. Drop in ramen noodles and boil for a minute, then reduce heat. Cook another 2–3 minutes, or until tender. Remove from heat, drain, add a chili flavor packet and oil, toss well and set aside.

In a small bowl mix yogurt, ginger, garlic, one packet chili ramen flavoring, coriander, lime juice and oil. Thread chicken onto short bamboo skewers and pour yogurt mixture over skewered chicken. Turn to coat completely in marinade. Place skewered on a baking sheet and bake about 15 minutes in a preheated, 425°. Serve hot over a bed of seasoned ramen.

SUBSTITUTIONS & OMISSIONS

Use lemon juice for lime. And substitute onion for meat on your skewers.

4 packages chili ramen	.40
1 cup chicken thigh meat, diced	.45
1 teaspoon coriander	.10
1 onion, quartered	.25
2 tablespoons lemon juice	*
2 cloves garlic, minced	.10
1 teaspoon ginger, grated	.10
2 tablespoons oil	.05

1 cup yogurt	.50
	Total: $1.95

$$$ BIG SPLURGE $$$

Use breast meat—and double the amount. Use white rice for ramen noodles.

CHICKEN, AVOCADO AND ROASTED GARLIC RAMEN

Serves four

Notes: Good fresh avocados are the key here. Use more or less garlic according to taste. Or depending on whether or not you wish to remain single.

3 packages chicken ramen	.30
½ pound chicken breast meat, cooked and cubed	1.25
1 red bell pepper, cut into 1-inch pieces	1.00
¼ cup olive oil	.30
5 cloves garlic, minced	.10
2 avocados, seeded and sliced	.75
	Total: $3.70

Bring 3–4 quarts of water to a boil and add ramen noodles. Cook approximately 3 minutes, or until noodles are just tender. Do not overcook. Remove, drain and set aside.

On a baking sheet or baking pan, roast the garlic and red bell pepper in the oven for 45 minutes at 425° or until brown. Remove and set aside.

In a large bowl, toss together cooked pasta, roasted vegetables, chicken, olive oil, one flavor packet and avocado. Serve.

SUBSTITUTIONS & OMISSIONS

Green bell pepper for red and go easier on the chicken.

3 packages chicken ramen	.30
¼ pound chicken thigh meat, cooked and cubed	.25
1 red bell pepper, cut into 1-inch pieces	.25
¼ cup olive oil	.30
5 cloves garlic, minced	.10
2 avocados, sliced	.75
	Total: $1.95

$$$ BIG SPLURGE $$$

Use grilled breasts, extra virgin olive oil and fettuccine for ramen.

ORANGE CHICKEN AND MUSHROOM PASTA

Serves four

Notes: You can also use tuna or chicken thigh meat or any other light main ingredient in place of breast meat. Use less and the orange flavor will still come out.

3 packages mushroom ramen	.30
1 tablespoon olive oil	.10
1 pound boneless, skinless chicken breasts, diced	3.50
1 cup fresh mushrooms, sliced	.50
1 cup heavy cream	1.00
1 cup orange juice	.25
6 cloves garlic, minced	.10
¾ cup Parmesan cheese, grated	.85
1 orange, peeled and sectioned	.25
½ teaspoon orange peel, grated	.00
black pepper to taste	.05
	Total: $6.90

Boil about six cups of water and toss in the ramen noodles. Cook one minute, then reduce the heat. Cook another 2-3 minutes, drain and set aside.

Heat the oil in a large skillet and sauté garlic for a half a minute, then add chicken. Cook about 5 minutes, searing the chicken. Reduce heat and add the mushrooms, the cream, pepper, two flavor packets and Parmesan. Add the orange juice and orange peel. Cook another three or four minutes, then pour over ramen, mixing well. Serve immediately.

SUBSTITUTIONS & OMISSIONS

Use cheapy thigh meat for breast meat, use less cream and mix with same amount of water. And use less dried Parmesan for fresh. Add ramen.

4 packages mushroom ramen	.40
1 tablespoon vegetable oil	.05
¼ cup chicken thigh meat, diced	.45
1 cup fresh mushrooms, sliced	.50
5 tablespoons cream	*
1 cup orange juice	.25

6 garlic cloves, minced	.10
½ teaspoon pepper	*
3 tablespoons Parmesan cheese, grated	*
½ teaspoon orange peel, grated	.05
1 orange, peeled and sectioned	.25
	Total: $2.05

$$$ BIG SPLURGE $$$

Use shrimp instead of chicken and use tagliatelle in place of ramen noodles.

RAMEN WITH TURKEY AND ALMONDS

Serves four

Notes: Use anything in place of almonds—peanuts to hazelnuts. Just don't omit them totally. You have to have the nuts to try this one.

3 packages chicken ramen	.30
½ cup almonds, toasted and slivered	.50
2 teaspoons margarine	.20
1 cup smoked turkey, cut into strips	1.50
1 cup green beans (canned or frozen is fine)	.75
½ onion, sliced	.45
½ cup carrot, shredded	.10
½ teaspoon dried tarragon leaves	.10
¼ cup Italian salad dressing	.50
	Total: $4.40

In a large pot of boiling water, prepare ramen noodles, cooking 3–4 minutes or until tender. Do not overcook. Drain and set aside.

In a skillet, sauté almonds in butter until golden. Remove and set aside. In same skillet, heat oil. Add smoked turkey, green beans, onion and carrot and cook over high heat until vegetables are tender. Stir in almonds and tarragon.

Add ramen noodles, salad dressing, one packet chicken ramen flavoring and stir well to mix. Serve immediately.

SUBSTITUTIONS & OMISSIONS

Use peanuts if nothing else is available, and use boiled chicken thighs for smoked turkey. Add ramen for bulk.

4 packages chicken ramen	.40
¼ cup sliced almonds, toasted	*
2 teaspoons margarine	.30
1 cup, cut into strips	.50
1 8-ounce can cut green beans	.35
½ medium yellow onion, thinly sliced	.15
½ cup carrot, shredded	.10
½ teaspoon dried tarragon leaves	.10
¼ cup non-fat Italian salad dressing	*
	Total: $1.90

$$$ BIG SPLURGE $$$

Add a touch of Brie cheese (without the rind) and use tagliatelle for ramen noodles.

RAMEN AND GROUND TURKEY AND MUSHROOM MEATBALLS

Serves four

Notes: Ground turkey is cheap and nutritious. Look for it in the frozen foods section, not the meat section of your supermarket for the bargains. Fill out the ground turkey with more bread crumbs or ramen noodles or add an onion.

3 packages chicken ramen	.30
1 teaspoon butter	.20
1 cup mushrooms, chopped	1.00
1 pound ground turkey	1.50
1 cup bread crumbs	.25
2 egg whites	.20
¼ cup Parmesan cheese, grated	.50
1 teaspoon dried oregano	.10
1 teaspoon rosemary	.10
pepper to taste	.05
	Total: $4.20

In a large non-stick skillet, warm the butter or margarine over medium-high heat. Add the mushrooms and sauté until very soft, about five minutes. Add ½ cup water, one mushroom flavor packet and flour; cook until mixture becomes thick. Remove and let cool.

Stir the mushroom mixture, ground turkey, bread crumbs, egg whites, cheese, oregano, rosemary, pepper and one flavor packet together in a mixing bowl. Knead the mixture together thoroughly and form into 1-inch balls.

Brown meatballs in a skillet

Put the tomato sauce into a large saucepan and bring to a simmer over low heat, then spoon the meatballs into the tomato sauce.

While sauce is simmering, Bring water to a boil in a large pot, and add ramen noodles. Cook for approximately four minutes, or until tender. Drain and transfer to a large serving bowl. Remove bay leaves from sauce; pour meatball sauce over ramen and serve.

SUBSTITUTIONS & OMISSIONS

Lighten to half of turkey amount; use real bread for your own bread crumbs and eliminate rosemary if none available. Add ramen if you need more filler.

4 packages chicken ramen	.40
½ teaspoon vegetable oil	.05
½ cup mushrooms, chopped	.30
½ pound ground turkey	.75
½ cup genuine day-old bread crumbs	*
2 egg whites	.20
3 tablespoons Parmesan cheese, grated	*
1 teaspoon oregano	.10
1 teaspoon rosemary	.10
pepper to taste	*
	Total: $1.90

$$$ BIG SPLURGE $$$

Use fresh rosemary and oregano. And use spaghetti for ramen noodles.

Chapter 9

SEAFOOD MAIN COURSES

BLACK PEPPER AND TUNA RAMEN

Serves four

Notes: A lot of black pepper—not a lot of tuna—is the secret here. Although the recipe calls for peppercorns, it's okay to use regular old ground black pepper. It should be sharp and spicy when you're finished.

3 packages shrimp ramen	.30
2 cups heavy cream	2.00
1 cup clam juice	.75
1 cup dry white wine	.75
6 whole garlic cloves, minced	.10
2 teaspoons whole black peppercorns	.10
2 tablespoons dill weed, chopped	.10
1 tablespoon vinegar	.10
¾ cup Parmesan cheese, grated	.85
2 cups tuna	1.25
1 cup sour cream	.50
3 tablespoons fresh dill weed, chopped	.50
	Total: $7.30

Boil about six cups of water and toss in the ramen noodles. Cook one minute, then reduce the heat. Cook another 2-3 minutes, drain and set aside.

Combine cream, tuna (including water from tuna can), wine, garlic, pepper, dill, vinegar, clam juice and one shrimp ramen flavor packet. Bring to a boil then reduce and simmer about five minutes. Toss with ramen, making sure to coat. Serve immediately.

SUBSTITUTIONS & OMISSIONS

Use five or six tablespoons cream and the same amount of water, using a teaspoon of cornstarch for the thickening agent. Use ground pepper instead of peppercorns and lose the wine and clam juice. Use less cheese and dried dill instead of fresh. Add ramen for lost bulk.

4 packages shrimp ramen	.40
¼ cup cream, mixed in ¼ cup water	*
6 whole garlic cloves, minced	.10
2 tablespoons dried dill weed	.10
1 tablespoon vinegar	.10
3 tablespoons dried Parmesan cheese, grated	*
½ cup tuna	.25
1 cup sour cream	.50
black pepper to taste	*
Total:	$1.45

$$$ BIG SPLURGE $$$

Use fresh trout. And use spaghetti for ramen noodles.

SALMON AND CARAMELIZED ONION RAMEN

Serves 4

Notes: What you want here is the seafood taste. You can get by with just a quarter of the amount of fish—even substituting tuna for it if necessary.

3 packages Oriental flavor ramen	.30
1 tablespoon butter	.30
1 onion, halved and sliced	.25
1 ½ cups milk	.75
¼ cup cream cheese	.50
¼ cup carrots, julienned	.25

¼ cup zucchini, julienned .25
1 can (6.5 ounces) salmon, drained and broken into chunks 1.00
Total: $3.60

Open ramen and cook the noodles with one packet of seasoning. When done, drain and set aside.

Melt butter in a frying pan and add sliced onion, sautéing until brown. Set aside.

In the same frying pan, add milk, cream cheese and another flavor packet. On low heat, stir continuously until smooth. Add carrots, zucchini and salmon and simmer for 3 minutes, or until tender. Add onion and simmer another two minutes.

Add ramen noodles to the warm mixture. Toss gently and serve immediately.

SUBSTITUTIONS & OMISSIONS

Substitute margarine for butter, cream for milk and reduce the amount of cream cheese.

3 packages Oriental flavor ramen	.30
1 tablespoon margarine	.05
1 onion, halved and sliced	.25
2 tablespoons cream, mixed with water	*
3 tablespoons cream cheese	.25
¼ cup carrots, julienned	.25
¼ cup zucchini, julienned	.25
½ can salmon, drained and broken into chunks	.50
Total:	$1.85

$$$ BIG SPLURGE $$$

Use cream for milk and double the amount. Use fresh ground pepper and substitute tortellini for ramen noodles.

RAMEN IN SALMON CREAM SAUCE

Serves four

Notes: The taste of salmon and dill is older than dirt. And although you don't want to screw around with this too much, you can use tuna or mackerel if you have to.

3 packages shrimp ramen	.30
½ teaspoon flour	.05

3 tablespoons sour cream	.30
1 teaspoon dried dill weed	.10
1 6-ounce can salmon	1.50
½ cup peas (frozen or canned is fine)	.30
½ cup red peppers, roasted and diced	.50
pepper to taste	.05
	Total: $3.10

In a large pot of boiling water, prepare ramen noodles, cooking 3–4 minutes or until tender. Do not overcook. Drain and set aside.

In a small mixing bowl, combine a ¼ cup of water with one packet shrimp ramen flavoring and flour. Whisk with a fork until flour is dissolved. Add sour cream and dill and mix thoroughly.

Pour the mixture into a skillet and warm over medium-low heat, adding the salmon, peas, red peppers and ground pepper. Heat three or four minutes, stirring occasionally.

Add the ramen to the skillet and stir gently until coated with sauce. Serve immediately.

SUBSTITUTIONS & OMISSIONS

Use mackerel or tuna for salmon and green peppers for red.

3 packages shrimp ramen	.30
½ teaspoon flour	.05
3 tablespoons sour cream	.30
½ teaspoon dried dill weed	.10
1 can tuna	.50
½ cup frozen peas	.30
½ cup roasted red peppers, very coarsely chopped	.15
pepper to taste	*
	Total: $1.70

$$$ BIG SPLURGE $$$

Use fresh dill, smoked salmon, portobello mushrooms and three tablespoons cream. Use fettuccine for ramen noodles.

CATFISH AND RED PEPPER WITH RAMEN NOODLES

Serves four

Notes: Catfish is probably the cheapest fish out there (besides maybe whiting). Prepared right, catfish makes a filling meal. And it contains less fat than a dish with ground beef.

3 packages shrimp flavor ramen	.30
1 pound catfish nuggets, rinsed and drained	2.00
¼ cup butter	.40
¼ cup olive oil	.40
3 large red bell peppers, cut into slivers	3.00
2 cloves garlic, minced	.10
1 teaspoon crushed red pepper	.10
¼ cup parsley, chopped	.10
juice of 1 lemon	.10
	Total: $6.50

Bring water to boil and drop in ramen noodles. Cook for three or four minutes or until tender, but not over cooked. Drain and set aside.

Meanwhile, melt butter in a frying pan and add bell peppers, garlic, crushed red pepper and one seasoning packet. Cook, stirring for 1 minute. Add water if the mixture begins to dry out. Remove and set aside.

Add another flavor packet to the skillet along with a ¼ cup cold water and lemon juice. Bring to boil again. Add catfish and cover, cooking until fish is white through and through—about five minutes. Add the pepper mixture and toss over ramen noodles.

SUBSTITUTIONS & OMISSIONS

Substitute margarine for butter and eliminate the olive oil completely. Use green peppers for red and drop the amount. Lose the parsley altogether. Back off the catfish a half-pound and add another package of ramen for volume.

4 packages shrimp flavored ramen	.40
½ pound catfish nuggets, rinsed and drained	1.00
½ cup margarine	.10
1 large green bell pepper, cut into thin slivers	.25
½ onion, diced	.15
2 cloves garlic, minced	.10
¼ teaspoon crushed red pepper	*
juice of 1 lemon	*
	Total: $2.00

$$$ BIG SPLURGE $$$

Use angel hair pasta for ramen noodles, yellow and orange peppers and good olive oil.

SARDINES, GARLIC AND OLIVE OIL IN RAMEN NOODLES

Serves four

Notes: It doesn't do wonders for the breath, but it's relatively healthy and cheap. And you should be able to find the key ingredients almost anywhere.

3 packages shrimp ramen	.30
1 can sardines (in oil)	.70
6 cloves garlic, minced	.10
¼ cup olive oil	.40
1 cup Chinese cabbage, chopped	.40
1 cup red bell pepper, diced	1.00
	Total: $2.90

Cook the ramen noodles in slightly salted boiling water until *al dente*, 3–4 minutes. Drain well and set aside.

Sauté the garlic in oil until brown. Add the sardines and wait until the edges of the sardines just begin to bubble with the heat. Remove and toss into the ramen along with the peppers, the onions, the cabbage and one flavor packet. Mix well and serve.

SUBSTITUTIONS & OMISSIONS

Use green bell pepper for red, lose the olive oil, cabbage and add another package of ramen.

4 packages pork ramen	.40
1 cup red cabbage, chopped	.45
1 can sardines (in oil)	.70
6 cloves garlic, minced	.10
¼ cup vegetable oil	.05
1 cup red bell pepper, diced	.25
	Total: $1.95

$$$ BIG SPLURGE $$$

Try some smoked oysters instead of the sardines and use spaghetti in place of ramen noodles.

ANCHOVY RAMEN NOODLES

Serves four

Notes: This is a good way to get a fish dish without the hassle of looking for fish. Although tuna can be substituted, it's not really a good alternative. Use sardines if no anchovies are available, or try pickled herring.

3 packages shrimp ramen	.30
5 cloves garlic, minced	.10
6 tablespoons olive oil	.30
3 tablespoons fresh parsley, chopped	.10
3 2-ounce cans anchovy fillets	4.50
	Total: $5.30

Heat about six cups of water and toss in the ramen noodles once the water is at a good boil. Cook one minute, then reduce the heat. Cook another 2–3 minutes, drain and set aside.

Sauté garlic in olive oil for about a minute, then toss in parsley and anchovies, reducing heat. Add a cup of water and a shrimp flavor packet. Simmer for 8–10 minutes. Then toss noodles with anchovy sauce and serve immediately.

SUBSTITUTIONS & OMISSIONS

Reduce the amount of anchovies to one can—or use one can of sardines, reduce the parsley, and use vegetable oil for olive.

3 packages shrimp ramen	.30
5 cloves garlic, sliced	.10
6 tablespoons vegetable oil	.05
2 tablespoons fresh parsley, chopped	.05
1 2-ounce can anchovy fillets	1.50
	Total: $2.00

$$$ BIG SPLURGE $$$

Use extra-virgin olive oil and replace ramen noodles with linguine.

RAMEN NOODLES CALAMARI

Serves four

Notes: As fancy as it sounds, calamari is reasonably cheap. For a better deal, buy it whole and clean it yourself. The heads look unappetizing, but actually are quite tasty if they're cooked in with other ingredients. You can easily lose the artichokes, but keep the garbanzos and the black olives.

3 packages shrimp ramen	.30
1 pound fresh calamari (squid), cleaned and sliced	3.00
1 6-ounce jar marinated artichoke hearts, drained	.85
½ can garbanzo beans, drained	.65
¼ cup pitted black olives, halved	.50
1 large tomato, diced	1.00
3 tablespoons olive oil	.30
1 tablespoon fresh basil, chopped	.30
juice of 1 lemon	.10
Total:	$7.00

Bring five quarts of water to a boil and toss in the ramen noodles, cooking three or four minutes or until tender but not mushy. Drain and set aside.

To clean calamari, pull head and tentacles off; the guts and skeleton should come with it. If not, cut and scoop with your index finger. Rinse body sack under running water with your finger. Remove the purple skin by rubbing. Slice the body into rings. If you're feeling brave, keep the tentacles (without the plastic-like spine and guts) and put them in the mix of the cut rings.

Bring a small pot of water to boil, then boil calamari for 3-4 minutes, or until they turn white and the tentacles curl up. Drain.

Combine all ingredients (except ramen noodles) with two packets of shrimp ramen flavoring. Once thoroughly coated, mix in the ramen noodles. Serve with grated Parmesan cheese.

SUBSTITUTIONS & OMISSIONS

Use half the amount of squid, forget the artichokes, replace the olive oil with vegetable oil and use dried basil for fresh. Use another package ramen to fill out.

4 packages shrimp ramen	.40
¼ pound fresh calamari (squid), cleaned and sliced	.40
½ can garbanzo beans, drained	.65
¼ cup pitted black olives, halved	.25
½ cup tomatoes, diced	.30

1 tablespoon dried oregano	*
1 teaspoon lemon juice	*
	Total: $2.00

$$$ BIG SPLURGE $$$

Use Greek or Spanish olives, capers and use large calamari pieces in orzo, not ramen noodles.

DTOM KAH TALAY

Serves four

Notes: Coconut makes this one, squid gives it a twist and chilies spice it up. This is also good as a cold leftover.

3 packages shrimp ramen	.30
2 stalks lemon grass, chopped	.20
3 cups coconut milk	1.50
4-5 whole squid	1.50
1 small onion, sliced	.25
3-4 jalapeno peppers, minced	.10
2 cups fresh mushrooms, sliced	1.30
juice of 2 limes	.20
2 tablespoons sugar	.05
	Total: $5.40

Bring about five quarts of water to boil in a large pot. Drop in ramen noodles and boil for a minute, then reduce heat. Cook another 2–3 minutes, or until tender. Remove from heat, drain and set aside.

In a small saucepan, bring coconut milk to a boil. Throw in onion, chilies, mushrooms and one packet of ramen flavoring. Add spices then reduce heat and simmer.

In the meantime, clean the squid, cutting the body into rings and pulling off the heads. Discard the plastic-like spine. Drop cleaned squid into the coconut mix, cooking approximately three minutes.

Serve over a bed of ramen noodles.

SUBSTITUTIONS & OMISSIONS

Reduce the amount of coconut milk and ease off the mushrooms. Use lemon juice for lime juice and use a little less lemon grass. Add another package of noodles for volume.

4 packages ramen	.40
1 stalk lemon grass, chopped	.10
1 cup rich coconut milk	.50
4-5 whole squid	.50
½ onion, diced	.10
4 teaspoons crushed red peppers	*
2 cups fresh mushrooms, sliced	.40
2 teaspoons lemon juice	*
2 tablespoons sugar	*
	Total: $2.00

$$$ BIG SPLURGE $$$

Use good calamari and skiitake mushrooms and serve over white rice instead of using ramen noodles.

RAMEN NOODLES IN CLAM SAUCE

Serves four

Notes: If linguine in clam sauce makes you week-kneed, this should do the same. Use a lot less clams and the sauce will still have the same flavor—just less chewy.

3 packages shrimp ramen	.30
2 6½-ounce cans minced clams	3.00
1 red bell pepper, diced	1.00
2 green onions, sliced	.10
¼ teaspoon dried basil	.10
¼ teaspoon crushed red pepper	.10
2 cloves garlic, minced	.10
¼ cup dry white wine	.40
4 teaspoons cornstarch	.10
1 tablespoon butter	.10
2 tablespoons fresh parsley, chopped	.10
2 tablespoons Parmesan cheese, grated	.30
	Total: $5.70

Heat about six cups of water and toss in ramen noodles once the water is at a good boil. Cook one minute, then reduce the heat. Cook another 2–3 minutes, drain and set aside.

Open the clams, but make sure you don't pour out the clam juice. In a skillet, sauté the garlic, onion, pepper, basil and crushed red pepper. Add the clams with the clam juice. Mix in one shrimp ramen flavor packet.

Simmer about 5 minutes or until onions are tender. Whisk the wine and cornstarch together in a small bowl or cup and pour mixture into saucepan, stirring continuously. Bring to a boil, then reduce heat and continue stirring until it has thickened and is bubbly.

In a large bowl, toss everything together and add Parmesan cheese and parsley. Serve immediately.

SUBSTITUTIONS & OMISSIONS

Use about a third of the clams and lose the wine. Use margarine in place of butter and use a half a green pepper. Use the appropriate amount of water in place of the wine to mix the cornstarch.

3 packages shrimp ramen	.30
½ 6½-ounce can minced clams	1.00
½ green bell pepper, diced	.15
2 green onions, sliced	.10
¼ teaspoon basil	.10
¼ teaspoon crushed red pepper	*
2 cloves garlic, minced	.10
4 teaspoons cornstarch, mixed in 4 teaspoons water	.10
1 tablespoon margarine	.05
2 tablespoons fresh parsley, chopped	.10
2 tablespoons Parmesan cheese, grated	*
	Total: $2.00

$$$ BIG SPLURGE $$$

Lots of butter, good fresh clams and young Asiago cheese.

THAI CLAMS IN RAMEN NOODLES

Serves four

Notes: Feeling poor? You need just a few clams to prepare this dish.

3 packages spicy shrimp ramen	.30
2 pounds fresh clams, still in the shells, scrubbed and rinsed	7.00
3 tablespoons peanut oil	.20
8 cloves garlic, minced	.20

6-10 Thai chilies, minced	.30
2 teaspoons sugar	.05
2-3 tablespoons crushed red chili peppers	.10
1 cup Thai basil leaves	.50
	Total: $8.65

Bring about five quarts of water to boil in a large pot. Drop in ramen noodles and cook for a minute, then reduce heat. Cook another 2-3 minutes, or until tender. Remove from heat, drain and set aside.

Heat oil in a large skillet and add oil, garlic and Thai chilies. Cook about three minutes, then add chili sauce, sugar, one ramen flavor packet and about a half-cup of water. Cook for another five minutes. Toss in the clams—whole and still in the shell—and stir-fry until the clams begin to open, about ten minutes.

Stir in basil, transfer to a serving dish and serve while hot.

SUBSTITUTIONS & OMISSIONS

Use fewer clams and use vegetable oil for peanut oil. Add another package of ramen.

4 packages spicy shrimp ramen	.40
½ cup fresh clams still in the shell, scrubbed and rinsed	.50
2 tablespoons peanut oil	.05
8 cloves garlic, minced	.20
6-10 Thai chilies, minced	.30
2-3 tablespoons crushed red chili peppers	*
2 teaspoons sugar	*
1 cup Thai basil leaves	.50
	Total: $1.95

$$$ BIG SPLURGE $$$

Spoon over fat Oriental noodles.

CRAB CAKES

Serves four

Notes: Crab is just for the flavoring. This one also works great with a little bit of tuna.

3 packages pork ramen	.30
3 eggs	.30

1 cup green onions, chopped	.10
1 cup celery, minced	.25
1 cup crab, shredded	3.00
¼ cup vegetable oil	.10
1 teaspoon garlic salt	.10
¼ cup flour	.10
black pepper to taste	.05
	Total: $4.30

Cook the ramen noodles in slightly salted boiling water until *al dente*, 3–4 minutes, omitting the flavor packets. Drain well and rinse under cold water. Chop into 1–2 inch pieces and set aside.

Mix the crab, green onions, celery and all the spices together. Add eggs and flour. Mix well. Form patties from the mixture and fry them in a skillet about five minutes each. Serve with your favorite condiment.

SUBSTITUTIONS & OMISSIONS

Use a can of tuna instead of crab.

3 packages pork ramen	.30
3 eggs	.30
1 cup green onions, chopped	.10
1 cup celery, minced	.25
1 can tuna	.50
¼ cup vegetable oil	.10
1 teaspoon garlic salt	.10
¼ cup flour	.10
black pepper to taste	.05
	Total: $1.80

$$$ BIG SPLURGE $$$

Use angel hair pasta for ramen and add some shrimp to the crab.

CRAB RAMEN

Serves four

Notes: Use imitation crab or shrimp and you'll get the same results. Cheddar will definitely add to the richness, but this dish won't deteriorate if you can't afford it.

3 packages shrimp ramen	.30

½ cup sour cream	.40
¾ cup mayonnaise	.40
½ pound sharp Cheddar cheese, grated	1.50
1 cup crab meat	2.00
1 onion, minced	.25
2 hard-boiled eggs, minced	.20
¼ teaspoon dry mustard	.10
½ teaspoon paprika	.10
pepper to taste	.05
	Total: $5.30

Mix sour cream with mayonnaise and blend until smooth. Add the rest of ingredients, plus one shrimp flavor packet. Mix well.

Bring four quarts water to boil. Add ramen noodles and cook until tender, about 4 minutes. Drain.

Add sour cream mix to noodles and toss well. Serve immediately.

SUBSTITUTIONS & OMISSIONS

Use cream and for sour cream, about half the cheese and half the crab, filling it out with another package ramen and another flavor packet.

4 packages shrimp ramen	.40
2 tablespoons cream mixed with water	*
½ cup mayonnaise	*
¼ pound sharp Cheddar cheese, grated	.70
¼ cup crab meat	.50
1 onion, minced	.20
2 hard-boiled eggs, minced	.20
pepper to taste	*
	Total: $2.00

$$$ BIG SPLURGE $$$

Increase the amount of crabmeat and use linguine in place of ramen.

CRAWFISH CREOLE RAMEN

Serves six

Notes: Although crawfish is the best way to go, you can use this recipe to make Chicken Creole by substituting a pound's worth of chicken. In that case, use chicken-flavored ramen instead of shrimp.

1 pound crawfish, washed and purged	**3.00**
¼ cup olive oil	**.30**
1 onion, diced	**.25**
¼ cup green bell pepper, diced	**.10**
¼ cup red bell pepper, diced	**.10**
2 jalapenos, minced	**.10**
3 stalks celery, sliced	**.10**
3 cloves garlic, minced	**.10**
2 tomatoes, diced	**1.00**
1 6-ounce can tomato paste	**.45**
½ teaspoon sugar	**.05**
½ teaspoon brown sugar	**.05**
2 teaspoons corn syrup	**.10**
1 teaspoon molasses	**.10**
1 teaspoon hot sauce	**.05**
2 tablespoons Worcestershire sauce	**.10**
1 teaspoon dried thyme	**.10**
2 bay leaves	**.10**
1 tablespoon lemon juice	**.10**
black pepper to taste	**.05**
	Total: $6.30

Purge the crawfish by adding the live crawfish to a pot of water and 2 cups salt. They will vomit themselves silly. Then wash twice and boil 'em up.

Add two flavor packets to all of the remaining ingredients except the crawfish and the ramen. Bring to a boil then reduce heat to a simmer for about ten minutes.

In another large pot, boil 4 quarts of water and drop in the ramen. Cook 2–3 minutes until tender and drain. Set aside.

Add the crawfish to the tomato mixture and simmer an additional 10 minutes. Then add the ramen to the tomato sauce and mix well. Serve hot.

SUBSTITUTIONS & OMISSIONS

Reduce the amount of peppers, onion and tomato and crawfish. Fill it back up by adding a fourth package of ramen and some more celery. Use tomato sauce for paste.

4 packages spicy shrimp ramen	**.40**
¼ cup vegetable oil	**.05**
½ onion, diced	**.15**
½ cup green bell pepper, diced	**.10**

2 jalapenos, minced	.10
6 stalks celery, sliced	.20
3 cloves garlic, minced	.10
1 tomato, diced	.50
1 8-ounce can tomato sauce	.20
black pepper to taste	*
½ teaspoon white sugar	*
2 teaspoons corn syrup	.10
1 teaspoon molasses	.10
1 teaspoon hot sauce	*
2 tablespoons Worcestershire sauce	.10
1 teaspoon dried thyme	.10
2 bay leaves	.10
1 tablespoon lemon juice	*
¾ pound crawfish, washed and purged	.70
	Total: $3.00

$$$ BIG SPLURGE $$$

Forget the ramen; use white rice or fettuccine instead.

RAMEN AND MUSSELS IN WHITE SAUCE

Serves four

Notes: Mussels are the oval-shaped, shiny black shellfish you find on pilings and piers all over the world. Now you're about to have them for dinner. If you find that offensive—or if you can't find them at the store (don't harvest them yourself, please)—use clams, which are generally cheaper anyway.

3 packages shrimp ramen	.30
1 pound mussels	4.00
2 tablespoons rice wine	.50
¼ cup milk	.20
1 teaspoon cornstarch. dissolved in 1 teaspoon water	.10
2 tablespoons oil	.05
2 stems of green onion, chopped	.10
¼ teaspoon fresh ginger, minced	.10
	Total: $5.35

Boil water in a large pot. Add ramen noodles and return to a boil for one minute, then reduce heat and cook another 2–3 minutes. Drain and set aside.

Thoroughly wash the mussels, then add them (shell and all) to hot oil in a skillet. Add onion and ginger, then stir-fry for 2 minutes. They should open on the heat and season the pan. Add rice wine, one shrimp flavor packet and ¼ cup water. Cover and cook another 3–4 minutes. Add milk and cornstarch. Wait until sauce boils and thickens, toss in ramen, coat and serve.

SUBSTITUTIONS & OMISSIONS

You can reduce the amount of mussels easily and still get the flavor and the look; or use stone clams and reduce. Reduce the amount of wine and use cream and water for milk.

3 packages ramen	.30
¼ pound mussels	1.00
1 tablespoon any white wine	.25
2 tablespoons cream, mixed with water	*
1 teaspoon cornstarch, dissolved in 1 teaspoon water	.10
2 tablespoons oil	.05
2 stems of green onion, chopped	.10
¼ teaspoon fresh ginger, minced	.10
	Total: $1.90

$$$ BIG SPLURGE $$$

Use all the mussels, more cream, some sherry and fettuccine for ramen noodles.

OYSTERS, LEEKS AND RAMEN NOODLES

Serves four

Notes: Two types of booze lend this dish its flavor, but tend toward extravagant. Ease off the wines, using just a touch of one or the other for the accent. Try not to use canned oysters, but don't fret if that's all you have.

3 packages ramen	.30
1 cup white wine	1.00
1 cup dry vermouth	1.50
1 bay leaf	.10

1 shallot, chopped	.20
1 cup spinach, chopped	.50
1 tablespoon heavy cream	.20
juice of 1 lemon	.10
2 tablespoons butter	.20
1 pound oysters	4.00
2 tablespoons leek, minced	.30
	Total: $8.20

Bring about five quarts of water to boil in a large pot, drop in ramen noodles and boil for a minute, then reduce heat. Cook another 2–3 minutes, or until tender. Remove from heat, drain and set aside.

Bring wine to a boil in a saucepan, combining vermouth, bay leaf and one flavor packet. Cook for about three minutes. Add cream and stir in butter. Add the lemon juice, stirring constantly and using care to keep the cream from curdling. Set aside.

Sauté oysters in a skillet with butter, quickly until soft but not completely cooked. Add leek pieces and cook another three minutes. Drain off extra liquid and add spinach. Stir-fry another minute. Toss with the ramen and serve immediately.

Substitutions & Omissions

Leave out all but 2 tablespoons wine, use green onion for shallot, and margarine for butter. Add a package of ramen for filler.

4 packages ramen	.40
2 tablespoons white wine	.30
1 bay leaf	.10
3 green onions, chopped	.10
1 cup spinach, shredded	.50
1 tablespoon cream	*
juice of one lemon	.10
2 tablespoons margarine	*
2 ounces oysters, diced into half-inch pieces	.40
	Total: $1.90

$$$ Big Splurge $$$

Use more cream, more shallots and linguine for ramen noodles.

KUNG-PAO SHRIMP RAMEN

Serves four

Notes: Shrimp and chili are the secrets here. You can also substitute chicken for shrimp and make Kung Pao Chicken. Use less shrimp if you need to, but don't mess with the chilies.

3 packages spicy shrimp ramen	**.30**
12 jumbo shrimp, peeled, de-veined and butterflied	**4.50**
1 cup onions, chopped	**.25**
2 tablespoons crushed red peppers	**.10**
2 cloves garlic, minced	**.10**
2 tablespoons green onions, chopped	**.10**
2 tablespoons soy sauce	**.20**
1 tablespoon vinegar	**.20**
2 tablespoons sugar	**.05**
1 teaspoon sesame oil	**.10**
¼ cup cornstarch, mixed with ¼ cup water	**.20**
1 egg	**.10**
½ teaspoon baking powder	**.10**
	Total: $6.30

Bring about five quarts of water to boil in a large pot. Drop in ramen noodles and boil for a minute, then reduce heat. Cook another 2–3 minutes, or until tender. Remove from heat, drain and set aside.

Sauté shrimp in oil about three minutes or until pink. Remove shrimp and add peppers, garlic, onions, soy sauce, vinegar, sugar, one flavor packet and cornstarch mixture. Stir-fry three minutes. Return fried shrimp to mix and stir-fry another minute. Serve over bed of ramen noodles.

SUBSTITUTIONS & OMISSIONS

Use less shrimp, and make them smaller (or use about a cup of chicken thigh meat) and use vegetable oil for sesame oil.

3 packages ramen	**.30**
2 jumbo shrimp, peeled, de-veined, sliced and butterflied	**.50**
1 cup onions, chopped	**.25**
2 tablespoons crushed red peppers	**.10**
2 cloves garlic, minced	**.10**
2 tablespoons green onions, chopped	**.10**
2 tablespoons soy sauce	*
1 tablespoon vinegar	**.20**

2 tablespoons sugar	*
1 teaspoon vegetable oil	.05
¼ cup cornstarch, mixed with ¼ cup water	.20
1 egg	.10
½ teaspoon baking powder	.10
	Total: $2.00

$$$ BIG SPLURGE $$$

Serve on white rice instead of ramen noodles.

RAMEN WITH KALE AND SHRIMP

Serves four

Notes: Lose the shrimp if you must, but the kale stays. The bitter aftertaste makes this a unique recipe. You can use as little as a third of the shrimp. Or try tuna. The result will be almost the same.

3 packages shrimp ramen	.30
1 cup fresh kale, chopped with stems removed	.50
1 pound medium shrimp, peeled and de-veined	5.00
½ cup fresh basil leaves	1.00
2 cloves garlic, minced	.10
¼ cup Parmesan cheese, grated	.50
1 cup plain yogurt	.50
1 teaspoon vegetable oil	.05
1 medium red bell pepper, diced	1.00
	Total: $8.95

In a large pot of boiling water, prepare ramen noodles, cooking 3–4 minutes or until tender. Do not overcook. Drain and set aside.

While pasta is cooking, place kale, basil, garlic, Parmesan cheese and one ramen flavor packet in a food processor or blender and blend until smooth, stirring in yogurt at the end of the cycle (if you don't have a blender or food processor, chop the kale finely and mix well).

In large skillet, sauté the shrimp and red bell pepper over medium-low heat for about three minutes or until shrimp is pink. Add the ramen, shrimp and bell pepper to the kale mixture and toss well. Serve immediately.

SUBSTITUTIONS & OMISSIONS

Use two tablespoons dried basil instead of fresh, use two tablespoons Parmesan instead of full amount, and ease way off the shrimp, using just a few ounces instead of a pound. Fill out the volume with another onion. Use green pepper for red.

3 packages shrimp ramen	.30
1 cup fresh kale, chopped with stems removed	.50
1 tablespoon dried basil	.10
2 cloves garlic, minced	.10
2 onions, minced	.50
¼ cup Parmesan cheese, grated	*
3 tablespoons cream, mixed in 3 tablespoons water	*
1 teaspoon vegetable oil	.05
¼ can cocktail shrimp	.30
½ green bell pepper, diced	.15
	Total: $2.00

$$$ BIG SPLURGE $$$

Not much you can do with kale. But try using more cream and serve over linguine instead of ramen.

PAD THAI RAMEN

Serves four

Notes: Tamarind juice is tough to find. However, tamarind seeds are available at most stores and tamarind powder (used as a drink) is available in the international aisle of any big supermarkets. It gives a lemony tang that makes this dish unique.

3 packages Oriental ramen	.30
¼ cup tamarind juice	.20
2 tablespoons sugar	.05
4 tablespoons peanut oil	.20
½ pound fresh shrimp, shelled, de-veined and butterflied	2.00
5 cloves garlic, minced	.20
3 shallots, minced	.30
¼ cup radishes, chopped	.30

2 teaspoons crushed red pepper	.10
3 eggs	.30
3 cups fresh bean sprouts	1.00
4 green onions, chopped	.20
	Total: $5.15

Bring about five quarts of water to boil in a large pot. Drop in ramen noodles and boil for a minute, then reduce heat. Cook another 2–3 minutes, or until tender. Remove from heat, drain and set aside.

Add 2 teaspoons oil to a heavy skillet. Stir-fry the shrimp until pink—about two minutes. Remove. Add the tamarind juice and one shrimp ramen noodle flavor packet.

Add garlic, radish and crushed red pepper to the skillet. Stir-fry a few seconds, then add the cooked ramen noodles. Toss well, stir-frying about two minutes. Push the mass up along one side of the pan and crack the eggs onto the cleared space; scramble lightly. Stir-fry again so egg is mixed in with the noodles.

Add the shrimp and tamarind mixture and stir well to evenly coat noodles. Serve immediately and top with green onion slices.

Substitutions & Omissions

Use only a half dozen or so shrimp, vegetable oil for sesame oil, lighten the garlic, lose the shallots and add another ramen package for volume.

4 packages ramen	.40
¼ cup tamarind juice (or use powder or fresh)	.20
2 tablespoons sugar	*
4 tablespoons vegetable oil	.05
4 or 5 small shrimp, shelled, de-veined and chopped into 1-inch pieces	.50
2 cloves garlic, minced	.10
3 green onions, minced	.10
2-3 radishes, chopped	.10
2 teaspoons crushed red peppers	*
2 eggs	.30
½ cup fresh bean sprouts	.25
	Total: $2.00

$$$ Big Splurge $$$

Use fat Oriental noodles instead of ramen noodles. And throw in more shrimp.

SHRIMP SAUTÉ RAMEN

Serves four

Notes: If you go Chinese—meaning you'll add a few big shrimp for flavor—you'll still get the taste of this dish.

3 packages shrimp ramen	.30
2 tablespoons olive oil	.20
2 cloves garlic, minced	.10
20 large shrimp, peeled and de-veined, tails on	4.00
¼ cup parsley, chopped	.25
juice of 1 lemon	.10
1 cup dry white wine	.50
half stick butter	.30
1 tablespoon capers	.30
	Total: $6.05

Bring a medium saucepan of salted water to a boil. Add ramen and cook until *al dente*, about four minutes. Drain, set aside.

Heat oil in a large skillet and add garlic. Cook over low heat for about a minute, then add shrimp, a packet of flavoring and parsley. Cook for 3 to 4 minutes or until pink. Set aside.

In a skillet, add lemon juice and wine and bring to a boil. Lower heat and reduce by half, about 2 minutes. Add parsley, butter, one flavor packet and capers, then the shrimp. Pour over ramen noodles on each serving plate.

SUBSTITUTIONS & OMISSIONS

Lighten up on the shrimp and add another package of ramen to fill out the volume. Use margarine for butter and lose the wine. Capers make this a nice deal, but omit them if they aren't in your budget.

4 packages shrimp ramen	.40
2 tablespoons olive oil	.20
2 cloves garlic, minced	.10
3 large shrimp, peeled and de-veined, tails on	.60
¼ cup parsley, chopped	.10
juice of 1 lemon	*
half stick margarine	.10
1 tablespoon capers	.30
	Total: $1.80

$$$ BIG SPLURGE $$$

Use some good flavored olives and use tomato and cheese tortellini in place of ramen noodles.

SPICY SHRIMP RAMEN ALFREDO

Serves four

Notes: Shrimp changes the basic Alfredo recipe, but if all you have is, say, chicken, crawfish, or tuna, use it in place of shrimp. Louisiana hot sauce is cheap and will warm you up on a winter's night. If you want to really crank it up, increase the hot sauce amount.

3 packages ramen, any flavor	.30
1 pound shrimp, cleaned and washed	4.00
½ stick butter	.75
1 cup cream	1.00
1 cup Parmesan cheese, grated	1.00
4 cloves garlic, minced	.10
1 teaspoon Louisiana hot sauce	.10
pepper to taste	.05
	Total: $7.30

In a large pot of boiling salted water, cook the ramen until tender but still firm, about 4 minutes. Drain well.

Cook ¼ pound small shrimp in a saucepan for 5 minutes with butter, garlic, hot sauce and black pepper. Add the Parmesan cheese and cream. Simmer until thick.

Stir in the ramen noodles, coating completely. Serve immediately.

SUBSTITUTIONS & OMISSIONS

Use margarine for butter, less cream mixed with water and dried Parmesan for fresh. Add another package of ramen.

4 packages ramen, any flavor	.40
1 can cocktail shrimp	.90
¼ cup margarine	.20
¼ cup cream, mixed with ¼ cup water	*
1 cup Parmesan cheese	*
4 cloves garlic, minced	.10

½ teaspoon pepper	*
1 teaspoon Louisiana hot sauce	*
	Total: $1.60

$$$ BIG SPLURGE $$$

Use lots of fresh Parmesan, lots of cream and Alfredo noodles for ramen noodles.

RAMEN SHRIMP-STUFFED MUSHROOMS

Serves four

Notes: This is really more an appetizer than a main course. But if you find large mushrooms, it can be served as a main course.

2 packages mushroom ramen	.20
1 pound mushrooms	2.00
1 can cocktail shrimp	1.75
¼ cup green onions, minced	.10
2 cloves garlic, minced	.10
¼ cup parsley, chopped	.10
½ stick butter	.45
1 cup Parmesan cheese, grated	1.00
black pepper to taste	.05
	Total: $5.75

Cook the ramen noodles in slightly salted boiling water until *al dente*, 3–4 minutes, omitting the flavor packets. Drain well and rinse under cold water. Chop into 1-inch pieces and set aside.

Remove the stems from the mushrooms, taking care not to tear the caps. Mince the stems and place them into a bowl. Add the shrimp, the green onions, two flavor packets, parsley, butter, pepper and eggs. Toss in the chopped ramen and mix well.

Form appropriate balls out of the mixture and place each one in the cap of the upturned mushrooms. Place them on a baking sheet, cap side down and bake for ½ hour. Serve hot.

SUBSTITUTIONS & OMISSIONS

Use slightly fewer mushrooms—or look for them on sale—and lose the shrimp and the butter. Add more ramen for volume.

3 packages mushroom ramen	.30
¾ pound mushrooms	1.40
¼ cup green onions, minced	.10
2 cloves garlic, minced	.10
¼ cup parsley, chopped	.10
½ cup Parmesan cheese	*
black pepper to taste	*
	Total: $2.00

$$$ BIG SPLURGE $$$

Use grilled, diced fresh shrimp for canned. And use extra large portobello mushrooms and angel hair pasta for ramen noodles.

RAMEN AND SHRIMP IN TOMATO CREAM

Serves four

Notes: Cream, tomato and shrimp make the rich taste. Don't eliminate any of the three, but reduce the required amount. Vermouth helps, but can be eliminated if unavailable.

3 packages tomato ramen	.30
½ cup sun dried tomatoes packed in oil, slivered	1.00
1 clove garlic, minced	.10
1 pound large shrimp, shelled and de-veined	5.00
¼ cup green onions, sliced, including tops	.25
1 tablespoon fresh basil, chopped	.10
¾ cup dry vermouth	1.00
1 cup heavy cream	1.00
2 tablespoons Parmesan cheese, grated	.30
black pepper to taste	.05
	Total: $9.10

Bring five quarts of water to a boil and toss in the ramen noodles, cooking three or four minutes or until tender but not mushy. Drain and set aside.

Add 2 tablespoons of olive oil, or oil from the tomatoes, in a skillet over medium-high heat and sauté garlic. Add shrimp and cook shrimp until pink. Add onions, chopped basil, tomatoes, pepper, one flavor packet, vermouth and cream.

Put ramen noodles on plates and pour sauce over. Garnish with Parmesan cheese.

SUBSTITUTIONS & OMISSIONS

Use a quarter of the listed amount of shrimp, rounding out the volume by using another packet of ramen. Lose the vermouth and all but one teaspoon of the sun-dried tomatoes. And use less cream, mixing what you have with water.

4 packages tomato ramen	.40
1 clove garlic, minced	.10
1 teaspoon sun-dried tomato, minced	.10
½ cup shrimp, diced	1.00
¼ cup green onions, sliced, including tops	.25
1 teaspoon dried basil	.10
3 tablespoons cream, mixed with equal parts water	*
2 tablespoons Parmesan cheese	*
black pepper to taste	
Total:	$1.95

$$$ BIG SPLURGE $$$

Use penne for ramen noodles and a lot of cream.

RAMEN AND SHRIMP WITH SWEET POTATOES

Serves four

Notes: Sweet potatoes (or yams) give this dish a new taste and a starch that gives it a great texture. Make sure you have enough garlic and chilies to set off the sweet taste of the potatoes.

3 packages ramen	.30
1 pound medium shrimp, cleaned and de-veined	5.00
1 pound sweet potatoes	.75
½ cup oil	.30
3 stalks lemon grass	.50
6 shallots	.50
4 cloves garlic, minced	.10
1 teaspoon dried ginger	.10
5 red chilies	.20
Total:	$7.75

Fill a large pot with enough water to cover 1 pound of sweet potatoes. Cook over high heat for approximately 45 minutes, or until potatoes are tender when piercing them with a fork. Run under cold water to remove skin. Once cleaned and cooled, mash into a paste with a fork or a potato masher.

Heat a skillet or wok and add a bit of oil with a package of shrimp ramen flavoring. Stir-fry the shrimp. As shrimp turn pink, stir in the mashed potatoes and continue stirring. Season the mix with a second flavor packet, sugar and pepper.

Bring about five quarts of water to boil in a large pot, drop in ramen noodles and boil for a minute, then reduce heat. Cook another 2-3 minutes, or until tender. Remove from heat, drain and set aside. Toss in hot potato and shrimp and mix well. Serve immediately.

SUBSTITUTIONS & OMISSIONS

Reduce the amount of shrimp dramatically, eliminate the lemon grass and use green onions for shallots. Go easy on the oil and slightly reduce the sweet potatoes. Add another package of ramen for volume.

4 packages ramen	.40
½ dozen small shrimp, cleaned and de-veined	.50
1 pound sweet potatoes	.75
2 tablespoons vegetable oil	.05
2 green onions, chopped	.10
4 cloves garlic, minced	.10
1 teaspoon ginger	.10
2 teaspoons hot sauce	*
Total:	$2.00

$$$ BIG SPLURGE $$$

Use more prawns, add a touch of sherry and use fettuccine for ramen noodles.

SEAFOOD PASTA STIR-FRY

Serves four

Notes: The orange peel and ginger make this interesting. If you have to, use canned tuna instead of scallops and shrimp.

3 packages spicy shrimp ramen	.30
2 tablespoons white wine vinegar	.20
2 tablespoons soy sauce	.20

2 cloves garlic, minced	.10
2 teaspoons fresh ginger, minced	.30
1 tablespoon orange peel, grated	.10
¼ cup orange juice	.20
8 ounces medium, fresh shrimp, peeled and de-veined	3.00
8 ounces fresh sea scallops	3.00
1 tablespoon vegetable oil	.05
½ teaspoon crushed red pepper	.10
1 cup fresh snow peas, cut in 1-inch pieces	.50
2 carrots, cut julienne	.10
1 red bell pepper, cut julienne	1.00
2 teaspoons cornstarch, mixed in 2 tablespoons water	.10
	Total: $9.25

Bring water to a boil in a large pot and add ramen noodles. Cook for approximately four minutes, or until tender. Drain and set aside.

Mix vinegar, soy sauce, garlic, ginger, orange peel and orange juice in a bowl; add shrimp and scallops and toss gently to coat seafood. Heat in a small saucepan and cook 2–3 minutes or until shrimp are pink and scallops are milk white.

Add cooled ramen and stir-fry about three minutes. Add crushed red pepper, one packet of ramen flavoring, snow peas, carrots and bell pepper. Stir cornstarch into wok. Cook another minute. Toss lightly and serve.

SUBSTITUTIONS & OMISSIONS

Use cocktail shrimp for medium shrimp; omit the scallops or reduce amount; or forget them both and use tuna. Use onion for volume; canned green beans for snow peas. And add one more package of ramen.

4 packages spicy shrimp ramen	.40
2 tablespoons white wine vinegar	*
2 tablespoons soy sauce	*
2 cloves garlic, minced	.10
2 teaspoons dried ginger	.10
1 tablespoon grated orange peel	.10
1 can tuna, drained	.50
1 tablespoon vegetable oil	.05
½ teaspoon crushed red pepper	*
1 cup fresh snow peas, cut in 1-inch pieces	.40
2 carrots, cut julienne	.10
½ green bell pepper, ribs and seeds removed, cut julienne	.15

2 teaspoons cornstarch, mixed in 2 teaspoons water	.10
	Total: $2.00

$$$ BIG SPLURGE $$$

Try a little heavy cream and some cognac for a different dish. And use fettuccine for ramen noodles.

RAMEN NOODLES WITH SCALLOPS

Serves four

Notes: Scallops tend to be on the high side of the budget. But they're a nice treat if you can afford them. Use less scallops, but try to keep them in the recipe.

3 packages shrimp flavor ramen	.30
½ pound sea scallops, sliced into ¼-inch pieces	3.50
1 medium tomato, diced	1.00
4 slices bacon, chopped	.30
3 cloves garlic, minced	.10
¼ teaspoon thyme	.10
	Total: $5.30

In a large pot of boiling salted water, cook the ramen until tender but still firm, about 4 minutes. Drain well.

Cook the bacon in a large skillet over medium heat, then sauté garlic in the drippings. Add scallops, cooking quickly to avoid browning, but cook thoroughly (this is facilitated by cutting into slices).

Put the tomatoes into the skillet, add a half packet of shrimp ramen flavoring and thyme and cook about 2-3 minutes, then drain. Remove and set aside.

Toss the pasta with the sauce and scallops and serve with freshly grated Parmesan cheese.

SUBSTITUTIONS & OMISSIONS

Use ¼ pound bay scallops, bacon bits for real bacon and add a package of ramen to fill out.

4 packages shrimp flavored ramen	.40
¼ pound bay scallops, sliced ¼ inch thick	1.00

½ medium tomato, diced	.30
4 tablespoons bacon bits	*
3 cloves garlic, minced	.10
¼ teaspoon thyme	.10
	Total: $1.90

$$$ BIG SPLURGE $$$

Go to a full pound of scallops, add some dry sherry and fresh thyme. Use a pound of linguine for ramen noodles.

THAI PRAWNS IN RAMEN NOODLES

Serves four

Notes: Prawns are great, but you might as well be cooking Krugerrands. You'll need to use a lot less. But with the lemon grass and lime, this is a nice meal.

3 packages spicy shrimp ramen	.30
2 pounds large tiger prawns with heads on	11.00
2 cloves garlic, minced	.50
6 shallots, minced	.50
3 stalks lemon grass, chopped	.30
8-10 dried red chilies	.30
8-12 Thai chilies, minced	.30
juice of 2-3 limes	.30
1-2 tablespoons sugar	.05
¼ cup short cilantro sprigs, chopped	.25
2 tablespoons peanut oil	.15
	Total: $13.95

Bring about five quarts of water to boil in a large pot. Drop in ramen noodles and boil for a minute, then reduce heat. Cook another 2-3 minutes, or until tender. Remove from heat, drain and set aside.

Sauté garlic and shallots in oil in a large skillet for about 10 minutes. Toss in dried chilies and cook about two minutes, then toss the entire mixture into a blender and mix to form a paste. Set aside.

Stir-fry prawns in a heavy skillet about 2-3 minutes. Toss in the pepper mash. Stir in chopped lemon grass and lime juice and stir-fry another minute.

Pour over a bed of ramen noodles.

SUBSTITUTIONS & OMISSIONS

Use just a few small prawns and add more ramen for lost volume. Omit the Thai chilies and use vegetable oil for peanut oil.

4 packages spicy shrimp ramen	.40
2 tiger prawns	.50
2 cloves garlic, minced	.10
3 green onions, chopped	.10
3 stalks lemon grass, chopped	.30
3 tablespoons crushed red chili peppers	*
3 tablespoons lemon juice	*
2 tablespoons sugar	*
¼ cup cilantro, chopped	.15
2 tablespoons vegetable oil	.05
	Total: $1.60

$$$ BIG SPLURGE $$$

Serve over fried fat Oriental noodles.

Chapter 10

BEEF MAIN COURSES

BAKED AMERICAN RAMEN

Serves four

Notes: Think mac and cheese with beef and you've got the hang of this one. It's filling, cheap and easy to make.

3 packages beef ramen	.30
1 large onion, chopped	.25
1 garlic clove, minced	.10
1 pound ground beef	1.50
1 ½ cups tomatoes, diced	.75
1 8-ounce can tomato sauce	.30
2 teaspoons Italian seasoning	.10
¾ cup Cheddar cheese, grated	1.00
	Total: $4.30

Boil approximately five quarts of water in a large pot and cook ramen noodles until tender, approximately 3-4 minutes. Drain and set aside.

Sauté onion, garlic and ground beef over medium heat in a large frying pan until browned. Drain grease. Add tomatoes, tomato sauce, a cup of water, Italian seasoning and one ramen flavor packet. Simmer for five minutes, stirring occasionally.

Place ramen noodles in a casserole dish. Add meat mixture and combine all ingredients. Bake at 350° for about 45 minutes.

SUBSTITUTIONS & OMISSIONS

Back off the beef by half, use onion and more ramen for volume and leave out the cheese (or add just a few tablespoons dried Parmesan for taste).

4 packages tomato ramen	.40
1 ¾ cup onions, diced	.40
1 garlic clove, minced	.10
½ pound ground beef	.50
½ tomato, diced	.25
1 8-ounce can tomato sauce	.20
2 teaspoons Italian seasoning	.10
	Total: $1.95

$$$ BIG SPLURGE $$$

Substitute rotini for ramen noodles and use good sharp Cheddar and some Gruyère for sharpness.

AUTUMN SQUASH AND CORNED BEEF RAMEN

Serves four

Notes: Horseradish, squash and beef. Call it Thanksgiving on a bed of ramen noodles.

3 packages vegetable ramen	.30
1 pound lean corned beef, cooked and sliced	3.50
1 cup acorn squash, peeled, seeded and diced	.50
½ teaspoon black pepper	.05
¼ teaspoon nutmeg	.10
¼ teaspoon mace	.10
1 bay leaf	.10
¼ teaspoon cloves	.10
2 teaspoons horseradish	.30
½ cup heavy cream	.50
	Total: $5.55

Heat about six cups of water and toss in the ramen noodles once the water is at a good boil. Cook one minute, then reduce the heat. Cook another 2-3 minutes, drain and set aside.

Cook the squash until tender and let cool. Purée in a blender or food processor (or mash well with a fork). Put the squash purée into a bowl and add cream, horseradish and one beef ramen flavor packet. Add the corned beef and toss into ramen noodles. Serve hot.

SUBSTITUTIONS & OMISSIONS

Use less beef and eliminate the mace. Use less cream and less horseradish. Add one more package ramen noodles for volume.

4 packages vegetable ramen	.40
¼ pound lean corned beef, cooked and sliced	.75
1 cup acorn squash, peeled, seeded and diced	.50
¼ teaspoon nutmeg	.10
1 bay leaf	.10
¼ teaspoon cloves	.10
2 teaspoons horseradish	*
3 tablespoons cream	*
black pepper to taste	*
	Total: $1.95

$$$ BIG SPLURGE $$$

Omit the ramen and use spaghetti.

BAKED BURGUNDY BEEF

Serves four

Notes: Burgundy Beef needs wine to be authentic, but wine costs a bit of cash. Use what you have, even if it's white wine or vodka, and you'll still have a nice taste—not to mention a buzz.

3 packages beef ramen	.30
1 pound chuck steak, cubed	2.00
1 cup burgundy	1.00
¼ cup bread crumbs	.30
1 bay leaf	.10
	Total: $3.70

Boil about six cups of water and toss in the ramen noodles once the water is boiling. Cook one minute, then reduce heat. Cook another 2-3 minutes, drain and set aside.

Fry the steak in a heavy skillet and shake in one packet of beef flavoring when beef is nearly done. Combine with wine and bay leaf, cook for about two minutes, then pour it all into the casserole dish. Add the bread crumbs, ramen, mix again, cover and bake about 90 minutes at 375°.

SUBSTITUTIONS & OMISSIONS

Use less beef and lose most of the wine.

3 packages beef ramen	.30
½ pound chuck roast, cubed	1.00
3 tablespoons burgundy	.60
¼ cup bread crumbs	*
1 bay leaf	.10
	Total: $2.00

$$$ BIG SPLURGE $$$

Use sirloin and elbow macaroni.

BARBECUE PEPPER STEAK AND RAMEN NOODLES

Serves four

Notes: Slop on your favorite steak sauce, add ramen noodles and you've got a good and filling meal. Make sure you coat the noodles with the steak sauce for the Full Monte.

3 packages spicy beef ramen	.30
½ cup steak sauce	.40
1 clove garlic; minced	.10
½ pound strip steak	1.50
black pepper to taste	.05
	Total: $2.35

Boil about six cups of water and toss in the ramen noodles. Cook one minute, then reduce the heat. Cook another 2-3 minutes, drain and set aside.

Combine steak sauce, one flavor packet and pepper in a small bowl and pour about a quarter of the mix over the steak. Let steak marinate for about an hour. Fry or broil steaks until done, brushing with sauce occasionally.

While hot, cut into strips. Pour the remainder into the skillet to heat about three minutes and toss the entire mix—sauce and meat—into the noodles. Stir to coat noodles. Serve immediately.

SUBSTITUTIONS & OMISSIONS

Use slightly less steak sauce.

3 packages spicy beef ramen	.30
¼ cup steak sauce	*
1 clove garlic; minced	.10
1 teaspoon black pepper	*
6 ounces strip steaks	1.50
	Total: $1.90

$$$ BIG SPLURGE $$$

Serve over tagliatelle pasta instead of ramen noodles.

BEEF AND BEER RAMEN

Serves four

Notes: Meat and alcohol? How could a man ask for anything more? Just don't use good beer.

3 packages beef ramen	.30
1 pound boneless chuck	2.00
¼ cup mushrooms, sliced	.30
½ can beer	.25

1 cup onions, thinly sliced	.25
2 tablespoons barbecue sauce	.10
1 green pepper, sliced	.25
1 tablespoon prepared mustard	.10
black pepper to taste	.05
	Total: $3.60

Boil about six cups of water and toss in the ramen noodles once the water is at a good boil. Cook one minute, then reduce the heat. Cook another 2-3 minutes, drain and set aside.

Brown beef in a large skillet, adding onions as the beef is cooking. Add pepper, one beef flavor packet and mushrooms. Cook for another two minutes or so. Pour in beer, stir in barbecue sauce and simmer, covered, for about 20 minutes or until meat is tender. Toss over ramen noodles and serve.

SUBSTITUTIONS & OMISSIONS

Use slightly less beer and half the beef. Add ramen for bulk.

4 packages beef ramen	.40
¼ pound chuck	.50
¼ cup mushrooms, sliced	.30
¼ teaspoon pepper	*
¼ can beer	.20
1 cup onions, thinly sliced	.25
1 ½ tablespoon barbecue sauce	*
1 green pepper, sliced	.25
	Total: $1.90

$$$ BIG SPLURGE $$$

Use portobello mushrooms and fettuccine for ramen noodles.

BAKED BEEF AND YOGURT RAMEN

Serves four

Notes: This is one of the few recipes in this book containing yogurt that isn't Indian. The cayenne makes it similar to an Indian taste, but less complicated. The ramen still makes it unique.

3 packages beef ramen	.30
1 pound chuck steak, cut into strips	2.00

3 tablespoons vegetable oil	.05
1 onion, chopped	.25
6 cloves garlic, minced	.10
½ teaspoon ginger	.10
¼ teaspoon cayenne	.10
1 tablespoon paprika	.10
1 cup plain yogurt	.50
	Total: $3.50

Boil about six cups of water and toss in the ramen noodles once the water is at a good boil. Cook one minute, then reduce the heat. Cook another 2-3 minutes, drain and set aside.

Brown meat in a heavy skillet. Add onion and garlic to the skillet and sauté about three minutes, then add ginger, cayenne, paprika, yogurt and simmer about five minutes. Remove and toss into the ramen noodles. Serve immediately.

SUBSTITUTIONS & OMISSIONS

Use less steak, and make it cheap beef. Use a fourth package of ramen and a spicy beef ramen flavor packet for cayenne.

4 packages beef ramen	.40
¼ pound steak, cut into strips	.50
3 tablespoons vegetable oil	.05
1 onion, chopped	.25
6 cloves garlic, minced	.10
½ teaspoon ground ginger	.10
1 tablespoon paprika	.10
1 cup plain yogurt	.50
	Total: $2.00

$$$ BIG SPLURGE $$$

Use shell pasta for ramen noodles.

BARBECUE BEEF CASSEROLE

Serves eight

Notes: Same principal here as lasagna, just use a beef-based taste rather than a tomato sauce base. It's filling and hearty.

4 packages spicy beef ramen	.40

1 pound ground beef	**1.50**
1 onion, diced	**.25**
2 tablespoons red wine vinegar	**.20**
¼ cup brown sugar	**.30**
3 tablespoons Worcestershire sauce	**.30**
1 tablespoon prepared mustard	**.10**
1 tablespoon barbecue sauce	**.20**
1 8-ounce can tomato sauce	**.25**
¼ teaspoon cayenne pepper	**.10**
1 cup corn (frozen or canned is fine)	**.50**
15-ounce container part-skim ricotta cheese	**2.00**
3 eggs	**.30**
¾ cup sharp Cheddar cheese, shredded	**1.50**
Total:	**$7.90**

Boil approximately five quarts of water in a large pot and cook ramen noodles until tender, approximately 3-4 minutes. Drain and set aside.

Sauté beef and onions in a large skillet over medium-high heat until beef is no longer pink and onions are soft. Drain well.

Combine tomato sauce, water, vinegar, brown sugar, Worcestershire sauce, mustard, two flavor packets and red pepper in a medium bowl. Add corn and the meat/onion mixture together and simmer for 5-10 minutes.

Spread about a half-inch of ramen noodles on the bottom a baking pan and cover with 1½ cups of meat sauce. Combine ricotta cheese and eggs and spread half the ricotta on top of the meat sauce. Arrange another layer of ramen noodles over ricotta and top with another 1½ cups meat sauce. Spread remaining ricotta on top. Arrange final bits of ramen noodles over ricotta and cover with remaining sauce.

Sprinkle cheese on top and bake 30 minutes at 375°. Serve immediately.

SUBSTITUTIONS & OMISSIONS

Use cottage cheese for ricotta, and lighten the amount by half; same with the Cheddar. Use a chili ramen flavor packet for the cayenne.

6 packages spicy beef ramen	**.60**
½ pound ground beef	**.50**
1 onion, diced	**.25**
¼ cup brown sugar	**.30**
3 tablespoons Worcestershire sauce	**.30**
1 tablespoon prepared mustard	*
1 tablespoon barbecue sauce	*
1 8-ounce can tomato sauce	**.25**
1 cup corn (frozen or canned is fine)	**.50**

1 cup cottage cheese	.50
3 eggs	.30
¼ cup sharp Cheddar cheese, shredded	.50
	Total: $4.00

$$$ BIG SPLURGE $$$

Use 2 pounds beef brisket, slow cooked. Use good Cheddar and substitute good herbed linguine or fettuccine.

BEEF BOURGUIGNON RAMEN

Serves four

Notes: Dark, rich sauce is the goal with this dish. The beef and onions make this hearty; the noodles make it a meal, the French name makes it sound a little too sophisticated.

3 packages beef ramen	.30
1 carrot, shredded	.10
1 10-ounce bag frozen pearl onions	1.50
1 pound beef tenderloin tips or steaks, cut into ½-inch pieces	3.50
¼ cup all-purpose flour	.10
2 tablespoons margarine	.10
2 teaspoons garlic, minced	.10
¼ cup red wine	.75
1 teaspoon dried thyme leaves	.10
2 teaspoons fresh parsley, chopped	.10
pepper to taste	.05
	Total: $6.70

Boil approximately five quarts of water in a large pot and cook ramen noodles until tender, approximately 3-4 minutes. Drain and set aside.

In a medium bowl, sprinkle flour, two packets beef ramen flavoring and pepper to taste. Add beef (in fact, you may do this in a paper or plastic bag, shaking the meat inside the bag to coat it).

In a large skillet, melt a teaspoon of margarine over medium-high heat, adding the floured beef. Brown the beef about five minutes. Remove from skillet and set aside.

Add garlic to drippings in skillet and cook 2 minutes, stirring occasionally. Add any remaining flour mixture, a cup of water, the final flavor packet and bring to a boil. Add pearl onions, wine and thyme to skillet and stir in cooked beef. Simmer about five minutes until sauce has thickened slightly.

Arrange ramen noodles on individual plates and spoon beef mixture on top. Sprinkle with fresh parsley and serve.

SUBSTITUTIONS & OMISSIONS

Pearl onions are nice, but pricey. Use chopped yellow onion instead and ease off the beef. Forget the thyme and wine if cash is tight.

3 packages beef ramen	.30
1 carrot, shredded	.10
2 cups onion, diced	.50
½ pound beef, cut into ½ inch pieces	.50
¼ cup all-purpose flour	.10
2 tablespoons margarine	.10
2 teaspoons garlic, minced	.10
1 teaspoon dried thyme leaves	.10
pepper to taste	*
3 tablespoons parsley, chopped	.10
	Total: $1.90

$$$ BIG SPLURGE $$$

Use sirloin, sweet Vidalia onions and use linguine for ramen noodles.

BEEF AND BULGUR RAMEN NOODLES

Serves four

Notes: Bulgur, or cracked wheat, is quite nutritious. It also adds volume and fills the stomach. Although it's cheap, it may also be tough to find. You can also use seven-grain breakfast cereal or brown rice instead. Also, you can use lamb, turkey or pork in place of beef.

3 packages beef ramen	.30
1 onion, diced	.25
1 clove garlic, minced	.10
1 ½ cups tomatoes, diced	.50
1 tablespoon oil	.05
¼ teaspoon thyme	.10
½ cup bulgur	.50
¾ pound ground beef	1.00
2 tablespoons parsley, chopped	.10
1 red pepper, diced	1.00

black pepper to taste	.05
	Total: $3.95

Heat about six cups of water and toss in the ramen noodles once the water is at a good boil. Cook one minute, then reduce the heat. Cook another 2-3 minutes, drain and set aside.

In a large skillet, sauté garlic, onion, red pepper, parsley, and cook about two minutes, until tender. Add spices, ground beef and cook until brown, then add bulgur. Reduce heat and cook about five minutes.

Pour into a casserole dish and bake for 1 hour at 350°. Serve immediately.

SUBSTITUTIONS & OMISSIONS

Reduce the amount of onion, tomatoes, bulgur, green pepper and beef. Add another package of ramen to fill out volume.

4 packages beef ramen	.40
1 onion, minced	.10
1 clove garlic, minced	.10
½ cup tomatoes, diced	.25
1 tablespoon oil	.05
¼ teaspoon thyme	.10
¼ cup bulgur	.25
½ pound ground beef	.50
2 tablespoons parsley, chopped	.10
½ green pepper, diced	.10
black pepper to taste	.05
	Total: $2.00

$$$ BIG SPLURGE $$$

Use orzo noodles for ramen noodles and add fresh thyme.

CHINESE PINEAPPLE BEEF AND RAMEN NOODLES

Serves four

Notes: Pineapple mixed with the beef makes this dish unique. Mix the salty soy with the sweet fruit and you have a crazy combination.

3 packages beef ramen	.30
1 pound ground chuck	2.50
1 can pineapple	1.25
2 teaspoons cornstarch, dissolved in two teaspoons water	.10
1 teaspoon sugar	.05
¼ teaspoon baking soda	.05
2 tablespoons soy sauce	.10
1 tablespoon oyster sauce	.20
1 teaspoon sesame oil	.20
1 tablespoon dry sherry, gin or vodka	.50
3 tablespoons vegetable oil	.05
1 clove garlic, minced	.10
2 tablespoons green onions, chopped	.10
black pepper to taste	.05
	Total: $5.55

Heat about six cups of water and toss in the ramen noodles once the water is at a good boil. Cook one minute, then reduce heat. Cook another 2-3 minutes, drain.

In a heavy skillet, sauté garlic in oil for a few seconds then add beef, pineapple, sugar, pepper, baking soda, soy sauce, oyster sauce, alcohol, one flavor packet and green onions. Stir-fry for 2-3 minutes or until beef is browned. Add cornstarch dissolved in water, add to noodles and mix to coat. Serve immediately.

SUBSTITUTIONS & OMISSIONS

Replace steak with ground beef and reduce the amount of pineapple. Add a package of ramen and eliminate the alcohol and the sesame oil.

4 packages beef ramen	.40
½ pound ground chuck	.50
¼ can pineapple	.45
2 teaspoons cornstarch, dissolved in 2 teaspoons water	.10
1 teaspoon sugar	*
¼ teaspoon baking soda	.05
2 tablespoons soy sauce	*
1 tablespoon homemade oyster sauce (see page 56)	.20
3 tablespoons vegetable oil	.05
1 clove garlic, minced	.10
2 tablespoons green onions, chopped	.10
black pepper to taste	*
	Total: $1.95

$$$ BIG SPLURGE $$$

Use fat Oriental noodles for ramen noodles. Also add a few tablespoons vodka and sherry.

SAVORY, SPICY BEEF RAMEN

Serves four

Notes: This is a good combination of ingredients—a lot of which can be eliminated. Keep the basic framework, which is beef-flavored ramen and stew beef, and you can do a lot of things here. Just keep it simple.

3 packages beef or spicy beef ramen	.30
1 pound beef, cut into 1-inch cubes	2.00
½ onion, chopped	.20
1 cup peas	.50
2 carrots, sliced	.25
½ red pepper, diced	.50
1 cup mushrooms, sliced	1.00
2 tomatoes, cut into wedges	1.00
1 cup red wine	1.50
1 bay leaf	.10
¼ cup fresh parsley, chopped	.25
¼ teaspoon crushed red pepper	.10
black pepper to taste	.05
	Total: $7.75

In a large pot, boil water and drop in ramen. Cook approximately 3-4 minutes, or until tender. Drain and remove from heat.

Combine beef, onion, carrots, red pepper, mushrooms, tomatoes, peas, wine, bay leaf, parsley and red pepper flakes with about 3 cups water in a large heavy pot. Cover and simmer over low heat for approximately one hour, stirring occasionally. Mix in 1-2 flavor packets, depending on your taste, black pepper and cooked ramen noodles. Cover and cook five minutes, stirring occasionally. Add peas and mix once again. Serve hot.

SUBSTITUTIONS & OMISSIONS

Use cheap meat here. Use green pepper for red. Eliminate the bay leaf and use corn instead of peas. Lose the wine. Add ramen to fill it out.

4 packages ramen	.40
¼ pound beef cut into 1-inch cubes	.50
1 onion, chopped	.25
2 carrots, sliced	.10
½ green pepper, diced	.15
¼ cup mushrooms, sliced	.25
½ tomato, diced	.25
¼ cup fresh parsley, chopped	.10
¼ teaspoon crushed red pepper	*
black pepper to taste	*
	Total: $2.00

$$$ BIG SPLURGE $$$

Use pearl onions, portobello mushrooms, keep the wine and use rigatoni for ramen.

BEEF RAMEN IN CASHEW SAUCE

Serves four

Notes: You need nuts for this one. But it will be worth the effort. Cumin, yogurt and cardamom finish it off.

3 packages ramen: 2 sesame, 1 curry	.30
1 pound chuck steak	2.00
4 tablespoons vegetable oil	.05
¾ pound potatoes, peeled and diced into ½-inch cubes	.30
1 bay leaf	.10
1 teaspoon crushed red pepper	.10
5 whole cardamom pods	.30
2 cinnamon sticks	.20
2 whole cloves	.20
2 cups onion, chopped	.50
2 tablespoons fresh ginger, minced	.20
1 tablespoon garlic, minced	.10
1 teaspoon green chili, seeded and chopped	.10
½ teaspoon turmeric	.10
2 teaspoons ground cumin	.10

¼ teaspoon sugar	.05
2 tablespoons plain yogurt	.10
1 tablespoon cashews, finely chopped	.30
	Total: $5.10

Bring about five quarts of water to boil in a large pot. Drop in ramen noodles and boil for a minute, then reduce heat. Cook another 2-3 minutes, or until tender. Remove from heat, drain and set aside.

Fry the potatoes in a skillet over medium heat until they turn golden brown—around 15 minutes. Remove potatoes and set aside.

Stir-fry bay leaf, red chili, cardamom, cinnamon, cloves and onion for approximately 10 minutes. Stir in ginger, garlic, green chili, turmeric, cumin, sugar and one ramen flavor packet.

Cut beef into 1-inch cubes and add to the ginger and spice mixture. Add potatoes again, cover and simmer 30 minutes. Blend in yogurt, nuts and one flavor packet. Remove from heat. Blend with ramen noodles and serve immediately.

SUBSTITUTIONS & OMISSIONS

Use less beef, less onions and lighten up on the cinnamon, the bay leaf, cloves, and the potatoes. Add a package of ramen for volume.

4 packages ramen: 2 sesame, 2 curry	.40
¼ cup beef	.30
4 tablespoons vegetable oil	.05
1 teaspoon crushed red pepper	*
5 whole cardamom pods	.30
½ cup onions, chopped	.15
2 tablespoons dried powdered ginger	.10
1 tablespoon garlic, minced	.10
1 teaspoon crushed red chili peppers	*
½ teaspoon turmeric	.10
2 teaspoons ground cumin	.10
¼ teaspoon sugar	*
1 tablespoon cashews, finely chopped	.30
2 tablespoons cream	*
	Total: $1.90

$$$ BIG SPLURGE $$$

Serve over fat Oriental noodles instead of ramen noodles.

BIG CHEESY RAMEN

Serves four

Notes: If you simmer this a long time, the cheese will melt throughout and it will end up quite filling.

3 packages tomato ramen	.30
½ pound mozzarella cheese, grated	2.00
½ pound provolone cheese, grated	2.50
1 pound ground beef	1.50
1 cup mushrooms, sliced	.50
1 pint sour cream	1.50
1 32-ounce jar spaghetti sauce	1.50
	Total: $9.80

Cook ground beef until brown. Drain fat. Mix spaghetti sauce with ground beef, adding one packet flavoring.

Put the mixture in a large pot. Pour sour cream over this and then add the grated provolone and mozzarella. Cook on low heat for about a half-hour. Pour over noodles and serve.

SUBSTITUTIONS & OMISSIONS

For the spaghetti sauce, use 2 12-ounce cans tomato sauce mixed with 1 teaspoon each of oregano, basil, garlic powder, two flavor packets and pepper to taste. Cut cheese amount in half and omit the provolone. Use Monterey jack if neither is available. Forget the sour cream and use a bit of real cream with some lemon juice for tartness instead (make sure you blend the lemon with the other ingredients before adding the cream). And use one extra ramen package.

5 packages tomato ramen	.50
¼ pound mozzarella cheese, shredded	.50
¼ pound ground beef	.30
1 can (8 ounces) mushrooms	.50
3 tablespoons cream, mixed with water	*
1 6-ounce can tomato sauce	.20
	Total: $2.00

$$$ BIG SPLURGE $$$

Use a Stilton or Glouster as well as the mozzarella. Substitute fettuccine for ramen noodles.

CHEESEBURGER RAMEN NOODLES

Serves four

Notes: Cheeseburger and pasta. What could be more pedestrian? Fill out ground beef with more bread crumbs or another onion.

3 packages beef ramen	.30
1 pound ground beef	1.50
¼ cup bread crumbs	.25
½ teaspoon onion powder	.10
1 egg	.10
2 teaspoons vegetable oil	.05
¼ cup ketchup	.30
½ cup sour cream	.50
1 cup Cheddar cheese, shredded	1.00
	Total: $4.10

Bring water to a boil in a large pot and add ramen noodles. Cook for approximately four minutes, or until tender. Drain and set aside.

Combine ground beef, bread crumbs, onion powder, one flavor packet and egg; mix well. Shape into approximately 20 small patty-shaped burgers. Heat oil in a large skillet and cook patties until browned on each side. Drain grease.

Combine another packet beef ramen flavoring in a ½ cup water, then mix in ketchup. Bring the mix to a boil in a skillet, remove from heat and stir in ramen noodles, sour cream and cheese.

SUBSTITUTIONS & OMISSIONS

Reduce Cheddar cheese amount and leave out the sour cream, using yogurt or cream, flour and lemon. Add an onion for extra bulk.

3 packages beef ramen	.30
¼ pound ground beef	.30
¼ cup genuine day-old bread crumbs	*
½ teaspoon onion powder	.10
1 onion, minced	.25
1 egg	.10
2 teaspoons vegetable oil	.05
¼ cup ketchup	*
½ cup cream, mixed with water	*
1 cup Cheddar cheese, shredded	.50
	Total: $1.60

$$$ BIG SPLURGE $$$

Use ground sirloin for hamburger and spaghetti for ramen noodles.

CHEESY BEEF RAMEN

Serves four

Notes: American cheese and ground beef provide a familiar taste. Kraft Velveeta (or a similar generic cheese loaf) can also be used in place of American cheese slices. Use a beef flavor packet to enhance the beef flavor.

3 packages tomato ramen	.30
1 pound ground beef	1.50
1 cup American cheese, diced	.75
¼ cup ketchup	.40
	Total: $2.95

Heat about six cups of water and toss in the ramen noodles once the water is at a good boil. Cook one minute, then reduce the heat. Cook another 2-3 minutes, drain and set aside.

In a large skillet, brown the beef and drain. Stir in the ketchup, a half cup water, one flavor packet and bring to a boil. Reduce heat and cover. Uncover and stir in ramen noodles, two flavor packets and cheese. Serve immediately.

SUBSTITUTIONS & OMISSIONS

If you have to, use grated Parmesan for American. Add one package ramen.

4 packages tomato ramen	.40
½ pound lean ground beef	.75
1 cup American cheese, diced	.75
¼ cup ketchup	*
	Total: $1.90

$$$ BIG SPLURGE $$$

Use shells for ramen noodles.

RAMEN CHILI-MAC

Serves six

Notes: This is another filling yet inexpensive recipe. And if you're single and fairly close to the AMA height/weight standards, this will last a week or more. If you're a fatso, a little less.

3 packages ramen: 2 tomato and one chili	.30
1 pound ground round	2.00
3 tablespoons olive or vegetable oil	.05
1 28-ounce can chili without beans	1.00
1 20-ounce can red kidney beans, drained	.50
1 16-ounce can tomato sauce	1.25
2 cups onions, diced	.50
3 cloves garlic, minced	.20
1 teaspoon chili powder	.10
1 teaspoon cumin	.10
½ teaspoon oregano	.10
½ teaspoon pepper	.05
1 bay leaf	.10
black pepper to taste	.05
	Total: $6.30

In a large pot, boil water and drop in ramen. Cook approximately 3-4 minutes, or until tender. Drain and remove from heat.

Brown beef in a large skillet. Add chili, onions, garlic, tomato sauce, two flavor packets and remaining seasonings. Cover and simmer for 45 minutes. Stir in kidney beans. Cook for an additional 30 minutes. Remove bay leaf. Add cooked ramen noodles to the chili then serve.

SUBSTITUTIONS & OMISSIONS

You can do without the canned chili, using only one can of beans, but you must add more spices to cover it. Leave out the bay leaf and the tomato sauce, adding instead another tomato ramen flavor packet and two cups water. You can also halve the ground beef. Use more onion and ramen for volume.

4 packages chicken ramen	.40
½ pound lean ground beef	.75
3 tablespoons vegetable oil	.05
1 20-ounce can red kidney beans, drained	.50

3 cups onions, minced	.75
3 cloves garlic	.20
1 teaspoon ground cumin	.10
½ teaspoon dried oregano	.10
1 bay leaf	.10
black pepper to taste	.05
	Total: $3.00

$$$ BIG SPLURGE $$$

Use elbow macaroni for ramen. Increase beef to 1 ½ to 2 pounds and reduce the beans. Top with sharp Cheddar.

RAMEN FIESTA LASAGNA

Serves eight

Notes: Another big meal. Although not expensive per serving, the entire dish tends to cost a little more than you'll normally find in this cookbook—but then it feeds more people, too. To save money, check out substitutes and omissions or just plan on eating Ramen Fiesta Lasagna all week.

5 packages chicken or spicy chicken ramen	.50
2 4-ounces cans diced green chilies	1.00
2 cups cottage cheese	1.50
½ teaspoon ground cumin	.10
1 teaspoon chili powder	.20
1 18-ounce can tomato sauce	.75
1 pound ground beef, browned and drained	1.50
1 8-ounce jar/can picante sauce	1.00
1 cup corn (frozen or canned is fine)	.50
1 bunch green onions, sliced	.25
2 cups sharp Cheddar cheese, grated	2.00

1 cup sour cream	1.00
¼ cup green olives, chopped	.50
	Total: $10.80

Boil water in a large pot and drop in ramen. Cook approximately 3-4 minutes, or until tender. Drain and remove from heat.

Stir the diced chilies into the cottage cheese, then mix in cumin, chili powder, tomato sauce and picante sauce, adding two chicken ramen flavor packets.

Spread about a half-cup of the mixture over the bottom of a casserole dish. Cover with ramen noodles. Spread half of the remaining cottage cheese on the ramen noodles and sprinkle half each of the ground beef, corn, green onions and Cheddar cheese.

Repeat layering, beginning with sauce. Place a layer of ramen noodles on top. Pour remaining sauce over. Top with sour cream, Cheddar cheese and olives.

Bake for 45 minutes at 425° and serve immediately.

SUBSTITUTIONS & OMISSIONS

Use half or less of the cottage cheese, omitting altogether if it's not in your budget. Ease up on the Cheddar, using less that one cup and go easy on the sour cream. For salsa, use any hot sauce you can scrounge and one spicy chicken ramen flavoring packet. Use a second spicy chicken ramen packet for the chili powder, and omit the olives if necessary.

6 packages ramen	.60
1 fresh jalapeno, diced	.10
½ teaspoon ground cumin	.10
1 16-ounce can tomato sauce	.35
½ pound ground beef, browned and drained	.50
¾ cup corn (frozen or canned is fine)	.35
1 onion, diced	.25
1 bunch green onions, sliced	.25
1 cup grated sharp Cheddar cheese, reserving ¼ cup for the top	1.00
1 cup low-fat sour cream	.50
	Total: $4.00

$$$ BIG SPLURGE $$$

Use cubed steak, good sharp Cheddar with some double Glouster for extra taste, and use lasagna for ramen noodles.

FRIED RAMEN

Serves four

Notes: Easy to make, easy to eat, easy to afford. This will be a ***Brother, Can You Spare a Dime*** *regular.*

3 packages ramen	.30
1 egg	.10
¼ pound ground beef	.30
¼ cup broccoli (frozen is fine)	.25
¼ cup green beans, cut into 1-inch pieces (frozen or canned is fine)	.25
3 tablespoons oil	.05
½ teaspoon ginger	.10
¼ cup green onions, sliced	.10
3 tablespoons sesame oil	.20
3 tablespoons soy sauce	.10
	Total: $1.75

Boil water in a large pot. Add ramen noodles and return to a boil for one minute, then reduce heat and cook another 2-3 minutes. Drain and set aside.

Heat a skillet to high heat and brown ground beef. Drain. In a bit of remaining oil, sauté ginger, scallion, one beef-flavored ramen flavor packet and meat two minutes. Add frozen vegetables, stir-fry again two minutes, then remove. Scramble the egg in the same pan, then return the other ingredients to the ramen noodles and mix everything. Serve immediately.

SUBSTITUTIONS & OMISSIONS

Use ham, pork, or chicken in place of ground beef.

$$$ BIG SPLURGE $$$

Use fat Oriental noodles for ramen and steak for ground beef.

RAMEN MEATLOAF

Serves four

Notes: Sure, you hated meatloaf when you were a kid. But mom made it to save some cash—and so will you. It won't taste a hell of a lot different, but it should be a hell of a lot cheaper.

3 packages beef ramen	.30
1 pound ground beef	1.25
2 eggs	.20
2 tablespoons milk	.10
¼ cup ketchup	.20
1 onion, diced	.25
½ green bell pepper, diced	.15
1 clove garlic, minced	.10
2 tablespoons steak sauce	.20
2 tablespoons Worcestershire sauce	.20
1 cup Cheddar cheese, grated	.75
	Total: $3.70

In a large pot of boiling salted water, cook the ramen until tender but still firm, about 4 minutes. Drain well then chop into small pieces.

Mix ramen with the ground beef and other ingredients, adding all three flavor packets. Mix until uniformly blended. Shape into a loaf and place in a large loaf pan or baking dish. Cover with aluminum foil and bake at 350° for 1 hour. Then uncover and bake an additional ½ hour. Serve with your favorite condiment.

SUBSTITUTIONS & OMISSIONS

Lose the cheese and the Worcestershire sauce, adding more steak sauce for the Worcestershire sauce. You can also lighten up on the beef, using about ¾ pound—but not much less. Fill out volume with another package of ramen.

4 packages beef ramen	.40
¾ pound ground beef	.90
2 eggs	.20
2 tablespoons milk	*
¼ cup ketchup	*
1 onion, diced	.25
½ green bell pepper, diced	.15
1 clove garlic, minced	.10
2 tablespoons steak sauce	*
	Total: $2.00

$$$ BIG SPLURGE $$$

For meatloaf? What are you, crazy?

OYSTER BEEF RAMEN

Serves four

Notes: Oyster sauce is the principal ingredient of this dish. It can be purchased at Asian grocery stores—or you can make your own (see page 56).

3 packages beef ramen	.30
1 pound beef, thinly sliced	1.50
½ cup green onions	.25
½ teaspoon soy sauce	.20
1 teaspoon cornstarch, mixed in 1 teaspoon water	.10
1 teaspoon sugar	.05
2 tablespoons vegetable oil	.05
2 tablespoons oyster sauce	.20
	Total: $2.65

Boil about six cups of water and toss in the ramen noodles. Cook one minute, then reduce the heat. Cook another 2-3 minutes, drain and set aside.

Combine soy sauce, one beef ramen flavor packet, a ½ cup of water and cornstarch. Mix well and add green onions and oyster sauce. Pour into a pan coated with oil and stir-fry beef for about five minutes until gravy becomes thick. Serve over a bed of ramen noodles.

SUBSTITUTIONS & OMISSIONS

Use less beef. Add ramen.

4 packages beef ramen	.40
½ pound beef, thinly sliced	.75
½ cup green onions, sliced	.25
½ teaspoon soy sauce	*
1 teaspoon cornstarch, mixed in 1 teaspoon water	.10
1 teaspoon sugar	*
2 tablespoons vegetable oil	.05
2 tablespoons oyster sauce	.20
	Total: $1.75

$$$ BIG SPLURGE $$$

Use sirloin with fat Oriental noodles instead of ramen noodles.

RAMEN PASTITSIO

Serves eight

Notes: This filling meal with last you a few days—more if you're a light eater. Cream sauce on top makes it a different dish from lasagna. Eliminate the cheese and you'll still be okay.

5 packages beef ramen	.50
4 cups milk	1.25
¼ cup flour	.10
4 eggs	.40
2 onions, diced	.35
¼ teaspoon ground cinnamon	.10
2 pounds ground beef	3.00
4 tablespoons butter	.50
2 cloves garlic, minced	.10
2 cups tomatoes, diced	1.00
1 8-ounce can tomato sauce	.25
½ cup bread crumbs	.30
1 cup fresh Romano cheese, grated	1.50
1 teaspoon fresh oregano, chopped	.20
	Total: $9.55

In a large pot of boiling salted water, cook the ramen until tender but still firm, about 4 minutes. Drain well and set aside.

Beat egg yolks together in a small bowl with the milk, then pour into a saucepan with butter and flour. Cook until mixture boils, then remove the pan from the heat.

Sauté onions in butter. Add meat, tomatoes, tomato sauce, spices and seasonings. Cover and simmer for 30 minutes.

Preheat oven to 350° and sprinkle bread crumbs into a buttered baking pan. Place a layer of ramen noodles in the baking pan; then add half the cream sauce. Add meat and sprinkle with grated cheese then cover with remaining sauce.

Bake for 1 hour, or until cream on top is golden. Since you cannot cut the pastitsio easily unless you cool it, let it stand 10-20 minutes, then cut into squares.

SUBSTITUTIONS & OMISSIONS

Mix about a half-cup of cream with two cups water and flour. Blend into the mix. Use half the ground beef, adding another package of ramen instead. Use margarine for butter, make your own bread crumbs and leave out the Romano cheese (or use Monterey jack).

6 packages beef ramen	.60
¼ cup flour	.10
4 eggs	.40
1 ½ cups onions, diced	.35
¼ teaspoon ground cinnamon	.10
1 pound ground beef	1.50
4 tablespoons margarine	.10
1 clove garlic, minced	.10
½ cup tomatoes, diced	.25
1 cup tomato sauce	.25
½ cup bread crumbs	*
1 teaspoon dried oregano	.10
Parmesan cheese	*
	Total: $3.85

$$$ BIG SPLURGE $$$

Replace milk with cream, use fresh Parmesan and replace the ramen with about four cups good elbow macaroni.

PHILLY STEAK RAMEN NOODLES

Serves four

Notes: White American cheese, fried onions and beef ramen flavoring make this dish. If you're from out West, you'll want to use mozzarella cheese. Resist the urge. It's not authentic.

3 packages beef ramen	.30
¼ cup mushrooms, sliced	.30
1 cup cube steak, thinly sliced	1.50
1 cup white American cheese, chopped into small pieces	1.00
1 cup onion, sliced	.25
black pepper to taste	.05
	Total: $3.40

Sauté the onion in a skillet and add the steak, cooking until tender. Add the mushrooms and one beef ramen flavor packet.

Heat about six cups of water and toss in the ramen noodles once the water is at a good boil. Cook one minute, then reduce the heat. Cook another 2-3 minutes, drain and set aside.

Toss the steak, mushrooms and onions into the hot ramen, than add the cheese and mix well. Serve immediately.

SUBSTITUTIONS & OMISSIONS

Use cheaper beef and less cheese. Use yellow onion and add another package ramen for volume. Also, if you can't find white American cheese, use yellow. Or use Velveeta or some other similar American cheese loaf.

4 packages beef ramen	.40
1 cup cube steak, thinly sliced	1.00
¼ cup American cheese	.50
¼ cup onion, diced	.10
black pepper to taste	*
	Total: $2.00

$$$ BIG SPLURGE $$$

Add mushrooms and use fettuccine or linguine for ramen noodles. Or do it right—forget the noodles and get a few hoagie rolls.

WEST TEXAS CASSEROLE

Serves four

Notes: Olives, sour cream and diced tomatoes make this what it is—a Mexican casserole. Try to leave at least those ingredients in tact.

3 packages beef ramen	.30
1 pound beef tips	3.50
2 tablespoons vegetable oil	.05
1 onion, diced	.25
1 green pepper, diced	.25
1 clove garlic, diced	.10
1 14.5-ounce can pinto beans, drained	.75
1 cup tomatoes, diced	.50
1 tablespoon cilantro, chopped	.10
½ cup Cheddar cheese, grated	1.00
1 teaspoons hot sauce	.10
black pepper to taste	.05
	Total: $6.95

Bring water to a boil in a large pot. Add ramen noodles and broccoli. Cook for approximately four minutes, or until tender. Drain and set aside.

While the ramen is cooking, cut beef into bite-sized pieces and brown in oil, stirring frequently, about 10 minutes. Remove meat, set aside. Cook onion and green pepper in skillet about five minutes.

Add garlic and return beef to skillet. Stir in tomatoes, pinto beans and one packet flavor packet and simmer until beef is tender.

Add meat to cooked ramen. Add cilantro, black pepper, one flavor packet and Tabasco. Simmer for 5 minutes. Transfer to casserole dish. Bake for 45 minutes at 375° or until brown on top. Sprinkle with cheese and serve.

SUBSTITUTIONS & OMISSIONS

Forget the beef tips. Get cheap stew meat for this one then reduce the amount. Add a package of ramen for the lost volume.

4 packages beef ramen	.40
¼ pound round	.50
2 tablespoons vegetable oil	.05
1 onion, diced	.25
½ green pepper, diced	.10
1 clove garlic, minced	.05
1 14.5-ounce can pinto beans, drained	.25
½ cup tomatoes, diced	.25
1 tablespoon cilantro, chopped	.10
1 tablespoon black pepper	*
¼ cup Parmesan cheese, grated	*
1 teaspoon hot sauce	*
	Total: $1.95

$$$ BIG SPLURGE $$$

Barbecue the beef first. Add a ¼ cup of tequila and use shell pasta for ramen noodles.

ROAST BEEF IN PORT MARINADE AND RAMEN NOODLES

Serves four

Notes: Port wine, white wine, tenderloin and French herbs. Sounds fancy-pants. It's a rich taste, for sure. Unfortunately, for the price, it's also likely not in the budget. Use a lot less wine and beef, reduce the herbs and enjoy.

3 packages beef ramen	.30
1 pound beef tenderloin or steak	4.00

¼ cup brown sugar	.20
¼ cup olive oil	.30
1 cup pineapple juice	.25
1 cup port wine	1.50
1 cup white wine	1.50
1 pinch Herbes de Provence	.20
pepper to taste	.05
	Total: $8.30

Bring about five quarts of water to boil in a large pot. Drop in ramen noodles and boil for a minute, then reduce heat. Cook another minutes, or until tender. Remove from heat, drain and set aside.

Marinate meat in brown sugar, pineapple juice, half the po wine, white wine, herbs, pepper, olive oil and one packet beef flavoring Let sit for a few hours.

Roast tenderloin for about an hour at 325°. Remove and slice into strips. Place the pan with the drippings on the stove and turn on one burner, add the other ½ cup of the port wine and stir. This will deglaze the pan and create natural gravy. Add half of the marinade and add pepper to taste. Boil the mixture, reduce heat.

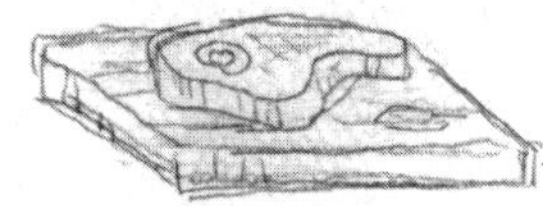

Mix the strips of beef with the ramen noodles and toss in the boiled marinade and deglazed drippings. Serve immediately.

SUBSTITUTIONS & OMISSIONS

Lose all but a few tablespoons of wine (and make it cheap wine at that).

4 packages beef ramen	.40
3 ounces chuck steak	.50
¼ cup brown sugar	.20
1 cup pineapple juice	.25
2 tablespoons white wine	.30
tiny pinch Herbes de Provence	.10
2 tablespoons olive oil	.25
pepper to taste	*
	Total: $2.00

$$$ BIG SPLURGE $$$

Use good-quality steak, some Cointreau liquor and penne for ramen noodles.

RADICCHIO AND SIRLOIN STEAK RAMEN NOODLES

Serves four

Notes: Again, to do this right you need to spend some cash. But if you had the cash in the first place you'd be reading something by Martha Stewart or Julia Child, right? So use cheaper cuts of beef and either lose the radicchio or use a lot less of it.

3 packages beef ramen	**.30**
1 pound sirloin steak	**4.00**
1 head radicchio	**1.25**
½ cup orange segments	**.10**
¼ cup soy sauce	**.30**
¼ cup sesame oil	**.30**
3 tablespoons olive oil	**.20**
1 tablespoon rice vinegar	**.20**
2 teaspoons soy sauce	**.10**
2 teaspoons rice vinegar	**.20**
3 teaspoons sesame oil	**.20**
pepper to taste	**.05**
	Total: $7.20

Bring about five quarts of water to boil in a large pot. Drop in ramen noodles and boil for a minute, then reduce heat. Cook another 2-3 minutes, or until tender. Remove from heat, drain and set aside.

Marinate the flank steak for 20 minutes to one hour in a bit of vinegar, sesame oil, pepper and one packet spicy beef ramen. Roast for 45 minutes at 325° (or pan fry for 15 minutes on medium heat).

Slice the meat into strips and add another packet of ramen flavoring. Mix until coated.

Cut radicchio and mix with the orange segments. Mix strips of beef with the ramen, then toss in the citrus and radicchio. Toss well with a bit more olive oil, some black pepper and a pinch of vinegar.

SUBSTITUTIONS & OMISSIONS

Reduce the amount of the steak and buy chuck or round. Add a fourth ramen package for volume. Use a few radicchio leaves if you can get them, or try it with green cabbage. Use half of the citrus blend, less soy sauce and vegetable oil for sesame.

4 packages beef ramen	**.40**
¼ pound cheap round or chuck steak	**.40**
5 radicchio leaves	**.45**

¼ head green cabbage	.35
½ cup orange segments	.25
¼ cup soy sauce	*
3 tablespoons vegetable oil	.05
1 tablespoon rice vinegar	*
2 teaspoons soy sauce	*
pepper to taste	*
	Total: $1.90

$$$ BIG SPLURGE $$$

Use more sirloin steak, a shot of triple sec, and fettuccine for ramen noodles.

ROAST BEEF AND SPINACH RAMEN

Serves four

Notes: Beef with horseradish makes this familiar. You can skimp on a few things and still retain the spirit of this dish.

3 packages Oriental flavor ramen, broken up while dry	.30
1 cup fresh spinach, torn	.50
½ cup onion, sliced	.25
½ pound roast beef, sliced	2.00
2 tablespoons rice vinegar	.30
2 tablespoons vegetable oil	.05
1 tablespoon prepared horseradish	.20
	Total: $3.60

Open both packages of ramen. Cook the noodles 3-4 minutes in boiling water without the seasoning packets. When done, drain and set aside.

Combine spinach, onion and roast beef in serving bowl. Mix beef ramen flavor packet with vinegar, oil and horseradish. Pour mixture over noodles and toss. Add beef onion and spinach and mix again.

SUBSTITUTIONS & OMISSIONS

Omit the vinegar, use less roast beef and add a package of ramen to fill out.

4 packages Oriental flavor ramen, broken up	.40
1 cup fresh spinach, torn	.50

½ cup onion, sliced	.25
¼ cup roast beef, cooked and sliced	.60
2 tablespoons vegetable oil	.05
1 tablespoon prepared horseradish	*
	Total: $1.80

$$$ BIG SPLURGE $$$

Substitute a pound of penne for ramen.

SLOPPY JOE RAMEN NESTS

Serves four

Notes: This takes patience to make, but is well worth the effort. It's also going to give you a nice change of routine.

3 packages tomato ramen	.30
1 egg, lightly beaten	.10
½ cup sour cream	.50
¾ cup sharp Cheddar cheese, grated	1.50
¾ pound ground beef	1.25
1 cup barbecue sauce	1.00
1 8-ounce can tomato paste	.50
	Total: 5.15

Boil approximately five quarts of water in a large pot and cook ramen noodles until tender, approximately 3-4 minutes. Drain and set aside.

Mix together egg, sour cream and ½ cup cheese. Add mixture to the ramen noodles and toss until well mixed. Set aside.

Cook beef in skillet until browned. Drain well and one package of ramen seasoning, tomato sauce and water. Cook over medium heat 10 minutes, stirring frequently. Set aside.

Grease a 12-cup muffin pan and divide spaghetti mixture evenly among muffin cups (about ¼ cup ramen noodles each). No muffin tins? You can make your own cups using aluminum foil, rolling the bottom edge to create a firm bottom. Press ramen firmly into cups with back of spoon. Spoon beef mixture into center of each cup (about 1 ½ tablespoons each), dividing evenly among cups. Top each with 1 teaspoon cheese.

Bake at 350° until firm and heated through, about 20 minutes. Let stand about ten minutes and loosen edges with a knife to remove from muffin cups. Serve immediately.

SUBSTITUTIONS & OMISSIONS

Use cream and lemon for sour cream. Lighten up the cheese amount.

3 packages tomato ramen	.30
1 egg, lightly beaten	.10
¼ cup sour cream	.25
¼ cup sharp Cheddar cheese, grated and divided	.50
½ pound ground beef	.50
1 8-ounce can tomato sauce	.20
¼ cup barbecue sauce	*
	Total: 1.85

$$$ BIG SPLURGE $$$

Use spaghetti for ramen.

SPICY BEEF AND BROCCOLI RAMEN

Serves four

Notes: Use whatever beef is available here—as long as it isn't ground beef. You're looking for the essence of the beef, not a great cut of steak here. You want great steak, get another cookbook.

3 packages beef ramen	.30
1 pound flank steak, cut into very thin strips	3.00
2 teaspoons vegetable oil	.05
3 cups broccoli florets (frozen is fine)	1.50
2 cups tomato sauce	.50
1 cup tomato, diced	1.00
½ cup red wine vinegar	.30
½ teaspoon crushed red pepper	.10
¼ cup brown sugar	.20
¼ teaspoon cayenne pepper	.10
3 cloves garlic, minced	.10
	Total: $7.15

In a large pot of boiling water, prepare ramen noodles, cooking 3-4 minutes or until tender. Do not overcook. Drain and set aside.

While pasta is cooking, stir in the vinegar, crushed red pepper, brown sugar, cayenne pepper and garlic. Add beef strips to the marinade.

Heat a large skillet and toss in beef mixture, sautéing until nicely browned. Remove.

Add broccoli to the same pan and sauté about 5 minutes. Add tomato sauce and one flavor packet, cooking another 2-3 minutes.

Spoon steak and sauce over ramen and garnish with diced tomatoes. Serve immediately.

SUBSTITUTIONS & OMISSIONS

Use less beef, less broccoli and more tomatoes (depending on which is cheaper) and eliminate vinegar.

3 packages beef ramen	.30
¼ pound round steak, cut into very thin strips	.50
2 teaspoons vegetable oil	.05
1 cup broccoli florets (frozen is fine)	.50
¼ cup tomato sauce	.05
1 cup tomatoes, diced	.50
½ teaspoon crushed red pepper	*
¼ cup sugar	*
3 cloves garlic, minced	.10
	Total: $2.00

$$$ BIG SPLURGE $$$

Add sherry or brandy and good sirloin. Serve over fettuccine instead of ramen noodles.

RAMEN NOODLE WITH VIETNAMESE-STYLE BEEF AND LEMON GRASS

Serves four

Notes: Lemon grass adds a depth to a normally straightforward dish. If you don't have steak, use stewing beef or some other cut.

3 packages ramen: 2 beef, 1 shrimp	.30
½ pound flank steak, cut into slivers	2.00
2 cloves garlic, minced	.10
1 green onion, chopped	.10
1 tablespoon lemon grass, chopped	.20
1 tablespoon sugar	.05
2 tablespoons oil	.05
1 onion, sliced into rings	.25
	Total: $3.05

Mix garlic, green onions, lemon grass, sugar and one packet of shrimp ramen flavoring into a bowl with the beef. Let sit for about 30 minutes.

In a heavy skillet or wok, heat oil and sauté onions about three minutes. Add the beef and marinade and stir-fry over high heat until beef is well browned and the marinade boils.

Bring about five quarts of water to boil in a large pot, drop in ramen noodles and boil for another minute, then reduce heat. Cook another 2-3 minutes, or until tender. Remove from heat, drain and toss with cooked beef mix.

SUBSTITUTIONS & OMISSIONS

Reduce the amount of meat. No lemon grass? Use green onions and lemon juice.

3 packages ramen: 2 beef, 1 shrimp	.30
¼ pound flank steak, cut in slivers	1.00
2 cloves garlic, minced	.10
1 green onion, chopped	.10
1 tablespoon lemon grass, chopped	.20
1 tablespoon sugar	*
2 tablespoons oil	.05
1 onion, sliced into rings	.25
	Total: $2.00

$$$ BIG SPLURGE $$$

Use more lemon grass, double the amount of steak and serve on linguine instead of ramen noodles.

Chapter 11

PORK AND LAMB MAIN COURSES
(INCLUDING BACON, SAUSAGE AND HAM)

BACON AND EGG RAMEN NOODLES
Serves four

Notes: Hung over? Try this one—a classic morning taste that doesn't have to be served at breakfast. For a twist, throw in some green onions or some bell peppers. Then have a Bloody Mary and find the dog that bit you.

3 packages ramen: two pork, one mushroom	**.30**
½ pound mushrooms, sliced	**1.00**
1 cup Cheddar cheese, grated	**2.00**
4 eggs, beaten	**.40**
2 tablespoons vegetable oil	**.05**
6 to 8 slices of bacon, fried crisp and crumbled	**1.00**
Total:	$4.75

Boil about six cups of water and toss in the ramen noodles once the water is at a good boil. Cook one minute, then reduce the heat. Cook another 2-3 minutes, drain and set aside.

In a heavy skillet, drop in the egg mixture and cook, adding mushrooms and cheese until the egg reaches desired consistency. You'll not likely get runny eggs in this dish, but if you want them extra firm, keep cooking.

Toss the eggs with the cooked ramen noodles and throw in the crumbled bacon. Serve immediately.

SUBSTITUTIONS & OMISSIONS

Don't worry about the cheese at all. This dish is fine without it. If you want to increase volume lost by the cheese add another egg or two, or another package of ramen—or both. Use an 8-ounce can of mushrooms instead of fresh and less bacon.

3 packages ramen: two pork, one mushroom	**.40**
½ pound mushrooms, sliced	**.50**
5 eggs, beaten	**.50**
2 tablespoons vegetable oil	**.05**
3 to 4 slices of bacon, fried crisp and crumbled	**.50**
Total:	$1.95

$$$ BIG SPLURGE $$$

Add shallots, 2 tablespoons brandy and an extra egg white. Toss into bow tie pasta instead of ramen noodles.

RAMEN NOODLES WITH BACON, GARLIC AND COLLARDS

Serves four

Notes: Don't forget the garlic, but you can use bacon bits in a pinch. Eliminate the red peppers if needed.

3 packages spicy chicken ramen	**.30**
1 pound collards	**1.00**
¼ pound sliced bacon, cut into ½ inch pieces	**.50**
4 cloves garlic, minced	**.10**
1 large onion, sliced	**.25**
¼ teaspoon crushed red peppers	**.10**
1 tablespoon red wine vinegar	**.20**
3 tablespoons fresh Parmesan, grated	**.50**
Total:	$2.95

In a large pot of boiling salted water, cook the ramen until tender but still firm, about 4 minutes. Drain well and set aside.

Discard the coarse stems of the collard greens and wash the leaves well. Chop greens into three-inch pieces and place in a pot of boiling water. Cook for 10 minutes, drain.

In a large skillet, cook the bacon over moderate heat. In half the drippings, sauté the garlic, onion, and the crushed red pepper flakes over moderately low heat until the onion is softened and the garlic is golden brown. Drain grease.

Add the collards, the bacon and the onion/garlic mixture and heat again, mixing in one flavor packet and the vinegar. Stir for one minute over medium heat and toss the mixture into the ramen noodles. Sprinkle each serving with a touch of Parmesan.

SUBSTITUTIONS & OMISSIONS

Use bacon bits for real bacon and dried Parmesan cheese for fresh.

3 packages spicy chicken ramen	.30
1 pound collards	1.00
¼ pound sliced bacon, cut into ½ inch pieces	*
4 cloves garlic, minced	.10
1 large onion, sliced thin	.25
¼ teaspoon crushed red peppers	.10
1 tablespoon vinegar	.10
3 tablespoons Parmesan	*
	Total: $1.85

$$$ BIG SPLURGE $$$

Use some cream, and exchange spaghetti for ramen noodles.

CABBAGE AND SAUSAGE WITH RAMEN NOODLES

Serves four

Notes: Cabbage and sausage are a nice earthy taste that will put you in a basic down-to-earth state of mind. It's also cheap.

3 packages ramen: two pork, one vegetable	.30
¼ cup olive oil	.40
4 cloves garlic, minced	.20
1 pound Italian sausage	3.00

1 pound cabbage, cut into ½-inch strips	**.75**
3 8-ounce cans tomato sauce	**.60**
¼ cup fresh Parmesan cheese, grated	**.50**
	Total: $5.75

Boil about six cups of water and toss in the ramen noodles. Cook one minute, then reduce the heat. Cook another 2-3 minutes, drain and set aside.

Sauté garlic in oil and add sausage. Cook until tender. Reduce heat and add the cabbage and one flavor packet. Cook for another three minutes, stirring constantly. Add tomato sauce, simmer about ten minutes and pour over a bed of ramen noodles. Top with grated cheese.

SUBSTITUTIONS & OMISSIONS

Buy bulk breakfast sausage and add some Italian seasoning. Use one cup of tomato sauce instead of three, adding two tomato ramen flavor packets and water. Reduce the amount of grated cheese. Add another package ramen for lost volume.

4 packages ramen: two pork, two tomato	**.40**
¼ cup olive oil	**.05**
2 cloves garlic, minced	**.10**
¼ pound sausage	**.35**
1 pound cabbage, cut into ½-inch strips	**.75**
1 cup tomato sauce	**.35**
¼ cup Parmesan cheese, grated	*
	Total: $2.00

$$$ BIG SPLURGE $$$

Use good Italian sausage, good extra-virgin olive oil and try an aged Swiss for Parmesan. Use spaghetti for ramen noodles.

CHINESE CAULIFLOWER WITH HAM AND RAMEN NOODLES

Serves four

Notes: Rice wine brings out the cauliflower nicely. Ham is along for the ride, but gives the savory flavor the dish needs.

3 packages ramen	**.30**
1 whole cauliflower, about ¾ pound (frozen is fine)	**2.00**

½ teaspoon rice wine .30
1 teaspoon cornstarch, mixed with 1 teaspoon water .10
½ cup ham, diced .75
Total: $3.45

Boil water in a large pot. Add ramen noodles and return to a boil for one minute, then reduce heat and cook another 2-3 minutes. Drain and set aside.

Boil cauliflower five minutes. Remove and drain. Set aside.

Add one flavor packet to a half-cup of water and dissolve. Pour half over the cauliflower then cut into 1-inch pieces. Chop the ham (should be precooked) into small pieces then stir into the cornstarch.

Pour the other half of the water and one flavor packet ramen noodle mixture into a skillet or wok and bring to a boil. Add ham. Cook, stirring, until thickened and toss in the cauliflower, mixing well over the heat. Remove, pour over a bed of ramen noodles and serve immediately.

SUBSTITUTIONS & OMISSIONS

Use a lot less ham. And add ramen.

4 packages ramen .40
1 ½ cups cauliflower (frozen is fine) .95
1 tablespoon cornstarch, dissolved in 1 tablespoon water .10
½ teaspoon rice wine .20
3 tablespoons ham, diced .35
Total: $2.00

$$$ BIG SPLURGE $$$

Use fat Oriental noodles for ramen and add smoked ham.

BAKED BEANS AND RAMEN NOODLES

Serves four

Notes: "Bahhsthhn" baked beans and a little ham, mixed with ramen, gives you a filling and tasty meal. Pick your own best tasting can of baked beans. Or forget the Boston accent and use ranch beans.

3 packages pork ramen .30
1 can Boston baked beans .60
1 cup ham, diced 1.00

1 cup onions, chopped	.25
1 cup tomatoes, diced	.50
2 tablespoons brown sugar	.05
1 tablespoon dry mustard	.10
1 tablespoon chili powder	.10
1 teaspoon Worcestershire sauce	.10
black pepper to taste	.05
	Total: $3.05

Boil about six cups of water and toss in the ramen noodles once the water is at a good boil. Cook one minute, then reduce the heat. Cook another 2–3 minutes, drain and set aside.

Add onion to the beans and pour into a small saucepan. Heat until onion is tender. Add ham, tomatoes, sugar, mustard, Worcestershire sauce, ramen flavoring and pepper. Cook another three minutes, then pour over ramen noodles and serve.

SUBSTITUTIONS & OMISSIONS

Reduce the amount of ham.

3 packages pork ramen	.30
1 can Boston baked beans	.60
¼ cup ham, diced	.25
½ cup onions, chopped	.10
1 cup tomatoes, diced	.50
2 tablespoons brown sugar	.05
1 tablespoon mustard, dry	.10
1 teaspoon Worcestershire sauce	.10
1 teaspoon pepper to taste	*
	Total: $2.00

$$$ BIG SPLURGE $$$

Not much you can do with baked beans, but change the ramen for shell pasta.

CHORIZO AND BEANS RAMEN NOODLES

Serves six

Notes: Chorizo is cheap and has a very unique taste. It's hard not to like it. Make sure, however, you don't read the ingredients (it's pretty revolting). Also, drain well when cooking; it's greasy (make sure you take the sausage from the casing and discard casing). Don't fret if it seems to fall apart in the pan; it's supposed to. Once you've made this one, it will feed you for a while.

3 packages vegetable or creamy chicken ramen	.30
1 pound chorizo	1.10
1 16-ounce container sour cream	1.50
1 teaspoon garlic salt	.10
1 tablespoon green chilies, chopped	.10
1 15.5-ounce can red kidney beans, rinsed and drained	1.00
1 15-ounce can garbanzo beans, rinsed and drained	1.25
1 3.8-ounce can black olives, sliced	.50
4 green onions (whites and tops) chopped	.15
2 cups tomatoes, diced	1.00
1 cup tortilla chips (optional)	.25
	Total: $7.25

Brown the chorizo in a skillet, breaking it up with a fork while cooking thoroughly. Drain well. Cool, then add sour cream, garlic, one flavor packet and green chilies.

In a large bowl, combine the other ingredients, mixing the chorizo and sour cream at the end.

Bring water to boil and drop in ramen noodles. Cook three or four minutes or until tender, but not overcooked. Drain and toss with the sauce. Serve immediately.

SUBSTITUTIONS & OMISSIONS

Use less sour cream by half, less chorizo by half and only one tomato (you've got enough food already with the ramen noodles).

4 packages vegetable or creamy chicken ramen	.40
½ pound chorizo	.60
1 8-ounce container sour cream	.75
1 teaspoon garlic salt	.10
1 tablespoon green chili, chopped	.35
2 15.5-ounces can red kidney beans, rinsed and drained	1.00
1 4-ounce can sliced black olives	.50
4 green onions, whites and tops, chopped	.15
1 medium size tomatoes, diced	.50
	Total: $4.35

$$$ BIG SPLURGE $$$

Use angel hair pasta for ramen and sprinkle with either crumbled *queso ranchero* or grated Oaxaca cheese.

RED BEANS AND RAMEN

Serves four

Notes: Use leftover ham or even some sausage if that's what you have and you'll still have a nice dish that tastes down-home.

3 packages ramen	.30
1 pound dried red beans or kidney beans (let soak four to six hours then simmer 2–3 hours)	.75
1 cup ham, diced	.75
2 tablespoons margarine	.05
1 large onion, finely chopped	.25
2 cloves garlic, minced	.10
¼ teaspoon red pepper	.10
1 bay leaf	.10
½ teaspoon oregano powder	.10
2 large tomatoes, diced	1.00
	Total: $3.50

In a large saucepan, boil 1 ½ quarts water. Drop in the beans, boil 1 hour. Set aside until they cool.

In another large pot, boil 4 quarts of water and drop in the ramen. Cook 2–3 minutes until tender. Drain and set aside.

Sauté onion until tender. Add to beans. Also add garlic, ham, tomatoes, bay leaf, pepper and one flavor packet. Cook over high heat, then reduce to simmer until tender, about 15 minutes.

Combine the two, mix and serve.

SUBSTITUTIONS & OMISSIONS

Reduce the amount of beans and ham and add one package of ramen to fill it back out.

4 packages ramen	.40
½ cup dried red beans or kidney beans	.25
¼ cup ham, diced	.25
2 tablespoons margarine	.05
1 large onion, chopped	.25
2 cloves garlic, minced	.10
¼ teaspoon dried red pepper	*
1 small bay leaf	.10
½ teaspoon oregano powder	.10
1 tomato, diced	.50
	Total: $2.00

$$$ BIG SPLURGE $$$

Forget the ramen. Use white rice and let it all simmer an hour or so before serving.

SAUSAGE WITH CRANBERRIES AND RAMEN NOODLES

Serves four

Notes: Dried cranberries add a nice tang to this filling and easy-to-prepare dish. If you don't have dried, use a cup of fresh cranberries cooked with the ramen noodles.

3 packages pork ramen	.30
½ pound mild sausage links	1.25
1 onion, chopped	.25
1 ½ cups orange juice	.30
½ cup dried cranberries, chopped	.50
½ teaspoon dried sage	.10
	Total: $2.70

Heat about six cups of water and toss in the ramen noodles. Cook one minute, then reduce the heat. Cook another 2-3 minutes, drain and set aside.

Brown sausage and onion in a large skillet about five minutes, stirring frequently. When cooked, drain and stir in cooked ramen. Add one ramen flavor packet, orange juice, cranberries and sage. Toss and serve.

SUBSTITUTIONS & OMISSIONS

Use half the required OJ and onion. Leave the rest as is.

3 packages pork ramen	.30
¼ pound mild sausage links	.85
1 small onion, chopped	.15
1 ½ cups orange juice	.10
½ cup dried cranberries	.50
½ teaspoon dried sage	.10
	Total: $2.00

$$$ BIG SPLURGE $$$

Use orzo instead of ramen noodles and fresh sage.

CREAMY HAM RAMEN

Serves four

Notes: Dill lends the flavor here, so try to keep it. Use dried dill if no fresh is available.

3 packages chicken ramen	.30
2 cups ham, cut into bite-size pieces	2.00
1 red bell pepper, diced	1.00
1 cup sour cream	.90
1 cup spinach, chopped (canned or frozen is fine)	1.00
1 cup milk	.30
¼ cup Dijon mustard	.20
¼ cup fresh parsley, chopped	.25
2 tablespoons fresh dill, chopped	.10
½ teaspoon vegetable oil	.05
1 tablespoon lemon juice	.10
1 teaspoon hot sauce	.10
pepper to taste	.05
Total:	$6.35

In a large pot of boiling water, prepare ramen noodles, cooking 3-4 minutes or until tender. Do not overcook. Drain and set aside.

While ramen noodles are cooking, add the ham and red pepper to a large skillet and cook until browned.

In a small bowl, mix the sour cream, spinach, milk, mustard, parsley, dill, lemon juice, one chicken flavor packet and hot sauce together with a fork until very smooth. Add the purée to the ham and red pepper. Heat and simmer ten minutes. Toss noodles with sauce, season with a portion of another flavor packet and pepper and serve.

SUBSTITUTIONS & OMISSIONS

Use less ham, green pepper for red and dried dill for fresh. Yogurt is cheaper than sour cream (add a teaspoon sugar if using yogurt), so use it. Also use a little cream and some water for the milk; and eliminate the parsley.

3 packages chicken ramen	.30
¼ cup ham, cut into bite-size pieces	.50
1 red bell pepper, diced (about 1 cup)	.25
¼ cup cream, mixed with ¼ cup water	*
1 cup spinach, chopped (canned or frozen is fine)	.50
¼ cup Chinese mustard	*

¼ cup fresh parsley, chopped	.15
2 tablespoons dried dill	.10
½ teaspoon vegetable oil	.05
¾ teaspoon hot sauce	*
pepper to taste	*
	Total: $1.85

$$$ BIG SPLURGE $$$

Use cream with the sour cream, fresh ground white pepper for black and prosciutto for ham. Use bow tie pasta for ramen noodles.

FIVE-SPICE FLAVORED SPARERIBS AND RAMEN NOODLES

Serves four

Notes: There's nothing like Chinese spareribs—and these can be created for just a couple bucks. Try to keep the spices as requested in the recipe. For a change, double cook (boil and then fry) the ramen noodles.

3 packages ramen	.30
1 pound pork spareribs, chopped into 1 ½-inch long pieces	2.00
1 tablespoon fresh ginger, minced	.20
3 tablespoons soy sauce	.10
1 teaspoon rice wine	.20
1 teaspoon fennel seeds	.10
2 tablespoons sugar	.05
2 tablespoons rice vinegar	.30
1 teaspoon brown sugar	.10
½ cup green onions, chopped	.10
	Total: $3.45

Boil water in a large pot. Add ramen noodles and return to a boil for one minute, then reduce heat and cook another 2-3 minutes. Drain and set aside.

Marinate the ribs in a little soy sauce for 15 minutes. Drain and rub with sugar. Set aside.

Heat the oil in a skillet or wok. Add the spareribs and deep-fry until golden brown. Remove, drain, and set aside again.

Remove the oil from the skillet, leaving only enough to coat the bottom. Reheat and add green onions, ginger, rice wine, fennel seeds, brown sugar, vinegar, one flavor packet and the remaining soy sauce. Stir-fry about 30 seconds, then return the spareribs to the skillet.

Lower heat and simmer until the sauce thickens and the meat falls from the bones—approximately 8–10 minutes. Remove and serve over a bed of ramen noodles.

SUBSTITUTIONS & OMISSIONS

Use fewer spareribs, and omit the wine.

3 packages ramen	.30
½ pound pork spareribs, chopped into 1½ inch-long pieces	1.00
1 tablespoon dried ginger	.10
3 tablespoons soy sauce	*
¼ teaspoon fennel seeds	.10
2 tablespoons sugar	*
2 tablespoons rice vinegar	.30
1 teaspoon sugar	*
½ cup green onions, chopped	.10
	Total: $1.90

$$$ BIG SPLURGE $$$

Barbecue the spareribs first, use more spareribs and use fat Oriental noodles for ramen noodles.

STIR-FRIED PORK SLIVERS WITH GINGER

Serves four

Notes: Sliced ginger creates a nice counterpoint to slivered pork. If you must use powdered ginger, go ahead—it won't spoil it. But try to keep it fresh.

3 packages ramen	.30
¼ pound lean boneless pork, cut into ¼-inch slivers	.75
2 teaspoons soy sauce	.20
3 tablespoons fresh ginger, minced	.10
1 teaspoon sugar	.05
¼ cup green bell pepper, chopped	.15
¼ cup large bean sprouts	.50
2 teaspoons cornstarch, dissolved in 2 tablespoons water	.10

¼ cup vegetable oil	.10
1 teaspoon rice wine	.20
	Total: $2.45

Boil water in a large pot. Add ramen noodles and return to a boil for one minute, then reduce heat and cook another 2-3 minutes. Drain and set aside.

Heat half the oil in a skillet or wok until very hot. Add the pork slivers and stir-fry until cooked, about 3-4 minutes. Add the rice wine, soy sauce, and sugar. Stir to blend. Pour into a bowl and set aside

Add the remaining oil to the wok. Add the ginger, green peppers and bean sprouts. Stir-fry about 2 minutes. Return the pork mixture to the skillet and stir in one ramen flavor packet with the cornstarch mixture. Cook until liquid thickens. Remove and serve over a bed of ramen noodles.

SUBSTITUTIONS & OMISSIONS

Get rid of the rice wine.

3 packages ramen	.30
¼ pound lean boneless pork, cut into ¼-inch slivers	.75
2 teaspoons soy sauce	*
3 tablespoons fresh ginger, minced	.10
1 teaspoon sugar	*
¼ cup green bell pepper, chopped	.15
¼ cup large bean sprouts	.50
2 teaspoons cornstarch, dissolved in 2 teaspoons water	.10
¼ cup vegetable oil	.10
	Total: $2.00

$$$ BIG SPLURGE $$$

Use fat Oriental noodles for ramen and add more pork.

HAM AND VEGGIE RAMEN NOODLE CASSEROLE

Serves four

Notes: This is one few cooks can screw up. You can even buy pre-mixed frozen vegetables to make this easy. Add some cheese—either cream cheese or grated Cheddar—and you have a completely different meal.

3 packages ramen: one mushroom, two ham	.30
1 pound cooked ham, diced	3.50
½ cup green beans (frozen or canned is fine)	.35
½ cup broccoli (frozen is fine)	.35
½ cup corn (frozen or canned is fine)	.35
½ cup peas (frozen or canned is fine)	.35
	Total: $5.20

Cook ramen for 4-6 minutes until tender, but not overdone. Remove and drain. Set aside.

Combine all ingredients, plus one ham and one mushroom flavor packet and pour into a baking or casserole dish. Bake at 350° until done.

SUBSTITUTIONS & OMISSIONS

Use a lot less ham, one more package of ramen noodles and less vegetables.

4 packages ramen: two mushroom, two ham	.40
3 tablespoons cooked (cheap) ham, diced	.35
½ cup green beans (frozen or canned is fine)	.35
½ cup broccoli (frozen is fine)	.35
¼ cup corn (frozen or canned is fine)	.20
½ cup peas (frozen or canned is fine)	.35
	Total: $2.00

$$$ BIG SPLURGE $$$

Use some thick-sliced, smoked ham, cut into chunks. You can also try some asparagus in place of the peas. And use tagliatelle instead of ramen noodles.

HOT DOG RAMEN CASSEROLE

Serves four (or eight medium-sized kids)

Notes: Hot dogs are cheap and kids love them. If you're an adult, just tell the people at the grocery store that your nieces and nephews are coming to visit.

3 packages chicken ramen	.30
1 cup hot dogs, sliced	.50
¾ cup peas (frozen or canned is fine)	.40

¾ cup carrots (frozen is fine)	.35
1 cup bread crumbs	.20
	Total: $1.75

Boil about six cups of water and toss in the ramen noodles. Cook one minute, then reduce heat. Cook another 2-3 minutes, drain and set aside. Preheat oven to 375° and lightly grease a casserole dish.

Slice hot dogs—which are completely cooked when you buy them—and mix with the ramen, the peas and carrots and two chicken ramen flavor packets. Mix in the bread crumbs. To make things simpler, you can toss in ramen and serve as is, or pour into the casserole dish. Bake at 375° about a half an hour.

SUBSTITUTIONS & OMISSIONS

Use other crackers or saltines for bread crumbs.

3 packages chicken ramen	.30
1 cup sliced hot dogs	.50
1 ½ cups frozen peas and carrots, thawed	.75
1 cup saltine crackers, crushed	.20
	Total: $1.75

$$$ BIG SPLURGE $$$

Drop the hot dogs and use bratwurst and add some sauerkraut. Use spaghetti for ramen noodles.

MU SHU PORK RAMEN

Serves four

Notes: Egg and pork combined make for a traditional Asian flavor. This recipe also happens to be cheap and easy to prepare.

3 packages pork ramen	.30
¼ cup vegetable oil	.05
1 tablespoon rice wine	.30
¼ cup lean pork, cooked and cubed	.75
½ teaspoon fresh ginger, minced	.20
1 cup spinach, cut into 3-inch pieces	.50
1 teaspoon cornstarch, dissolved in one teaspoon water	.10

2 teaspoons soy sauce	.20
3 eggs	.30
	Total: $2.70

Boil water in a large pot. Add ramen noodles and return to a boil for one minute, then reduce heat and cook another 2-3 minutes. Drain and set aside.

Mix cooked pork with the soy sauce, ginger and cornstarch and set aside.

Beat the eggs and mix in one packet of pork ramen flavoring. Scramble the eggs in a hot skillet with oil. Remove and set aside.

In the same skillet, heat more oil and add the wine and the pork mixture. Stir-fry again for about five minutes. Add the ramen needles and stir-fry for about a minute before adding spinach pieces and the cooked egg. Stir-fry another few seconds to blend the ingredients. Serve immediately.

SUBSTITUTIONS & OMISSIONS

Lose the rice wine, ease up on the eggs and use powdered ginger in place of fresh.

3 packages pork ramen	.30
¼ cup vegetable oil	.05
¼ cup lean pork, cooked and cubed	.75
½ teaspoon powdered ginger	.10
1 cup spinach, cut into 3-inch pieces	.50
1 teaspoon cornstarch	.10
2 teaspoons soy sauce	*
2 eggs	.20
	Total: $2.00

$$$ BIG SPLURGE $$$

Use thin rice noodles for ramen noodles.

PEPPERY PORK RAMEN

Serves four

Notes: Three types of pepper make this different. Use crushed red chili peppers, black pepper and jalapeno peppers. Eliminate whichever of the three you wish to lose—or all three if you tend toward being a sissy.

3 packages pork ramen	.30
½ pound pork, cut into ¼-inch slivers	1.50

1 egg, beaten slightly and mixed with a little flour	.15
1 cup vegetable oil for deep-frying	.50
1 tablespoon hoisin sauce (page 49)	.30
½ teaspoon crushed red peppers	.10
1 tablespoon soy sauce	.10
1 onion, diced	.25
1 tablespoon hot chili oil	.20
1 teaspoon sugar	.05
2 teaspoons sesame seeds, roasted	.20
½ teaspoon fresh ginger, chopped	.10
black pepper to taste	.05
	Total: $3.80

Boil water in a large pot. Add ramen noodles and return to a boil for one minute, then reduce heat and cook another 2-3 minutes. Drain and set aside.

Mix pork with egg white and one flavor packet. In a small skillet or wok heat a bit of oil and add the pork. Add hoisin sauce. Mix with soy sauce, sugar, ginger, cornstarch and one flavor packet. Add sesame seed and heat everything until the sauce thickens.

Pour meat and sauce over the ramen noodles and serve.

Substitutions & Omissions

Reduce the amount of pork. Eliminate the hot chili oil and the sesame seeds.

3 packages pork ramen	.30
¼ pound lean boneless pork, cut into ¼ inch slivers	.75
1 egg, beaten slightly and mixed with a little flour	.15
2 tablespoons vegetable oil for frying	.05
1 tablespoon hoisin sauce (page 49)	.30
1 onion, diced	.25
½ teaspoon crushed red peppers	*
1 tablespoon soy sauce	*
1 teaspoon sugar	*
½ teaspoon fresh ginger, chopped	.10
black pepper to taste	*
	Total: $1.90

$$$ Big Splurge $$$

Use fat Oriental noodles for ramen, grind some fresh green, red and black peppercorns and add more pork.

RAMEN ITALIAN SAUSAGE PIE

Serves four

Notes: Italian sausage is the big-ticket item here. You can always use less, but why not make your own? Get a couple of pounds bulk breakfast sausage, add some oregano, basil, crushed red chili peppers and maybe some fennel and you have a pretty good substitute for about 25¢ worth or spices. In this dish, cheese is essential, but if you can't get mozzarella, use Monterey jack or Cheddar. Forget about the fresh Parmesan; use a pinch of dried.

4 packages tomato ramen	.40
3 eggs, beaten	.30
½ cup Parmesan cheese, grated	.50
4 tablespoons butter	.35
½ cup onion, minced	.20
1 ½ cups sour cream	.85
1 pound Italian sausage	3.00
1 12-ounce can tomato paste	.75
1 cup mozzarella cheese, grated	1.00
	Total: $7.35

Bring 4 quarts water to boil. Add ramen noodles and cook until tender, about 4 minutes. Drain and combine with the eggs and Parmesan cheese. Pour into the bottom of a pie tin or casserole dish and pat the mixture up the sides with a spoon.

In a skillet, melt the butter and sauté the onion. Stir in sour cream. Set aside then cook the sausage in the same skillet until fully crumbled and done. Drain. Add tomato paste and water.

Simmer 10 minutes. Mix the sour cream mixture with the sausage. Arrange the mozzarella on top and bake at 350° for 30 minutes, or until the cheese melts. If using a casserole dish, let cool for ten minutes before slicing.

SUBSTITUTIONS & OMISSIONS

Use less Parmesan, omit the mozzarella, use margarine for butter and create your own sausage; also and use cream and water for sour cream.

4 packages tomato ramen	.40
3 eggs, beaten	.30
3 tablespoons Parmesan cheese, grated	*
4 tablespoons margarine	.05
½ cup onion, minced	.20
¼ cup cream	*

½ pound homemade Italian sausage	.50
1 12-ounce can tomato sauce	.35
	Total: $1.80

$$$ BIG SPLURGE $$$

Use filo or pastry shells for the crust, macaroni in place of ramen and fresh Parmesan for dried.

STIR-FRIED HOT DICED PORK

Serves four

Notes: Yellow bean sauce and chilies make the flavor in this recipe. If you don't have yellow bean sauce, use black bean sauce or make your own (see pages 33–34).

3 packages pork ramen	.30
1 cup boneless pork, cut into ½-inch cubes	.75
1 teaspoon bean sauce	.10
2 teaspoons cornstarch, dissolved in 2 teaspoons water	.10
1 cucumber, diced	.25
1 teaspoon crushed chili peppers	.10
½ cup vegetable oil	.20
1 teaspoon green onions, minced	.10
½ teaspoon ginger, minced	.10
2 teaspoons rice wine	.30
	Total: $2.30

Boil water in a large pot. Add ramen noodles and return to a boil for one minute, then reduce heat and cook another 2-3 minutes. Drain and set aside.

Mix raw pork with the bean sauce and the cornstarch. In a medium saucepan, heat the oil and deep-fry the pork cubes, stirring the pieces to keep them from sticking together.

Add the green onions, ginger, salt, cucumber, chili peppers and one packet of pork ramen flavoring. Stir-fry about two minutes. Cook until the sauce thickens. Pour over ramen noodles and serve.

SUBSTITUTIONS & OMISSIONS

Leave out the wine, make your own bean paste.

3 packages pork ramen	.30
1 cup boneless pork, cut into ½-inch cubes	.75
1 teaspoon bean paste	.10
2 teaspoons cornstarch, dissolved in 2 teaspoons water	.10
1 cucumber, diced	.25
1 teaspoon crushed chili peppers	*
½ cup vegetable oil for deep-frying	.20
1 teaspoon green onions, minced	.10
½ teaspoon ginger, minced	.10
	Total: $1.90

$$$ BIG SPLURGE $$$

Use fat Oriental noodles for ramen and add more pork.

SAUSAGE AND CREAM IN RAMEN NOODLES

Serves four

Notes: Sausage and cream will be filling and tasty, and will give you more cholesterol than drinking butter. But you're looking for cheap and filling here, not diet dishes. Enjoy. And when you get rich, you can look for a cookbook with expensive dishes that don't kill you, but taste like crap.

3 packages creamy chicken ramen	.30
8 sweet Italian sausages, removed from their casings	4.00
1 medium onion, diced	.25
2 cups heavy cream	2.00
2 tablespoons cognac	1.00
	Total: $7.55

Boil about six cups of water and toss in the ramen noodles. Cook one minute, then reduce the heat. Cook another 2-3 minutes, drain and set aside.

Fry the sausage in a skillet over medium heat until brown. Drain grease. Add the cream, the flavor packet and cook until slightly thickened. Add cognac if you have it and stir for another half minute, then remove from the fire and toss with the ramen noodles. Serve immediately.

SUBSTITUTIONS & OMISSIONS

Lose the cognac and reduce the amount of sausage requested. Add a package of ramen for filler.

4 packages creamy chicken ramen	.40
8 sweet Italian sausages, removed from their casings	1.25
1 medium onion, finely chopped	.25
5 tablespoons cream	*
	Total: $1.90

$$$ BIG SPLURGE $$$

Keep the cognac and use good Italian sausage. Serve in penne instead of ramen noodles.

RAMEN WITH HOT SAUSAGE AND SPICY TOMATO SAUCE

Serves four

Notes: Tomato is the key here, and you can easily swap fresh for canned, or improvise otherwise on your tomato derivatives. The sausage can range from good Italian to cheap breakfast sausage with a few spices (sage, oregano, crushed red pepper and salt mostly).

3 packages spicy chicken ramen	.30
½ pound Italian sausage, casings removed	1.50
1 large onion, chopped	.25
1 green bell pepper, diced	.25
2 cloves garlic, minced	.10
2 cups tomatoes, diced	1.00
1 8-ounce can tomato sauce	.25
½ cup mushrooms, sliced	.50
1 teaspoon basil	.10
1 teaspoon thyme	.10
½ teaspoon chili powder	.10
½ cup mozzarella cheese, shredded	.75
	Total: $5.20

In a large pot of boiling water, prepare ramen noodles, cooking 3-4 minutes or until tender. Do not overcook. Drain and set aside.

In a large skillet, cook sausage, onion, green pepper and garlic over medium heat until sausage is brown. Drain grease and stir in tomatoes, tomato sauce, mushrooms, basil, thyme, chili powder and one packet of spicy chicken ramen flavoring. Add one cup of water and simmer uncovered 10 minutes.

Pour over ramen noodles and top with cheese, serve.

SUBSTITUTIONS & OMISSIONS

Use bulk breakfast sausage, adding one packet of spicy chicken ramen flavoring to make it into a decent replica of Italian sausage. If the cheese is a problem, use a small bit of Parmesan. And if you're having trouble rounding up all the spices separately, use Italian seasoning, available at most grocery stores. Use 2 8-ounce cans tomato sauce, about a cup of water and one packet tomato ramen flavoring.

3 packages ramen: 2 spicy chicken ramen, 1 tomato	**.30**
½ pound bulk sausage	**.40**
1 large onion, chopped	**.35**
1 medium green bell pepper, seeded and chopped	**.25**
2 cloves garlic, minced	**.10**
2 cans tomato sauce	**.50**
1 tablespoon Italian spice	**.10**
	Total: **$2.00**

$$$ BIG SPLURGE $$$

Use good Italian sausage and fresh thyme. Use a yellow pepper for the green and serve over penne instead of ramen noodles.

SWEET AND SOUR PORK

Serves four

Notes: Okay, now *you can use tomato ketchup—it gives Sweet and Sour its color. Cornstarch, egg, sugar and soy sauce give it its texture and taste.*

3 packages ramen	**.30**
1 pound pork, cut into 1-inch pieces	**3.00**
4 tablespoons sugar	**.10**
2 eggs, beaten	**.20**
3 tablespoons vinegar	**.30**
¼ cup cornstarch, mixed with ¼ cup water	**.30**
2 teaspoons soy sauce	**.20**
1 medium green pepper, cut in 1-inch pieces	**.25**
2 tablespoons tomato ketchup	**.30**
½ cup bamboo shoots, cut in 1-inch pieces	**.75**
2 tablespoons oil	**.05**
4 cloves garlic, minced	**.10**

¼ cup green onions, chopped	.10
	Total: $5.95

Boil water in a large pot. Add ramen noodles and return to a boil for one minute, then reduce heat and cook another 2-3 minutes. Drain and set aside.

Heat the oil in a skillet or wok over medium heat until very hot. Add oil and stir-fry the pork slices until they turn golden brown. Drop the bamboo shoots into the skillet and stir-fry another minute. Remove from pan and set aside.

Add the garlic, green onions and green pepper to the skillet. Cook, stirring, until thickened then add the pork again. Stir to coat thoroughly. Remove, mix all and serve.

SUBSTITUTIONS & OMISSIONS

Lose the bamboo chutes, reduce the amount of pork and add one more package of ramen, reducing slightly the amount of cornstarch.

4 packages ramen	.40
¼ pound pork, cut into ½-inch pieces	.75
4 tablespoons sugar	*
2 eggs, beaten	.20
3 tablespoons vinegar	*
¼ cup cornstarch, mixed with ¼ cup water	.15
2 teaspoons soy sauce	*
1 medium green pepper, cut in 1-inch pieces	.25
2 tablespoons tomato ketchup	*
2 tablespoons oil	.05
4 cloves garlic, minced	.10
¼ cup green onions, chopped	.10
	Total: $2.00

$$$ BIG SPLURGE $$$

Serve on white rice instead of ramen, and use more pork.

THAI FLAVORED PORK AND RAMEN

Serves four

Notes: Coconut milk creates a creamy sweet sauce that brings the flavor of the pork out, so you can use a lot less pork and still be in good shape.

3 packages pork ramen	.30
1 14-ounce can coconut milk	1.25

2 tablespoons curry powder	.10
1 pound pork, cut into ¼-inch slivers	3.00
2 zucchinis, sliced	.50
½ cup peas (frozen or canned is fine)	.50
2 teaspoons sugar	.05
½ cup fresh basil leaves	.10
1 teaspoon serrano chilies, diced	.10
	Total: $5.90

Add coconut milk to a small saucepan and heat over medium heat. When bubbly, add the curry powder and one curry ramen flavor packet. Set aside.

Bring about five quarts of water to boil in a large pot. Drop in ramen noodles and boil for a minute, then reduce heat. Cook another 2-3 minutes, or until tender. Remove from heat, drain and set aside.

In another pot, bring three cups of water to a boil and add the pork. Reduce heat and simmer about 10 minutes uncovered before adding the zucchini and peas. Add one shrimp flavor packet, sugar, basil and chilies and let simmer about three minutes. Pour all but a few teaspoons water out. Add the coconut milk mix, cook two more minutes and serve hot over ramen noodles.

SUBSTITUTIONS & OMISSIONS

Leave out the peas and basil and reduce the amount of pork.

4 packages ramen	.40
½ can coconut milk	.55
2 tablespoons cream, mixed with water	*
2 tablespoons curry powder	.10
¼ pound pork, cut into ¼-inch slivers	.75
½ zucchini, sliced	.10
2 teaspoons sugar	*
1 teaspoon serrano chilies, diced	.10
	Total: $2.00

$$$ BIG SPLURGE $$$

Use fat Oriental noodles instead of ramen noodles.

TWICE-COOKED PORK AND RAMEN NOODLES

Serves four

Notes: Pork gives a good flavor when mixed with twice-fried ramen noodles. You can also use ham, but do yourself a favor and fry the ham a few moments before mixing with the other ingredients.

3 packages pork ramen	.30
1 pound pork, cooked and diced	3.00
2 tablespoons bean sauce	.30
¼ cup green onions, chopped	.15
1 tablespoon sweet bean sauce	.30
1 tablespoon vegetable oil	.05
	Total: $4.10

Boil water in a large pot. Add ramen noodles and return to a boil for one minute, then reduce heat and cook another 2-3 minutes. Drain and set aside.

Heat a skillet and put in the vegetable oil, adding the pre-cooked pork, soybean paste, bean sauce, green onions, one chicken ramen flavor packet and a bit of water. Stir-fry for 5 minutes, or until the green onions are tender and the bean sauce loses its raw taste. Remove and serve.

SUBSTITUTIONS & OMISSIONS

Reduce the amount of pork to one-quarter of the amount listed, and fill out the recipe with another ramen package. And make your own bean sauce (pages 33–34).

4 packages pork ramen	.40
¼ pound pork or ham	.75
2 tablespoons bean sauce	.30
¼ cup green onions, chopped	.15
1 tablespoon vegetable oil	.05
	Total: $1.65

$$$ BIG SPLURGE $$$

Use fat Oriental noodles in place of ramen noodles.

RAMEN NOODLES WITH FRIED BEAN PASTE

Serves four

Notes: This filling meal owes a good deal to the hoisin sauce. A recipe for homemade hoisin sauce can be found on page 49.

3 packages pork ramen	.30
1 cup lean pork, cooked and cubed	2.00
½ cup hoisin sauce	.30
¼ cup vegetable oil	.20

1 teaspoon green onions, chopped	.10
1 teaspoon fresh ginger, chopped	.10
¼ cup soy sauce	.20
1 tablespoon cornstarch, dissolved in 1 tablespoon water	.10
pepper to taste	.05
	Total: $3.35

Boil water in a large pot. Add ramen noodles, one flavor packet and return to a boil for one minute. Reduce heat and cook another 2–3 minutes. Drain and set aside.

In a skillet, heat oil and add cooked pork, green onions, ginger, soy sauce, pepper, one flavor packet, hoisin sauce and water. Stir-fry the mix about two minutes. Mix cornstarch, bring everything to a boil and cook, stirring, until thickened. Transfer to a serving bowl and serve on a bed of noodles.

SUBSTITUTIONS & OMISSIONS

Use less pork.

3 packages pork ramen	.30
¼ cup pork, minced	.50
2 tablespoons homemade hoisin sauce (page 49)	.10
5 tablespoons vegetable oil	.20
1 teaspoon green onions, chopped	.10
1 teaspoon fresh ginger, chopped	.10
5 tablespoons soy sauce	*
1 tablespoon cornstarch, dissolved in 1 tablespoon water	.10
pepper to taste	*
	Total: $1.40

$$$ BIG SPLURGE $$$

Use fat Oriental noodles for ramen noodles.

LAMB AND HERBS RAMEN NOODLES

Serves four

Notes: Lamb and herbs are an acquired taste, and it may not be a dish for everybody. If you like lamb and know lamb, you'll know how to spice it to your liking. If not, try the recipe the way it's presented. New Zealand lamb tends to be a little sharper than domestic, so if you aren't a lamb person stick to homegrown.

3 packages pork ramen	.30
¾ pound ground lamb	2.50
1 cup tomatoes, diced	.50
1 tablespoon olive or vegetable oil	.05
2 cloves garlic, minced	.10
1 medium onion, diced	.25
1 teaspoon rosemary	.10
½ teaspoon thyme	.10
1 cup dry red wine	1.50
¼ teaspoon ground nutmeg	.10
¼ cup Parmesan cheese, grated	.40
	Total: $5.90

Boil about six cups of water and toss in the ramen noodles. Cook one minute, then reduce heat. Cook another 2-3 minutes, drain and set aside.

Mix the tomatoes, lamb, one flavor packet and garlic and cook until the meat begins to brown, about three minutes. Add the onion, rosemary and thyme; cook 1 minute.

Add the lamb to the ramen noodles and stir, tossing in the Parmesan cheese. Serve immediately.

SUBSTITUTIONS & OMISSIONS

Leave out the wine, the rosemary and the nutmeg, use less Parmesan cheese, tomatoes, onion and lamb. And add a fourth package of ramen for filler.

4 packages pork ramen	.40
¼ pound lamb, ground	1.00
½ cup tomatoes, diced	.25
1 tablespoon vegetable oil	.05
2 cloves garlic, minced	.10
½ onion, finely chopped	.10
½ teaspoon dried thyme	.10
¼ cup grated Parmesan cheese	*
	Total: $2.00

$$$ BIG SPLURGE $$$

Use fresh rosemary and thyme and young Parmesan for dried Parmesan. Use linguine instead of ramen noodles.

RAMEN NOODLES WITH LAMB, YOGURT AND COCONUT MILK

Serves four

Notes: Lamb, coconut and a plethora of spices give dish this a lot of character. If you're not a lamb person, use beef or chicken—but the gaminess of the lamb is a nice counterpoint to the sweet of the coconut.

3 packages chicken ramen	.30
1 pound lamb chops, boned, trimmed and cubed	3.50
1 cup plain yogurt	.50
1 teaspoon caraway seeds	.10
½ teaspoon saffron	.10
2 sticks cinnamon	.30
¼ teaspoon cardamom seeds	.10
3 whole cloves	.20
1 cup onions, diced	.25
1 clove garlic, minced	.10
1 teaspoon fresh ginger, minced	.10
½ teaspoon crushed red pepper	.10
1 cup coconut milk, canned	.50
¼ cup unsalted almonds, slivered	.30
	Total: $6.45

Bring about five quarts of water to boil in a large pot. Drop in ramen noodles and boil for a minute, then reduce heat. Cook another 2-3 minutes, or until tender. Remove from heat, drain (keep the water for later) and set aside.

Put saffron into a small bowl or cup and add about a ¼ cup of the ramen noodle's boiled water. Stir in yogurt, caraway seeds and one packet of curry ramen flavoring. Drop in cubed lamb meat and mix thoroughly until all the pieces are evenly coated. Leave for about a half-hour.

In another bowl, combine the almonds with another ¼ cup of hot ramen noodle water. Pour the almonds and the ramen water mixture into a blender and blend until you have a smooth paste.

In a skillet, heat the mix and add cinnamon, cardamom, cloves, onions, garlic and ginger. Stir-fry for about five minutes, or until the onions are soft and golden brown.

In a skillet, add the lamb, coconut milk and the marinade. Cook until meat is browned evenly, about fifteen minutes. Add the almond purée and crushed red pepper and cook 10 more minutes.

Serve on a bed of ramen noodles.

SUBSTITUTIONS & OMISSIONS

Use just a few ounces of lamb (or use a cup or so of chicken thigh meat), get rid of the butter, lose the almonds, halve the onion, and use cream instead of yogurt.

4 packages chicken ramen	.40
3 tablespoons lamb	.30
2 tablespoons cream, mixed with water	*
1 teaspoon caraway seeds	.10
1 teaspoon cinnamon	.10
¼ teaspoon cardamom seeds	.10
1 teaspoon cloves	.10
¾ cup onions, chopped	.20
1 clove garlic, minced	.10
1 teaspoon dried ginger	.10
½ teaspoon crushed red chili pepper	*
1 cup coconut milk, canned	.50
	Total: $2.00

$$$ BIG SPLURGE $$$

Serve over white rice instead of ramen noodles.